CAIRO
Revitalising a Historic Metropolis

EDITED BY STEFANO BIANCA AND PHILIP JODIDIO

UMBERTO ALLEMANDI & C.
for

THE AGA KHAN TRUST FOR CULTURE

Preface

HIS HIGHNESS THE AGA KHAN

We stand today confronted with starkly different visions of the future of historic cities. At a time when our heritage, the anchor of our identity and source of inspiration, is being threatened with destruction, by war and environmental degradation, by the inexorable demographic and economic pressures of exploding urban growth, or by simple neglect, there can be no doubt that it is time to act. Will we allow the wealth that is the past to be swept away, or will we assume our responsibility to defend what remains of the irreplaceable fabric of history? My answer is clear. One of our most urgent priorities must be to value, and protect, what is greatest in our common heritage. Breathing new life into the legacy of the past demands tolerance, and understanding and creativity beyond the ordinary.

The Islamic world boasts roughly a third of the historic cities in the UNESCO World Heritage List. It appeared that this remarkable concentration of cultural history was not receiving the sort of economic, social and academic support that it deserved. A large proportion of the population of these cities typically lives in poverty, creating social problems that must be addressed, but also aggravating factors related to the preservation of their historic heritage. It was clear that it was necessary for the Islamic world to try to harness new resources to protect these historic cities, and to bring relief to their marginalised populations. When the Aga Khan Trust for Culture started its Historic Cities Support Programme, there was no agency that was committed to these goals. Academic knowledge about how to restore and revive historic cities in the Islamic world and bring support to their populations was lacking, because this work had not been done earlier and was unknown to development agencies, teaching centres, and universities.

The Aga Khan Trust for Culture has accordingly sought to identify three 'themes of concern' that correspond to the challenges we face. First, there must be an effort to protect, restore and skilfully reuse the heritage of the past. Second, we must address the pressing needs for social development and community buildings in a Muslim world all too beset by poverty. Third, it is essential to identify contemporary architectural expressions of quality, the best efforts at capturing the opportunities of the present and defining our dreams for tomorrow.

Since it was founded by my ancestors the Fatimids in 969 (AH 359), Cairo has been one of the great centres of Islamic culture and civilisation. Despite its rapid growth in modern times, it still boasts an unrivalled group of monuments and historic areas. These buildings and neighbourhoods stand as a nearly indelible testimony to Cairo's past, but I believe that they are also the key to its future. Today, with its sixteen million inhabitants, the contemporary metropolis clearly poses the full array of development problems. It raises in the most acute terms the question of how to create links between this rich heritage and the demands of today's world.

The exceptional density of the city of Cairo makes it obvious that there is an urgent need for new green spaces. Often overlooked, public open spaces have a great role to play in historic cities. Besides offering inhabitants relief from the pollution and pace of their everyday lives, a park can enhance a sense of civic responsibility and conceivably act as a catalyst for private initiatives in urban rehabilitation. Since I first evoked the idea of creating a new park in Cairo, almost twenty years ago, the needs of the city in this area have become even more pressing.

Close to the Citadel, near to the eastern limits of medieval Cairo, an opportunity did arise to act on all three 'themes of concern' of the Aga Khan Trust for Culture. At the outset the proposal was indeed to provide a much-needed green space, but on the site chosen, the progressive uncovering of more than a kilometre of the long-buried Ayyubid wall led to a major task of conservation. It soon became obvious that the wall was inseparable from the historic fabric of the Darb al-Ahmar neighbourhood. A combined rehabilitation process was elaborated, leading to the creation of a range of community-based improvement projects providing cultural, social, economic and institutional support. Though immediate improvements in living conditions in the vicinity of the park were surely a goal, the scope and breadth of this project implies an ongoing commitment to the monuments, of course, but above all to the people of the Darb al-Ahmar district.

It is within the confines of the new Azhar Park that the third theme of concern of the Aga Khan Trust for Culture has been acted upon. This thirty-one hectare expanse of trees, fountains and buildings was little more than dust just a few years ago. Calling on the talents of both Egyptian and foreign architects and landscape designers, Azhar Park combines a respect for Islamic tradition with a much needed breath of fresh air. From the hills and walkways of the park, not only the Ayyubid wall is visible, but also the Citadel, the Sultan Hasan Mosque and much more of Cairo's new and old skyline as well. Indeed, it is in order to re-establish the skyline as much as possible to its original appearence, and to retain restored mosques to the local population, that the Trust has restored the minarets of the Umm al-Sultan Shaaban and the Khayrbek complexes.

How can this project serve a wider purpose? Because of its scale, and its multiple ramifications, Azhar Park represents a case study situation that should be used for the broadest possible pedagogical purposes. The information thus gathered will be consolidated with the lessons that the AKTC is drawing from other similar projects such as that being undertaken in Zanzibar. Some of the information that will come out of this analytical process will be formatted and targeted to other countries and cities, such as those already on the UNESCO World Heritage List, so that decision makers such as government or local officials in these environments can learn from the experience we have had in Cairo, Zanzibar and elsewhere. The same thinking could be applied to civil society entities that are involved in the restoration of historic cities elsewhere, including local non-governmental organisations, micro-credit organisations, or service providers in health and education. The total package of information we will make available to the multiple stakeholders in the rehabilitation of historic cities should thus help to create a broad framework within which to advance.

Azhar Park, like the ongoing conservation of the Ayyubid wall or the rehabilitation of al-Darb al-Ahmar are not finished simply because the park has been inaugurated. The park requires maintenance, the wall requires continuous care by the skilled hands of masons and archaeologists, and the living community needs the full range of presence and assistance that we have begun to provide. For the work in al-Darb al-Ahmar, the Trust was fortunate to find committed partners such as the Ford Foundation and the Swiss Egyptian Development Fund to support the ongoing work. Similarly, the comprehensive conservation of the historic wall is going forward in collaboration with the Supreme Council of Antiquities in Cairo and will be managed by the Trust with the participation of other organisations, such as the French Institute for Archaeology.

The implementation of this complex undertaking would not have been possible without the active participation and support of the Egyptian authorities, under the leadership of Their Excellencies, President Hosni Mubarak and First Lady Mrs Suzanne Mubarak, who kindly agreed to lay the foundation stone of the park. My thanks go to them and to His Excellency the Minister of Culture, Mr Farouk Hosni, to the Secretary General of the Supreme Council of Antiquities, Dr Zahi Hawas and to his predecessor Dr Gaballa Ali Gaballa, and particularly to His Excellency the Governor of Cairo, Dr Abdel Rahim Shehata, as well as to his predecessor, His Excellency Mr Omar Abdel Akher, whose constant support and personal commitment have been essential to the work of the technical team in charge of carrying out the project.

Never more than now has it been so important to renew with vigour our creative engagement in revitalising our shared heritage. It is my hope that Azhar Park, set amidst the great monuments of Islamic Cairo, will become a symbol for visitors and residents alike, opening new vistas onto this unique city. The Ayyubid wall and al-Darb al-Ahmar are the living fabric of the historic city. Those who live here and those who pass through may now be more aware of the wealth that is within their grasp. It is our task, but theirs as well, to sustain and develop that wealth into the future.

Preface

HIS EXCELLENCY DR ABDEL RAHIM SHEHATA, GOVERNOR OF CAIRO

Many years ago, Cairo used to be a city of parks and gardens. Zamalek, Maadi, Garden City and Heliopolis consisted of green residential districts, where private gardens merged with planted public open spaces and the Nile riverbanks. At the heart of the urban extensions planned under the Khedives during the nineteenth century was the Azbakiyya Garden, which became the focal point for a series of important new avenues linking the old medieval city and the newly created districts of Cairo.

In the past decades, demographic pressures, technological progress and urban development have introduced massive changes in the townscape of the rapidly growing metropolis. Planners found it difficult to keep pace with this rapid transformation, and, land being one of the scarcest resources of Egypt, many orchards, gardens and green spaces have been sacrificed under the pressures of rapid urban development. Today, Cairo must be one of the most densely built agglomerations of the Middle East.

Yet a capital city owes it to its residents to provide places to breathe, to relax and to enjoy nature within the city. That is why the Cairo Governorate during the past few years has embarked on a series of important projects, including the creation of new parks, the enhancement of existing parks and gardens, and the establishment of pedestrian squares in the city centre.

Major public gardens created in recent years include the International Garden in Nasr City, with its different corners representing different countries; Fustat Garden, overlooking Cairo's last remaining lake; and Sayyeda Zeinab Park for Children. In parallel, well-established public green areas in the city have been revitalised. These include Merryland Park, with its numerous restaurants and leisure facilities, and the Fish Garden with its aquaria and grottos, Azbakiyya Garden and Horeyya Garden in Gazira. The importance of creating public space in the city centre has led to the pedestrianisation of two large areas in downtown Cairo: the Alfy Street area — a popular shopping and entertainment venue — and the area surrounding the Egyptian Stock Exchange, which has gone through extensive urban upgrading.

Azhar Park, of which we are celebrating the opening in spring 2004, fits into the framework of this general policy of urban enhancement and beautification, and yet it acquires a very special significance due to its sponsorship, to its location, to its design and to the positive change it has generated in this part of historic Cairo.

To assess the impact of this project one only needs to compare the images before and after the intervention. Used as a dumping area since the Fatimid era, this formerly barren site has now been converted into a centrally located public park, and the hills which have accumulated over centuries provide unique viewing points, unfolding a 360° panorama of historic and modern Cairo. The eastern edge of historic Cairo with its 1.5-kilometre-long Ayyubid city walls has come to light again and the Darb al-Ahmar district located behind it is being enhanced and revitalised. The combination of all these interventions provides visitors and residents with a new experience of their city. Azhar Park has indeed become the engine for a much larger urban renewal programme and undoubtedly qualifies for being called one of the "Grands Projets" of the City of Cairo in modern times.

I express my thanks and gratitude for the encouragement and continuous support received from President Hosni Mubarak and Mrs Mubarak all along the phases of implementation.

It is a pleasure for me to salute the vision and the generosity of the sponsor of this project, His Highness the Aga Khan. His contribution will leave an important mark on Cairo — as did the contributions of the Fatimid founders of this great city.

I would like to thank the joint team of Egyptian and international professionals for the efforts they have put into the park and the associated projects. Now that their work has come to fruition, I trust that the residents of Cairo will appropriate, appreciate, and enjoy this splendid new facility at the core of their historic town.

A Visionary Urban Project

LUIS MONREAL, GENERAL MANAGER, AGA KHAN TRUST FOR CULTURE

An international seminar entitled "The Expanding Metropolis: Coping with the Urban Growth of Cairo" was organised by the Aga Khan Award for Architecture in 1984. On that occasion, His Highness the Aga Khan visited once more the great Islamic city and met with some of the most prominent architects, urban planners and development experts attending the meeting. He had new opportunities to view old Cairo from various vantage points — from the terrace of Hassan Fathy's Mamluk house, Beit al-Fann, and from the top of the minarets erected in the Gamaliyya and al-Darb al-Ahmar districts. An anomaly in the urban landscape struck his eye: the existence of a barren land, a man-made heap of debris, the Darassa Hills, a surprisingly uninhabited piece of wasteland, to the east of al-Azhar Mosque, bordering on the vast metropolis of medieval Cairo, the City of the Dead. David Roberts had sketched his famous view of Cairo's Ayyubid walls from that vantage point, in 1839. But, by the end of the twentieth century, nothing could be seen of the old city ramparts, which had been covered by a thick layer of waste and rubble formed through a spontaneous process of rejection by an overpopulated metropolis — a process that was a norm in medieval times, when the lack of organised collection of solid waste caused cities to accumulate layers of debris.

That visit to Cairo was determinant in the Aga Khan's decision to propose the creation of a thirty-hectare park as a gift to the city. At that time, the question of how to reconcile conservation and development was a fairly new one. The notion of building a park on wasteland seemed outlandish. Nevertheless, it was clear that Cairo needed more green space. A study found that people had at that time an average of thirty square centimetres of green space per person, which is equivalent to the size of a footprint — one of the lowest proportions in the world.

Because of its sheer size and location near the historic centre of Cairo, the thirty-hectare Darassa Hills site offered a unique opportunity to create a new 'lung' for a megalopolis that was notably deficient in green spaces. What little greenery or park space that may have existed in the city had been in large part consumed by the pressures of urbanisation. At the same time, the site was in the neighbourhood of a community economically poor but rich in cultural heritage.

From the outset, it was recognised that a park in that location should not only be conceived as an environmental improvement, as a space for leisure, but also, and more importantly, as a catalyst for the social and cultural development of the community. The project would have to revitalise the heart of the medieval city, improving the quality of life of its residents and bringing new economic activities to the area. After an intense period of conceptualisation and planning, the Governorate of Cairo and the Aga Khan Trust for Culture signed a protocol in 1990 for the implementation of the project. This project was one of the pioneers of a movement to reclaim ancient city centres. Shortly after the Aga Khan's decision to create the Cairo park as an engine for environmental and socio-economic development, other cities also began to look at their derelict old centres and their industrial fringes, engaging in large-scale renovation projects that could impact the quality of life and the economy of their communities.

The location of the Cairo park was indeed exceptional in many ways, not least because it abutted the historic city walls. Though some parts of the Ayyubid walls remained visible, it was not possible to predict at that time how much of such a major architectural work had survived under the millions of cubic metres of rubble rejected by the metropolis over several hundred years. However, as a first survey of the site was conducted, it became clear that restoring these walls would also become a major element of the project.

The strategy of the project was based on the principle that the park could only be successfully developed with the participation of the principal beneficiaries of this operation, the Darb al-Ahmar community. The park would benefit all of Cairo, but it should be primarily both a catalyst and a strong stimulus for the development of the adjacent neighbourhood. As with similar programmes undertaken by the Aga Khan Development Network elsewhere in Asia and in Africa, the Cairo project would eventually gather momentum and sustain itself. Upgrading the socio-economic environment of the community while simultaneously restoring monuments and building a park was considered a bold experiment at that time. It was more than a commonplace matter of landscape design and historic preservation; it was an integrated programme designed to have a significant effect on the quality of life. It was also meant to serve as a catalyst for the development of other parts of the medieval city.

Landscaping a large barren area, while at the same time restoring a range of significant historic buildings and, contemporaneously, upgrading the local community's socio-economic environment was a bold initiative. Indeed, from its inception the project attempted to create a synergistic effect between the construction of the park, the restoration of the walls and the upgrading and renewal of the urban fabric in the Darb al-Ahmar area, its housing, public spaces and monuments. At the time it started, preservation of the medieval city was not yet perceived by public opinion as an asset. The prestige of modernity was a prevalent notion, and many could not conceive that the rehabilitation of old architectural structures, coupled with a judicious replacement of irretrievable buildings, would bring a new quality to the lives of the inhabitants, without compromising the best asset of the city, its Islamic heritage.

Al-Darb al-Ahmar was once the area where a certain gentry lived, a middle to upper-class population. Its nineteenth-century streets were occupied by the wealthy who by the turn of the twentieth century began to move to the new city along the banks of the Nile. They were replaced by a rural population, and this movement gained considerable momentum following the construction of the Aswan dam that triggered massive immigration to the urban centres of Egypt. Despite having been in the area for one or two generations, many of these former peasants in the old town still have difficulty adapting to the ways of the city. In an attempt to alleviate this problem, the Darb al-Ahmar project has devised a strategy aimed at providing tools for residents to become not only urban dwellers but also to gradually climb the social ladder. The goal is to provide new opportunities to improve the lives of the area's population. This is where the resources of the Aga Khan Development Network come into play, by promoting the establishment of associations of local residents, by creating training opportunities and by offering financial opportunities through a micro-financing programme that supports the upgrading of housing and the development of family businesses.

For several reasons, the creation of Azhar Park and its related project components should be interpreted as a symbol of hope. First of all, because it involves the visual rediscovery of Cairo itself. These now green hills are a new vantage point that allows visitors to take in the city at a simple glance. This metropolis offers one of the greatest concentrations of art and culture in the world, now visible as a scenic panorama from a breathtaking *mirador*. In this respect, the project will have a significant cultural impact, as it may help its own inhabitants rediscover the historical values of the city. In the near future this site will also house a new feature, the Visitors' Centre for Islamic Cairo, a gateway to the architectural heritage of the city built here in collaboration with the Supreme Council of Antiquities, that will serve both as an educational facility for the Cairene and provide the necessary information to foreign visitors about this unique urban ensemble. Since the park houses three great water tanks for the city, it is also Cairo's symbolic fountain, a source of fresh water in a city besieged by dryness. The park will be managed by the Aga Khan Cultural Services-Egypt under the supervision of a Park Authority Board presided over by His Excellency the Governor of Cairo. This experiment in the creation of an autonomous self-perpetuating entity, able to reinvest its own income in improvements and operations, mirrors the spirit that has presided over the entire project. The Aga Khan Trust for Culture and the Aga Khan Development Network have deployed their efforts not only to improve the environment, but rather to bring forth a new element of development and cultural pride that is expected to endure the test of time.

This book is an account for posterity documenting the rationale and the process followed in the creation of the Cairo park project, enriched by essays on relevant aspects of urban history and an outlook on the city's future. The Aga Khan Trust for Culture wishes to thank the distinguished specialists in various fields that have contributed to this volume, which is also a tribute of gratitude to the many people that have committed their personal effort to the implementation of this project: leaders of the community and simple citizens, architects, landscape architects, planners, development specialists, conservators, gardeners, masons, and many other professional trades that would be impossible to list exhaustively. These hundreds of people have made possible, each in his or her own area of competence and level of specialisation, the transformation into reality of what was, twenty years ago, a visionary dream.

Special thanks are due to the main donor agencies which joined the Trust's conservation and community development work in al-Darb al-Ahmar and provided continued support to specific projects. The World Monuments Fund, through the Wilson Challenge Award, has contributed yearly matching grants for the restoration of the Umm al-Sultan Shaaban Mosque and the Khayrbek complex. The Ford Foundation has participated significantly in the rehabilitation of the Darb Shoughlan community centre building and in various housing improvement initiatives along the Ayyubid wall. A generous four-year grant from the Egyptian Swiss Development Fund was essential for initiating the ongoing social and physical rehabilitation works in al-Darb al-Ahmar.

When His Highness the Aga Khan looked out from the terrace of Beit al-Fann, Hassan Fathy's house in 1984, he saw the great monuments of Islamic Cairo, silent witnesses to a glorious past. The creation of Azhar Park, the restoration of the Ayyubid wall and revitalisation efforts in al-Darb al-Ahmar are as much a celebration of the past as an expression of confidence in the future of the metropolis.

Contents

PAST

THE ROLE OF HISTORY

The history and the modern development of Cairo into one of the great cities of the world
is described here by Janet Abu-Lughod and Jim Antoniou.
Nasser Rabbat recounts the history of Cairo's green spaces, while Seif El Rashidi
gives an overview of the history of the Darb al-Ahmar area, the historic district
along the twelfth-century city wall facing Azhar Park.
These texts reveal how the contemporary urban situation has been formed by the past,
creating great cultural wealth but also a series of complex problems.
Indeed, any effort to improve living conditions in Cairo must necessarily take
this history into account.

Cairo, an Islamic Metropolis

JANET ABU-LUGHOD

The seed from which the modern metropolis of Cairo sprang dates in reality from the time of the Arab conquest. The ancient historic significance of the site and the continuity of settlement there from earliest times indicate that some great city would have emerged in the general location. The point where the wide Delta, embraced by the two downstream branches of the river, meets the narrowing Nile upstream has always endowed Cairo's site with enormous strategic advantages. There, and only there, could the soft underbelly of the Delta be defended against invaders, and there, and only there, could the source of the upstream floodwaters be protected.

The site, therefore, had been the choice of all successive rulers of the Nile Valley, who, since Pharaonic times, had built their cities in the vicinity. But modern Cairo is not just 'any' city; it is a *unique* city. The arrival of Islam in the seventh century, while it did not interrupt geographic continuity, created a marked break in cultural continuity. Contemporary Cairo stands pre-eminently as a Muslim city, bearing only slight traces of the physical and cultural imprint of its Pharaonic and Greco-Roman precursors.

The message of Islam was first brought to Egypt in AD 639 by Arab forces under 'Amr ibn al-'As, the commander who eventually conquered an Egypt much weakened by battles between contending Persian and Byzantine armies. By 641, his army had advanced to the northern edge of Babylon (in Egypt), a partially fortified port on the Nile. 'Amr had received instructions from Caliph Umar to establish his headquarters in the country's interior and to protect his *land* lifeline to Arabia. The strategic site of Cairo was his inevitable choice, both because of its central location and because it was on the firmer eastern bank of the Nile. This assured his access to Arabia by land and, later, by water as well, through the old Red Sea Canal (renamed Khalij Misri) which 'Amr reopened in 643. This preference for the eastern bank sealed forever the fate of Memphis (on the western shore of the river) and, until the present century, led to greater and greater concentrations on that bank. To understand how the Nile formerly constituted the insurmountable barrier that it no longer presents, a brief description of the regional terrain and of the changes in the course of that river is essential. Given the narrow cone of alluvial land on the eastern shore, wedged between the old channel of the Nile and the high ridges that divide it from the desert, the only path for urban expansion from Babylon was to its north (see fig. 1).

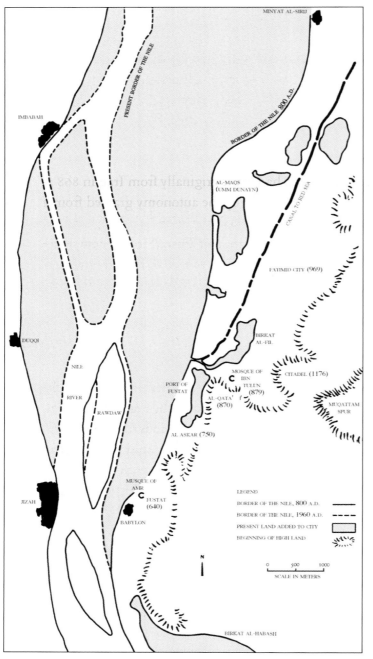

Fig. 1. The Cairo area showing the location of major settlements and the land added through shifts in the channel of the Nile since AD 800.

During the seven months that 'Amr besieged Babylon, his army's tents were pitched on the dusty plain north of Babylon. Once capitulation was achieved, the troops were arranged formally in a more permanent settlement called al-Fustat. Here, in the southern part of today's Cairo known as Misr al-Qadima (Old Cairo), 'Amr built the first mosque on the African continent. Over the ensuing almost fourteen hundred years, Islam spread its roots in the region. Cairo, the largest (and most Islamic) city of Africa, now contains some sixteen million inhabitants who occupy hundreds of square kilometres on both shores of the Nile. This chapter summarises its development, focusing primarily on the premodern phase.

At first, Babylon continued to serve as the port and commercial centre for al-Fustat, housing the original population of Copts and Jews. Over time, most but not all had converted to Islam, and the town and the army camp grew together, both physically and socially. But new additions to these nuclei lay ahead that reflected changing patterns of leadership and schismatic forces occurring within the expanding Islamic empire.

The new towns of Islam were of two major types: army camps such as al-Fustat that eventually developed into permanent cities; and princely towns founded to celebrate the hegemonic power of new dynasties. (The next few settlements marked significant political changes.) The final scene of an internal struggle between the Umayyads and the Abbasids for imperial supremacy was played out on the site of Fustat in AD 750. The Umayyad caliph had fled to Fustat in the hope of evading his pursuers but was apprehended there and killed. In the struggle, much of Fustat was burned. For the Islamic world outside Spain, this marked the end of Umayyad power and the removal of the seat of the Caliphate from Damascus to the new capital of Baghdad. For the smaller world of Egypt, it meant the displacement of local governing functions to a newly constructed suburb to the north of Fustat where Abbasid troops were quartered. This princely city, called al-Askar (the Cantonment), dominated rebuilt commercial Fustat and, as had its predecessor, eventually blended with it.

The next governor/builder was Ahmad ibn Tulun, who had come originally from Iraq in 868 as deputy for the Abbasid governor of Egypt. Aided temporarily by the autonomy granted from a fragmenting empire and presumably inspired by luxurious Samarra from which he hailed, he added his own princely city north and inland from the existing conurbation of Fustat. In this new settlement, called al-Qata'i (The Wards), Ibn Tulun assigned separate areas to each of the ethnic groups making up his army. Employing architects and builders who followed Byzantine/Coptic traditions, he had his mosque constructed (an acknowledged masterpiece completed in 878), with its ziggurat minaret patterned on that of Samarra. It stands today in the southern part of Cairo, now densely populated, marking the location of his long vanished town.

However, Cairo itself had not yet been built. It had to await a new set of rulers, followers of the Shi'ite branch of Islam, who arrived from Tunisia under the command of their talented general, Jawhar the Sicilian. In AD 969 Jawhar easily overcame the resistance of the previous ruling Ikhshids. He quartered his troops temporarily on the plain north of al-Qata'i until he could provide them with permanent quarters. He proceeded to lay out a new, rectangular, and even more glorious princely town on the flat land farther north, between the Khalij canal on the west and the beginning of the eastern desert, at first naming it al-Mansuriyya. This well-planned walled city was divided into four main quarters by its two intersecting thoroughfares.[1] The north-south processional route, named after the Fatimid caliph, Muizz al-Din (but later to be known in medieval literature simply as the *qasaba*) stretched from the centre of the northern wall to the centre of the southern wall, along which were built the palaces of the ruler (Bayn al-Qasrayn, or "between the two palaces"). The east-west thoroughfare led from the Khalij to al-Azhar Mosque, which was destined to become the world's first university. The remaining areas were assigned to various ethnic groups in his composite army. By 974 the city was ready (see fig. 2). Jawhar renamed it al-Qahira (the Victorious) to celebrate the ceremonial installation of Muizz al-Din as the caliph of the Fatimid dynasty under which the city would reach one of its historic and artistic high points. (The name Cairo was a later European-language distortion of the city's Arabic name.)

Despite the increasing beauty, luxury, and intellectual vitality of the Fatimid princely city, for close to two hundred years it remained a royal refuge within whose secure enclosure successive rulers

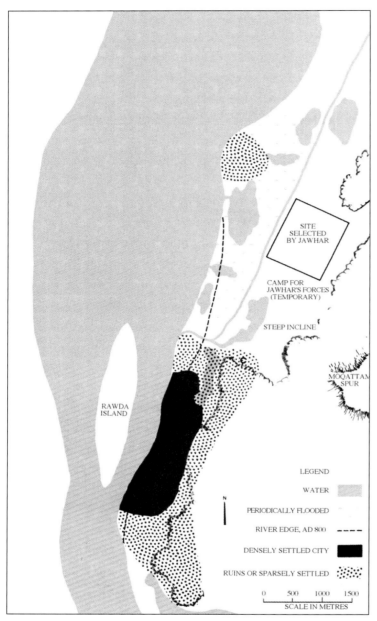

and their entourages governed the region and pursued their lives. As a royal enclave, it was closed to the masses. Fustat and its extensions, already known by the alternative name of Misr,[2] remained the dominant transport, productive, and commercial metropolis. Its population continued to inhabit the increasingly dense and prosperous conurbation, isolated from the artistic, architectural and intellectual achievements of the Fatimid capital.

During the eleventh century, then, we can reconstruct two thriving but symbiotic cities. Misr-Fustat, the larger of the two whose northern limit was the mosque of Ibn Tulun, was occupied by the indigenous population and devoted to commercial and industrial activities. Al-Qahira, instead, was a well-designed community serving the needs of a large and complex courtly society. Originally divided into ten separate quarters (*harat*) for the defending army and their dependents, it was liberally endowed with gardens, palatial residences and mosques, of which the new al-Hakim Mosque near the northern wall was one of its architectural treasures. The dual city was served by dual ports, the older one at Misr-Fustat, devoted to commercial shipping, and a newer one at al-Maqs (a revival of the pre-Islamic port of Tendunyas on the island of Bulaq, not yet joined to the mainland) where the powerful Fatimid navy was anchored. So secure did the Fatimids feel that apparently they neglected to maintain the defensive walls around al-Qahira, until they were repaired and strengthened by Badr al-Jamali towards the end of the eleventh century.

Fig. 2. The site of Cairo and its development at the time of the Fatimid invasion and the founding of al-Qahira.

LEGEND

WATER

PERIODICALLY FLOODED

RIVER EDGE, AD 800 — — — —

DENSELY SETTLED CITY

RUINS OR SPARSELY SETTLED

0   500   1000   1500
SCALE IN METRES

SITE SELECTED BY JAWHAR

CAMP FOR JAWHAR'S FORCES (TEMPORARY)

STEEP INCLINE

MOQATTAM SPUR

RAWDA ISLAND

The thriving dual city, however, was to experience setbacks over the course of the next century. Some were natural events (a plague that began in 1063, an earthquake in 1138) but the final blow was administered in 1168 by larger-scale religious and political events. The Europeans had launched their first crusade in the final year of the eleventh century, but Cairo's peripheral position *vis-à-vis* the Holy Land kept it relatively insulated from the battles being fought in the Fertile Crescent. Two-thirds of a century later, however, the city was disastrously drawn into them. Between 1164 and 1169 it was at best a pawn in the complex and shifting alignments of the rival powers in Syria (under Nur al-Din) and the Christian forces of Amalric (Amaury) in Jerusalem, her young Fatimid caliph a figurehead at the mercy of changing viziers.

When the campaigns that had wracked Egypt for five bitter years ceased temporarily in 1169, the future of Cairo had been completely altered. Al-Qahira had been transformed from a princely city in symbiotic competition with commercial Misr-Fustat to an overflowing metropolis inhabited by masters and masses alike. Although still nominally ruled by Fatimid Shi'ites, it was actually controlled by the new Sunni vizier, Salah al-Din (Saladin), who had participated in the campaign (led by his uncle, Shirkuh, whom he succeeded after the latter's death in 1169) that had rescued Egypt from the attempted conquest by the crusaders. The next few years witnessed the final overthrow of the Fatimids in Cairo and the establishment of a new dynasty of Sunni Ayyubids under the leadership of Saladin.

How had this remarkable transformation taken place? Quite simply, through the virtual destruction of Misr-Fustat, not the only but certainly one of the major casualties of the war. The crusader forces, in an unusual tactic, were approaching Cairo from the south. Fearing that they might occupy indefensible Fustat and use it to launch a fatal attack on the walled enclave of Cairo, in 1168 the Fatimid vizier ordered the city of the masses to be burned down. Burn it did — for fifty-four days and nights. The smoke, borne southwards by the prevailing winds, drove the crusaders into retreat. The people of Misr-Fustat fled northwards in great confusion, seeking protection within the walls of Cairo. By the following year, when the Syrian forces had routed Amalric and Saladin had assumed the role of vizier, much of Fustat lay in ashes; her population crowded within the former princely city or huddled in temporary camps outside her walls.

While the disaster was not total, the changes were irreversible. In the next fifteen years, parts of Misr-Fustat along the shores of the Nile were rebuilt, but the greatly reduced population no longer needed the higher lands, which were abandoned. The city of Misr-Fustat, formerly almost contiguous with al-Qahira and of at least equal importance, had become a community separated from, and definitely subordinate to, its northern neighbour. In contrast, the city of al-Qahira, now infused with population, industry, and commerce, had become the true centre of the region in every sense of the term. Having little interest in preserving al-Qahira as a sacrosanct refuge for the court and contemplating his own private domain in the citadel he was planning, Saladin had opened the city to the masses who, in their need for more space, constructed everywhere within the larger streets and *mayadin* (open spaces), gradually effacing the basic outlines of the original symmetrical design. The palaces were torn down and replaced by schools and mosques, and former Fatimid villas were converted to commercial uses.

Although Saladin was never to spend much time in Egypt because his campaigns against the crusaders demanded constant attention abroad, he invested efforts to strengthen and expand al-Qahira's walls, extending the northern wall all the way to al-Maqs, which encouraged some construction west of the Khalij. He also ordered the building of a fortified Citadel on the spur of the Moqattam Hills overlooking the city, from which he planned to govern.[3] Begun as early as 1174-1175, travellers' accounts noted that it was still under construction in 1183 (by crusader prisoners) and it remained unfinished at his death in 1193. Its construction, however, served as a magnet that encouraged settlements in the area between the existing southern wall and the approaches to it.

During the next few centuries, Cairo expanded into a world capital, becoming the most populous city of the world outside China. The medieval cycle of Cairo's growth and subsequent decline began essentially with the accession of Saladin to the leadership of Sunni Islam. It rose sharply within the next 175 years, reaching an apogee during the long reigns of the Mamluk sultan al-Nasir ibn Qalawun before the middle of the fourteenth century. The entire cycle was played out within the central section of contemporary Cairo (see fig. 3).

The expansion, begun towards the end of the twelfth century under Saladin, picked up speed after the middle of the thirteenth century when two events caused far-reaching changes in the shape of western Islam. The first was the rise to power in Egypt of the Mamluks, whose mounted cavalry, under their leader Baybars, routed Saint Louis' forces when his crusaders invaded the Egyptian Delta in 1250, and also wrested control of Palestine from the Europeans, adding that territory to their expanding empire.[4] Baybars was installed as sultan in 1260, and under his successors Egypt became the head of a large and flourishing empire. The second factor was the Mongol conquest of eastern Islam and the destruction of Baghdad, which resulted in the relocation of the Caliphate to the safety of Baybars' capital, Cairo.

The shift to Mamluk rule was much more than a simple change in dynasty, however. It represented, rather, a social revolution of deep significance that, while it facilitated a flowering of medieval Cairo, contained within it the seeds of its own (and Cairo's) eventual decline. Although from one point of view Egypt had rarely been ruled by indigenous elements, earlier conquerors had eventually been absorbed into or at least coalesced with the population they ruled. The Mamluks, on the other hand, remained a 'foreign' military caste, each generation recruited anew from abroad. Although inter-

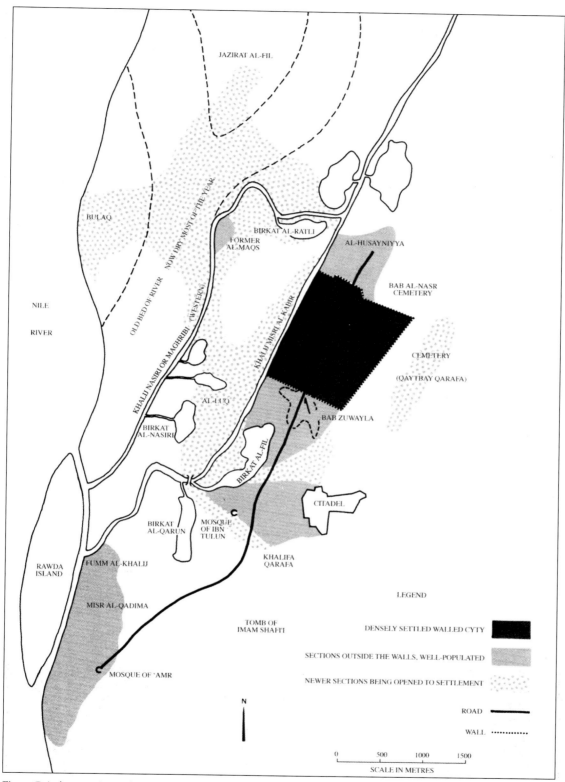

Fig. 3. Cairo's expansion at the time of Sultan al-Nasir ibn Qalawun *c.* 1340.

marriage and common belief in Islam bridged some of the distance, not since the early days of the Arab conquest, when Muslims governed a predominantly Christian populace, had so great a cleavage existed. But whereas the former split had been bridged by the gradual conversion of Egyptians to Islam, such assimilation was impossible during the later era when the ranks of the Mamluks were, by definition, closed to local recruits. Their unique form of feudal control over the countryside and their virtual monopoly over the spice trade, however, yielded enormous prosperity to the rulers who, in addition to recruiting and training more slaves from the Caucasus, invested it in endowing mosques, schools, hospitals and palaces in Cairo. They also began to build funerary mosques in the Cities of the Dead outside the city, especially in the cemeteries just east of the capital.

The city's fortunes closely reflected those of the empire, for as internal strife and external threats multiplied, the expansion of the city came to a temporary halt. The Black Death of 1353 onward, which spread along world trade routes from its point of origin in China all the way to north-west Europe, afflicted Egypt and Syria as well, causing Cairo's population to drop by about a third. As elsewhere, it precipitated a change in the ruling regime — from the Bahri (or Nile-based) Mamluks to the Circassian Mamluks of the Burj (Citadel). By the opening decades of the fifteenth century, Cairo's fortunes rose with the recovery of the larger world system, significantly enhanced by the virtual monopoly control her merchants, in league with their alien rulers, exercised over the trade between a rising Europe and a prosperous Far East.[5] It was then that the expanded city reached its maximum dimensions of the pre-modern era. It completed laying down the precious heritage we now seek to restore and revive. By then, Cairo's population may have reached half a million. This peak, however, was soon to pass.

The mirror image of the rise of Islam on the Anatolian plateau, signalled by the conquest of Constantinople in 1453 by the Ottoman Turks, represented a decline in Egypt's imperial wealth and autonomy. After the Ottoman conquest of Egypt in 1517, Cairo was reduced from its former status as centre of a vast empire to a mere provincial capital. Its talented cadre of architects and artisans were removed to Istanbul where they contributed to the transformation of that Byzantine Christian city into a magnificent Islamic capital. During the ensuing centuries, Egypt underwent a precipitous decline. Peasants fled the burdensome taxes imposed by a contracting economy, and peripheral lands went out of cultivation, the east-west spice trade found alternate routes, including those around the African continent, and Egypt and Cairo lost population. This was especially true in the 'old city', as developments west of the Khalij, including the zones around the interior lakes of Azbakiyya and Birkat al-Fil, began to be favoured by Mamluk aristocrats. These zones attracted some clients, residents, and businesses from the walled city's two dominant quarters, al-Jamaliyya north of al-Azhar Street, and al-Darb al-Ahmar south of it.

The arrival in 1798 of the Napoleonic expedition to Egypt brought the cycle to a close, the intrusion forming a bridge between a medieval Cairo much decayed and a modern Cairo yet to be. The *savants* who accompanied the brief occupation mapped the city, estimating its population at less than three hundred thousand. Although the French did not remain as colonisers, the processes of 'modernisation' and 'reform' had begun.

The first 'reformer' was Muhammad Ali, the Albanian soldier appointed by the Porte to govern Egypt. He first ruthlessly dispatched his remaining Mamluk rivals by a ruse. Then he reorganised the feudal system and introduced new crops (in particular, long staple cotton), and tried to modernise education, administration, and his army. In the later years of his rule, he also made some important revisions to Cairo's urban pattern. The rubbish mounds that had collected around the city walls were levelled and the residue used to fill in some of the disease-breeding interior lakes, including the one at Azbakiyya, which was drained. North of the city, in Shubra, he built a large palace, and Shubra Street was laid out to give access to it. Although not completed in his lifetime, he ordered two new thoroughfares to open the way for better circulation. The most striking was a broad diagonal thoroughfare that connected the Zuwayla Gate in the southern wall with the Citadel, to which he added new fortifications, a Turkish-style mosque, and additional barracks for his large army. He also ordered a new street (al-Sikka al-Jadida, later al-Muski Street) that cut laterally through the old city, parallel to the road that led to al-Azhar. Both these avenues required ruthless demolitions of existing houses and shops.

But all the same, these were minimal changes in comparison to those introduced by his successors, changes in the urban panorama increasingly influenced by European planning principles. Muhammad Ali was succeeded by his nephew Abbas who, during his brief reign, allowed the British to build railways to connect Alexandria with Cairo and Cairo with Suez, thus intensifying Cairo's links with the outside world. The Cairo terminus was at Bab al-Hadid, the gate in Saladin's wall extension that had been only recently demolished. In addition, Abbas set up a small military city in the desert outpost of Abbasiyya. Both developments tended to elongate the shape of the city to the north. After a brief interlude under the reign of Muhammad Ali's youngest son, Said, most noteworthy because he invited his old tutor, De Lesseps, to begin executing the latter's plan for the Suez Canal, Khedive Ismail, the ruler most committed to modernising Cairo along European lines, succeeded.

Ismail, assisted by his talented polymath chief engineer, Ali Mubarak, was responsible for setting in motion the most significant changes in the city during the latter third of the nineteenth century. Like many times before, the digging of a new canal (the Ismailiyya Canal parallel to but much farther west than the old Khalij Misri, which was dry for much of the year) opened a further gift of dry land between the built-up city and the newly stabilising banks of the Nile.

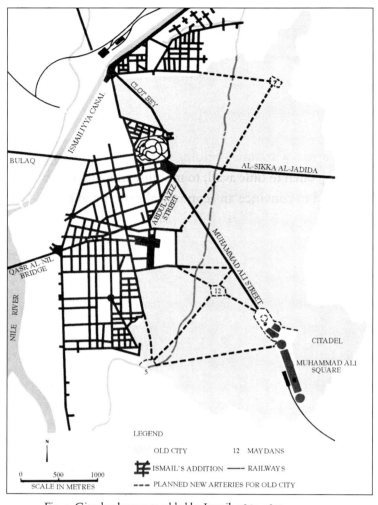

Fig. 4. City developments added by Ismail, 1869-1870.

Ali Mubarak, after visiting Paris where he much admired Hausmann's re-planning of that city, drew up his plans for a 'new' westernised addition to Cairo. On this *tabula rasa*, only sparsely occupied and newly rescued from flooding by the construction of the Ismailiyya Canal, he used his ruler to create a rough checkerboard suited to carriage travel that was becoming more popular among the wealthy. The latter were drawn to the new area by Ismail's new palace there and the incentive of cheap land for those willing and able to build. Thus began the creation of the dual city (see fig. 4), which would be carried to its extreme after Ismail's bankruptcy[6] and lead eventually to British colonial rule.[7]

The impact on the older quarters of Cairo was dramatic, although the full force of the change was not really felt until after British colonial rule brought numerous Europeans who pre-empted the space designed by Ali Mubarak. As elsewhere in other Third World colonised cities, the dual-city pattern eventually denuded the older quarters of wealthy natives who flocked to ape the new consumption patterns associated with the colonisers. In the process, the older quarters became neglected and degraded, as new migrants from the countryside joined the poorer population left behind, subdividing the large homes of the departed rich into cubicles, unable to maintain them, and eventually spilling out to the cemeteries east and south-east of the city. All resources were devoted to paving the streets in the new quarters, to providing them with gaslights, piped water and even sewers. While the old quarters did not lose their important economic functions — handicrafts and the processing and distribution of foods — these products were increasingly purveyed to people of similar social standing. In the new city, which increasingly stretched back to the western border of medieval Cairo at the Khalij Misri, the consumption needs of the indigenous rich and the foreigners who increasingly dominated the new districts were provided for by upmarket grocery stores and glass-windowed shops selling imported goods and luxuries. Medieval Cairo was alive with production and people, but its architectural heritage was condemned to death by neglect, poverty, and overcrowding.

It seemed that in the rush to be 'modern', few placed any value on the old; the Aladdin scam of 'new lamps for old' was too compelling. At first, it seemed, only mavericks cared. K. A. C. Cresswell, who had come to Egypt at the end of the nineteenth century with the British occupying army, came to care a great deal. A tiny man with enormous self-confidence and a tendency to bully, he devoted his life to surveying and mapping the hundreds of Islamic buildings left in the old city, to carefully documenting each monument, and trying, often to little avail, to mobilise more than the cadre of well-meaning *noblesse oblige* Westerners and to convince an economically-strapped government to preserve Cairo's breathtaking historic heritage. But he had little concern for, or interest in, the people who remained in the degraded urban setting and who he often seemed to blame for its destruction. One senses that his ideal solution would have been an urban landscape without people.[8] Without his work, however, the present efforts to rescue the living heritage of Cairo, together with its people, would have been even more challenging than it is.

As it was, the western edges of the pre-modern core city had already been redeveloped into the Central Business District of the early twentieth century, especially after 1898 when the Khalij Misri was finally filled in and street cars were introduced along the broad thoroughfare of Port Said Street: the division between old and new became concretised. Port Said Street was as impassable a barrier as any wall had ever been, separating the remnants of the original walled city and its northern and southern extensions from the nucleus of the new city. The area east of that divider remained for the most part on the older pattern, replete with neglected mosques and monuments and crumbling buildings, but also with major streets and out-pockets (notably the *qasaba* and the fifteenth-century Khan al-Khalili) still thriving as commercial centres, albeit more geared towards tourists.

Current efforts,[9] including those being assisted by the Aga Khan Foundation described in this publication, have built on the work of their non-Islamic predecessors, but with a real difference. More sensitive to the needs of living inhabitants, they have been trying to preserve not only the monuments and street patterns, but to upgrade housing while preserving much of the area's economic base in labour-intensive handicrafts. The Egyptian government, particularly the Ministry of Tourism, has been both supportive of these efforts and simultaneously pressing in an opposite direction as it seeks to enhance the exotic appeal of the areas in question.

Today, the historic city, while containing the largest remaining remnants of any Middle Eastern medieval-styled city, is dwarfed by the gigantic urban agglomeration that now surrounds it on all sides. The population has declined, not only because residences have crumbled from age, but also because they are being destroyed by natural events (the recent earthquake) and the works of man (new highways and tunnels, new colonies of informal settlements, the clearance of parts of the Cities of the Dead, such as al-Darrasah). Time is of the essence. Increased commitments to preserving not only monuments, but also the 'living city', are needed. The world's heritage embodied in this Islamic 'medieval city' is too precious to squander.

This chapter draws heavily on Janet Abu-Lughod, *Cairo: 1001 Years of the City Victorious*, Princeton University Press, Princeton 1971, from which the original maps have been taken. The author retains the copyrights to the original cartographic materials, which may not be reproduced without the prior written permission of the author.

[1] Although some have suggested that the plan was based on that of Mahdiyya, it seems to me that it was modelled more generally on Roman-origin cities in the North African region, for example, Tunis, Tunisia; Lepsis Magna, Libya; Timgad, Algeria.

[2] It was common for the capital of a province and its main city to bear the same name, for example: Dimashq, the name for the province of Syria and also of its capital city, Damascus. In the same fashion, the name Misr came to stand for the province of Egypt and its main city.

[3] Syrian cities such as Aleppo, with their strong citadels, were undoubtedly the inspiration, but Cairo's Citadel was relatively unique because of its location on elevated terrain and its separation from the centres of population.

[4] This effectively closed off the central trade route between Europe and Asia, forcing Italian merchants to deal with Egypt in pursuit of the increasingly profitable spice trade.

[5] See Janet Abu-Lughod, *Before European Hegemony: The World System AD 1250-1350*, Oxford University Press, New York 1989.

[6] European lenders were eager to provide loans to fund his ambitious schemes for modernising Egypt, but the main cause of the fiscal crisis was the expense of constructing the Suez Canal, opened with lavish ceremonies in 1869. When the Egyptian government was unable to repay the loans called in by European bankers, Ismail was forced to sell the country's shares in the Canal to Great Britain, which opened the door to colonial rule in 1881 as part of the 'grand empire'.

[7] See Janet Abu-Lughod, "Tale of Two Cities: The Origins of Modern Cairo", in *Comparative Studies in Society and History*, July 1965, pp. 429-457.

[8] The author was privileged to know Professor Cresswell a little (he was a diffident man) when we were both affiliated with the American University in Cairo. I have enormous respect for his scholarly devotion and erudition, and am eternally grateful for rare access to his library, his advice, and his offhand ability to answer the most obscure questions I could pose about Cairo's development.

[9] See the proposals, for example, of the joint study project by the United Nations Development Programme and the Egyptian Supreme Council for Antiquities, *Rehabilitation of Historic Cairo Final Report*, Technical Cooperation Office, Cairo December 1997.

Cairo's Urban Growth and Its Impact on the Historic City

JIM ANTONIOU

Cairo's clamour is partly attributed to the exuberance of its citizens, but mainly to rapid growth, leading to overcrowding and acute congestion. Over the last fifty years, Cairo has grown alarmingly, from a city of two million inhabitants to today's Greater Cairo agglomeration with a population of more than sixteen million. How has this explosive growth taken place in such a relatively short period of time in the capital's long history and what impact has this had on the historic city?

THE MAKING OF GREATER CAIRO

As defined in 1982 by the General Organisation for Physical Planning, the Greater Cairo Region is located within the jurisdiction of three Governorates, namely Cairo to the east of the River Nile, Giza to the west and Qalioubia to the north. Each Governorate is now administered by its own local government and is headed by an appointed Governor. The area allocated is vast and includes all of Cairo Governorate and most of the extensive Giza and Qalioubia Governorates. The latter two include rural areas and small towns, with little relation to the extent of Greater Cairo. Thus, the actual built-up area covers some three hundred square kilometres and is the fifteenth largest metropolis in the world.

At the beginning of the Second World War, Cairo was contained within its traditional core, consisting of the historic area and its expansion of the European developments on the west of the old city (that is, today's downtown area). Expansion also took place along two axes: Rod al Farag and Shubra to the north and Abbasiyya, Ain Shams and Heliopolis towards the north-east. Maadi and Helwan to the south were then small isolated settlements. Similarly, there were few developments across the River Nile, with growth restricted to the traditional villages of Giza to the south-west, and Dokki and Aguza to the west.

At the end of the war, as a result of free spending by the allied forces, Cairo's economy enjoyed a boom period. Basic infrastructure was by then in place, including roads and bridges, water and sanitation systems and power grids. The city was thus ready to begin expanding on a scale never before experienced in its history.

Fig. 5. Khayrbek Mosque seen from the eastern city wall, with the minaret under repair.

By 1947, migration to Cairo had been heavy and with the city's population expanding at an annual rate of four percent, the result was acute overcrowding in the existing housing stock. Yet, until that time, Cairo did not have an independent local administration; nor was there a planning framework with a guiding master plan. Various central ministries and utility concessions controlled urban affairs issues until the Municipality of Cairo was created in 1947. Later, in 1960-1961, the Municipality was transformed into the Housing and Utilities Directorate of the Governorate of Cairo.

Between 1947 and 1967, Cairo grew rapidly, mainly on private agricultural land. Public housing construction began in the early 1950s, carrying substantial direct subsidies. After the 1952 Revolution, new laws reduced rents on new, as well as existing, housing units. Large numbers of Cairo's residential units (some fifty-two percent) still remain under rent control at extremely low rates. In particular, many of the dwellings in the historic city are subject to rent controls, leading to a lack of care and maintenance.

In 1956, a master plan was prepared for Cairo, emphasising the need for expansion into the east and west desert flanks. Nasr City, an ambitious desert fringe project to the east was launched by the Government in 1958, followed by further urban expansions in Heliopolis, Ain Shams and Maadi.

By 1960, the city had grown to 3.4 million people (with Greater Cairo having a population of 4.5 million). The main axis of growth continued towards the north, where the wide Delta plain was suitable for urban use. Expansion also took place in new industrial areas such as Shubra El Kheima to the north and by way of public housing projects on agricultural land. Urbanisation also took place on the west bank of the Nile, with notable additions to Maadi and Helwan in the south.

Fig. 6. The Darb al-Ahmar sports club seen from the eastern city wall, with Aqsunqur, or the Blue, Mosque in the background.

The 1967 war with Israel and subsequent events had the crucial effect of freezing formal types of development in the capital by the Government. However, although urban plans were shelved, the demographic growth of Cairo continued unabated, with the informal sector gaining momentum. Small private land owners, independent contractors and would-be homeowners contrived to circumvent building and zoning regulations. The informal sector also included squatters on Government land in the desert. Eventually, due to the country's chronic housing shortage, this essentially illegal sector became so large that the Government turned a blind eye to much of its activity.

By the beginning of 1974, Egypt's economic condition changed dramatically for the better. The oil price rise provided opportunities for Egyptians to work in new wealthy countries in the Middle East, including Saudi Arabia, Iraq and Libya. Expatriate earnings created an unprecedented cash-based economy, allowing Egyptians at all levels of society to benefit, including blue-collar workers and their families and other groups who were attracted to live in informal areas. Over the next few years, an overwhelming eighty percent of additions to Cairo's housing stock were illegal. The Government was forced to take notice and a series of decrees also made it illegal to build on agricultural land and discouraged encroachment on State, mainly desert, land. Nevertheless, these interventions had little effect in controlling the informal growth of development.

In 1977, the New Town policy was launched and came to dominate both Egypt's urban development discourse and its budgetary allocations. With this policy, the Government hoped to reduce

Fig. 7. Aslam Mosque, an important community node in al-Darb al-Ahmar, was once at the forecourt of one of the city gates on the eastern wall.

overcrowding and improve the housing problem in Cairo and other urban centres, while at the same time protect agricultural land. Nevertheless, infrastructure costs for new towns were substantially higher than in Cairo. Similarly, the cost of living in new town housing was more than the typical household income in the capital and certainly much more costly than living on the periphery of the city. Consequently, the industrial blue-collar workers for whom these new towns were essentially intended found that such housing was too expensive for their needs. Ironically, new apartments are plentiful on the capital's market. However, prices are beyond the means of the average middle-income family and, hence, the mass of people with limited means.

By 1981, the housing deficit was officially estimated at 1.6 million dwellings, corresponding to the needs of more than a third of the city's population.[1] The lower income groups, being in fact outside the housing market, resorted to informal housing construction, through self-help on land without services. Some fifty percent of all private housing at that time was constructed on this basis.

However, as a result of a reduction in remittance incomes from Egyptians abroad, the number of informal developments began to fall. Greater Cairo's annual growth rates fell from 3.1 percent (1961-1975) to 2.7 percent (1976-1986), followed by 1.9 percent (1986-1996). Even so, by 1996, a total of over seven million inhabitants was estimated as residing in informal areas within Greater Cairo, representing sixty-two percent of the total population, corresponding to almost fifty-three percent of the total build up of residential land.[2] Over the last ten years, an area of thirty-seven square kilometres of agricultural land is taken annually for informal housing.[3] Industry is also moving away from the centre to the fringes of Cairo.

The main extent of informal settlements has occurred in the west and north parts of Greater Cairo (that is, Giza and Qalioubia Governorates respectively, amounting to a total of eighty-one percent) and less in the south-west, in Cairo Governorate where urban development is relatively stable (accommodating the remaining nineteen percent). These informal areas also suffer from a chronic lack of basic public services, including infrastructure and community facilities and also inadequate ac-

Fig. 8. Al-Darb al-Ahmar Street leading from the southern city gate, Bab Zuwayla, to the Citadel.

cessibility.[4] Moreover, due to the accommodation crisis, the decision on where to live for most families is one which is made once in a lifetime, making housing mobility marginal in Cairo.

THE METROPOLITAN AREA

A series of updated master plans were prepared over the last twenty years as part of an effort to address the capital's rapid growth through physical planning and urban management. The recurring themes of these plans have been the supply of housing, either through upgrading or new construction; the improvement of the traffic and transportation network; and the development of the socio-economic factors affecting employment and poverty.

Tramlines between the centre and the expanding suburbs first increased the extent of the city along transit routes. With the increase of vehicular traffic in the last three decades, the metropolitan area more than trebled. Over the last twenty years, more than one thousand kilometres of new roads have been constructed in Greater Cairo, with ninety percent in desert areas. As Cairo extended into the desert, reliance on flexible transport became essential. Today, twenty-five thousand mini-buses carry 1.2 million people every day, while private vehicles account for only thirteen percent of all daily trips. Cairo now relies for access on new thoroughfares, flyovers and the new Ring Road, the 100-kilometre-long perimeter of the city, thus changing the pattern of urbanisation in the desert.

Further improvements were initiated in 1990, with the Economic Reforms and Structural Adjustment Programme, aiming towards a rapid rate of self-sustaining growth. The Programme demanded critical structural reforms to the public sector, including the delivery of public utilities, as well as an appropriate urban management environment. To that end, the 'Homogeneous Sector' (HS) concept was conceived with the objective of organising Greater Cairo into smaller self-sufficient units, while encouraging decentralisation by creating within these units employment, transportation links and public or private centres.[5] However, rehabilitation plans and objectives for the various sectors did not reach an implementation stage.

Fig. 9. Khayrbek Mausoleum and Mosque seen from al-Darb al-Ahmar Street, before restoration of the minaret.

Within the metropolis, HS1 covers an area of 6.5 kilometres across and 9.5 kilometres from north to south and contains 1.5 million people. Its boundaries are within the railway line to Upper Egypt to the north and the Ring Road to the south, with the River Nile to the west and the Moqattam Hills to the east. This central area provides employment for a major part of Greater Cairo and most of the decision-making establishments in the country (government departments, company headquarters, business and trade activities, tourism and commerce). In addition, this sector contains the significant components of historic Cairo that make up the urban heritage. Transportation routes serve this sector along the Corniche Road and Qasr El Aini on the north to south direction, Port Said Street to the west and north-west and the Salah Salem Street and the Autostrade to the south and east. On an east to west axis, there are the streets of al-Azhar (and the new tunnel route), Salah Salem and the Ring Road. The Metro runs close to the Nile and continues in a north-east direction.

HISTORIC CAIRO

The historic components, which still survive to this day, consist of uniquely separate areas. This heritage includes to the south, Old Cairo, containing the city's pre-Islamic origins and al-Fustat, now an archaeological area and mainly uninhabited since its destruction in AD 1168. In addition, there is the Citadel, the largest and best-preserved fortification in the Middle East, and the south and north-east cemeteries, which contain significant architecture to Islam. In addition, the historic city has the largest concentration of Islamic monuments in the world. All these districts have been on the UNESCO International Heritage List since 1979. Alas, Bulaq to the north, once the commercial port for the Ottomans, with many important buildings of that time still standing, was inadvertently omitted from the List. Moreover, the areas listed by UNESCO are neither with demarcated boundaries, nor specific context.

Fig. 10. The Hawd of Sultan Qaytbay.

Each one of these areas has its own concentration of monuments. Old Cairo, located towards the south part of HS1, refers to the enclosure of the Roman fort. It covers an area of thirty-three hectares and today less than one hundred people live there. The numerous buildings and structures located on this site are from a variety of historic periods and include Roman remains, a synagogue and many important Coptic and Greek Orthodox churches, as well as the Coptic museum.

Today, al-Fustat covers an area of almost one hundred hectares and is considered by the Supreme Council of Antiquities (SCA) as an important archaeological site, representing the first Islamic city in Africa. It contains crucial information relating to living conditions during the early development of the city. Others, however, see it as a valuable piece of real estate in a city where demand for land is acute, particularly due to its vicinity to the capital's centre. Almost the whole site is surrounded by land already built on, or land prepared for building. Consequently, there is constant pressure to build in this area, which so far has been resisted.

The Citadel, with its location being a major focus to any overall design of the historic components, covers an area of about twenty-three hectares and dominates the historic city, while offering magnificent views as far as the Pyramids at Giza. Moreover, the Citadel, together with the Moqattam Hills, overlooks the city. Within the famous walls, there are several important listed buildings, making the Citadel a major tourist attraction.

The cemeteries are divided into two major areas. The south cemetery is to the east of al-Fustat and the north cemetery is to the north-east of the historic city. There has always been a tradition (for religious and scholastic reasons) of the living residing among the dead. Now, due to acute population pressures, more than two hundred thousand people are said to live and work around the tombs. Demographic pressures and a lack of housing have resulted in considerable building activity close to the monuments. Here, multi-storey constructions have taken place, with high densities, narrow streets, commercial and industrial activities, but with inadequate services.

Bulaq is at a distance of 1.5 kilometres north of the historic city, where today some forty thousand people live and are employed in workshops (often remnants of historic buildings associated with the port), now dealing with iron works and the motor trade. Here, too, there is considerable pressure for commercial redevelopment, due to the area's proximity to the Corniche Road, creating the most dramatic contrast between old and new architecture.

THE HISTORIC CITY

The historic city is at the heart of the metropolitan area and adjacent to the downtown business district. It has less than one percent of the sector's area (3.87 square kilometres) and twenty percent of its population (some 310,500 people). It is located within five *qisms* (security jurisdictions), namely, Bab al Sharia, Gamaliyya, al-Darb al-Ahmar, Khalifa and Sayyeda Zeinab. The city has experienced demographic changes during the last few decades (for example, from 433,000 in 1966 to 310,500 in 1996 and still declining). These shifts have been due to an initial population growth as a result of agricultural reforms in Egypt, followed by a significant decline due to a rapid housing expansion, both formal and informal.

Fig. 11. Outside the Zuwayla Gate, looking towards the street of the covered Tent Makers' bazaar.

Moreover, public management is fragmented, which implies that any unified and equitable administrative decision has to be taken at the Cairo Governorate level. Thus, public decision-making at the district level may be in conflict with the physical and socio-economic homogeneity of the historic city. Administrative reform, uniting the historic city in one municipal jurisdiction is therefore lacking.

Today, the historic city is poorly grafted into the downtown central area of Cairo and its thoroughfares. Major routes such as al-Azhar Street still divide the historic core into two parts and the unsightly overpass continues to facilitate east-west connections to and from central Cairo (in spite of a new 2.6-kilometre-long tunnel crossing in the same direction). The historic city's commercial and economic activities are not integrated and the urban character it offers is not qualitatively compatible with central Cairo's needs.

There is a long-term decline in the appearance of the historic city. Living conditions continue to deteriorate, with small-scale manufacturing industries, including metal welding, aluminium and copper smelting, timber yards, marble cutting and vehicle repair yards. These intrusions create air, noise and visual pollution, seriously affecting the quality of life and having a negative impact on the many monuments. Solid waste and debris are widespread on the streets, on various plots and around the ruins.

The majority of the entrepreneurs in the historic city are not environmentally orientated and their interests are limited to the use of the ground floor of buildings. Absentee landlords, as a result of rent control rules, do not maintain their houses, which are occupied by employees. In turn, residents, due to their low income and poor status, are more concerned with affordable housing and employment opportunities and less with the deterioration of their residential environment. The city contains some thirty thousand squatters (almost ten percent of the population), without security of tenure, living in shacks, on vacant plots and ruined buildings.[6]

The historic city also contains 313 listed monuments, with 274 such buildings owned by the Ministry of Waqf (MoW), responsible for religious trusts. Thus, although the SCA is obliged to restore the monuments, the MoW owns the land as well as the monuments, most of which are rented out to individuals. In addition, the Governor of Cairo has issued Decree No. 257 (1980), which requires fifty metres of empty space around each monument, thus exposing façades not meant to be exposed while allowing for the deterioration of the surrounding buildings. The overall impact of this Decree, if implemented, is likely to transform the unique urban qualities of the historic city into an archaeological park.

The city has attracted numerous rehabilitation, preservation and restoration studies, proposals and projects, through Governmental, bilateral, and multilateral efforts. Their success has been mainly limited to the restoration of individual monuments by various foreign missions and the SCA. Some forty-seven Government sponsored restoration projects are currently underway as part of a programme to restore 157 monuments over the next eight years, mainly executed by four large contractors. This sudden burst of restoration activity has left many buildings embraced in scaffolding. A limiting factor is that those responsible for the well-being of the monuments are reluctant to adopt the concept of sympathetic reuse and with limited funds and expertise there is little preventive maintenance. As a result, buildings are restored by a variety of sponsors but remain locked and empty.

Meanwhile, comprehensive attempts at area rehabilitation, both as master plans and action plans, with the involvement of the community have not had any implementation success to date. Moreover, a legally defined geographic area does not exist as a designated conservation and active zone on to which the Government and other agencies can focus.

At present, a major effort is being undertaken by the Aga Khan Trust for Culture to provide a model for community development in the Darb al-Ahmar area of the city. Here, the embodiment of community aspirations is combined with rehabilitation and restoration, with links to the adjoining Ayyubid wall and the new Azhar Park.[7]

Thus, the historic city remains the crumbling core of the largest city in Africa. Yet, literally hundreds of impressive monuments still remain standing along the thoroughfares, although many have already been lost. Here, liveliness, charm and a rich variety of visual delights are available to the visitor. With its medieval flavour, the historic city remains a place where local people take part as characters in a never-ending novel by Egypt's famous novelist, Naguib Mahfouz. Here are found noisy children from a nearby school, black-clad old women shuffling to and fro, men in rumpled *galabiyyas* making exaggerated gestures and pretty girls smiling shyly down from broken *mashrabiyya* windows.[8] Sadly, in Europe's historic cities, similar scenes have long since been 'restored' through gentrified façades and smart boutiques. But a walk through Cairo's medieval core can be the same exhilarating experience it must have been several centuries ago.

[1]Peter Wang, *Housing*, Middle East Construction Report on Egypt, November 1981.
[2]David Sims, *Residential Informality in Greater Cairo*, Egyptian Centre for Economic Studies, Cairo 2000.
[3]*Cairo Almanac, The Encyclopaedia of Modern Egypt*, 2003.
[4]Eric Denis and Marion Sejourne, *Information System for Informal Settlements: Predicting Growth through Comparing Satellite Imagery*, Observatorie Urbain du Caire Contemporain in the Centre de Recherche et de Documentation Economique, Juridique et Social, Cairo 2002.

[5]GOPP/IAURIF, *Implementation of the Homogeneous Sector Concept*, Final Report, Cairo 1988.
[6]United Nations Development Programme/Supreme Council of Antiquities, *Rehabilitation of Historic Cairo*, Technical Cooperation Office, Cairo 1997.
[7]Aga Khan Trust for Culture, *Darb al-Ahmar Project, Urban Rehabilitation and Community Development in Historic Cairo*, AKCS-E 2001.
[8]Jim Antoniou, *Historic Cairo: A Walk Through the Islamic City*, The American University in Cairo Press, Cairo 1998.

A Brief History of Green Spaces in Cairo

NASSER RABBAT

After the overwhelming first sight of the magnificent pyramids, the next impression a first-time visitor to Cairo receives when coming in by plane is of an ochre sea spreading below him/her on both sides of the Nile, with very small dots of darker colours that do little to alleviate the dull monotony of the landscape. This is modern Cairo, sprawling across miles and miles of former agricultural and desert land and made up of densely laid out buff-coloured buildings with few green spaces between them. The only green is along the banks of the river and on the island of Gazira. These unalleviated expanses of tan are perplexing, to say the least, for a city lying at the apex of the bountiful Nile, one of the mightiest rivers in the world and the greening agent of its own valley. It is also misleading, insofar as it convinces urban and landscape students that Cairo has always been a toneless city with no gardens or parks, when historical records unmistakably suggest otherwise.

In fact, the city of al-Qahira (Cairo) was originally founded around a *bustan*, which, in modern terminology, is the equivalent of a park. When the Fatimid army arrived in 969, its general Jawhar al-Siqilli was charged by his master, Caliph al-Muizz li-Din Allah who remained back in Ifriqiyya, to establish a new royal city. The general chose an area almost two miles north of the then capital of al-Fustat around the Bustan al-Kafuri and laid out the royal enclave that came to be known as al-Qahira. The Bustan al-Kafuri was a sizeable *jardin de plaisance* planned by Kafur al-Ikhshidi, the slave ruler of Egypt between 949 and 968, immediately before the Fatimid invasion, who was unjustly defamed by al-Mutannabi, the most eloquent master of Arabic poetry. This original siting of al-Qahira is rarely remembered, especially since the overcrowded area of al-Muski at the heart of historic Cairo,

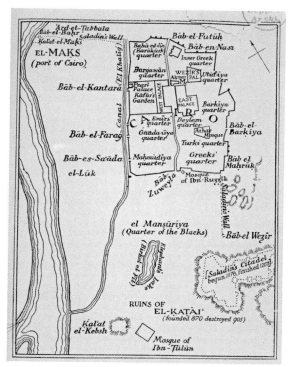

Fig. 12. Plan of Fatimid Cairo with the Bustan al-Kafuri, after Paul Ravaisse.

43

where the *bustan* once stood, today betrays no hint of its verdant past (fig. 12). The Bustan al-Kafuri was soon incorporated into the Fatimid Western Palace, built by Caliph al-Aziz (975-996), where it more or less maintained its function as a *jardin de plaisance*, this time in a genuine royal context. After the fall of the Fatimids in 1176, the palace enclosure was parcelled out and built over by the Ayyubids. In the next century and a half, at least four major charitable complexes (of the sultans al-Kamil, Qalawun, his son al-Nasir Muhammad, and Barquq) and two amirial palaces (those of Baysari and Salar), in addition to a number of *hammams* and *khans* (urban caravanserais), occupied the largest part of what used to be the Western Fatimid Palace and its gardens. The only vestiges that remained of the palace are found today in the ruined *iwans* (open-ended, vaulted spaces) and courtyard of the once prosperous Bimaristan of Qalawun, or hospital, built in 1284,

Fig. 13. *Shadirwan* from the Fatimid Western Palace, now in the Bimaristan of Qalawun.

whose coffered wooden ceiling with painted animals and floral motifs, and marble *shadirwan* (wall fountain) still stand in what is believed to be original Fatimid *iwans* (fig. 13). Of the Bustan al-Kafuri nothing remains.

But the Bustan al-Kafuri was not the only famous *bustan* in the history of medieval Cairo. The proximity of the Nile river allowed the powerful and wealthy during the Fatimid, Ayyubid, and Mamluk periods to exploit its eastern bank — and to a lesser extent its western one — and the borders of the several seasonal ponds that formed after its annual flood in the low land west of the city, to establish huge *basatin* for their recreation. Most famed are the Basatin of Sayf al-Islam (a brother of Salah al-Din al-Ayyubi) which lay to the west of where the two magnificent mosques of Sultan Hasan and al-Rifa'i stand today and extended towards the no longer extant Birkat al-Fil (Pond of the Elephant). The Basatin of Sayf al-Islam were called the gardens of Abbas in Fatimid times and were appropriated by Salah al-Din's family along with most other Fatimid properties. Other famous *basatin* existed on Rawda Island in the middle of the Nile facing al-Fustat which developed in the early Mamluk period on the ruins of a short-lived late Ayyubid citadel. The Rawda citadel was first built by the last Ayyubid sultan of Egypt, al-Salih Najm al-Din Ayyub (1240-1249), as a place for him and his loyal troops to retreat from the more official Citadel of Cairo. The majority of structures inside it and along its walls, including the towers which overlooked the Nile, were either residential or pleasure structures. The sources mention belvederes (*manazir*; sing. *manzara*), porches (*maqa'id*; sing. *maq'ad*), and residential halls (*qa'at*; sing. *qa'a*) located along the two sides of the Citadel facing the river. Opposite the Citadel, and later on its site after its abandonment, many *basatin* were developed in the early Mamluk period. The memory of these *basatin* is preserved primarily in the *waqf* (endowment) documents of buildings that were erected on their sites and in the accounts of literati, who describe many festive settings in them with ceremonial, recreational, literary, or amorous aims. From these descriptions emerges an image of verdant gardens with both decorative and fruit trees and some light pavilions scattered across the landscape.

Another type of open space, the *maydan*, flourished in the medieval period, especially under the Ayyubids and the Mamluks. *Mayadin* became essential urban spaces in Cairo — there were eight of them at one time or another — as everywhere else in the Islamic world where Turkic horsemen ruled and established an equestrian military elite after the Seljuks rose to power in the eleventh century. Although they were all large, open, and covered with grass (*najil* in medieval terminology), the *mayadin* were not meant for the use of the masses. They were royal establishments for polo games and equestrian exercises (*furusiyya*), the backbone of the Mamluk

Fig. 14. View of the Qaramaydan today from the minaret of Sultan Hasan Mosque.

military organisation upon which the new regime depended. Sultans Salah al-Din al-Ayyubi (1176-1193), al-Kamil Muhammad (1218-1238), al-Zahir Baybars (1260-1276), al-Nasir Muhammad (1293-1341), and Qansuh (1501-1516) are the most famous builders of *mayadin* in the history of Cairo. The most important of these *mayadin*, and the only one that still exists today, is the *maydan* under the Citadel. Planned along with the Citadel itself by the Ayyubid sultan al-Kamil Muhammad for military parades and training, the *maydan* sits almost on the same site as the parade ground built by Ibn Tulun around 876, more than three centuries earlier. To judge from the chroniclers' reports, it had at least three different and interchangeable names: the Maydan al-Qal'a (Citadel Maydan), the Qaramaydan (Turkish for Black Maydan), or the Maydan al-Akhdar (Green Maydan) (fig. 14). It was refurbished by many rulers after the end of the Ayyubid period, most notably by Baybars, al-Nasir Muhammad, and Qansuh al-Ghawri. Al-Nasir Muhammad took great care to ensure its usability all year round and to protect its grass from the scorching heat of Cairo in the summer. He had palm and fruit trees planted in it, presumably along the edges, and a number of wells dug and equipped with waterwheels (*sawaqi*; sing. *saqiya*) for its irrigation. He had it filled in with a special kind of rich black soil (called *al-ibliz*), whence perhaps the origin of

Fig. 15. The Sabil-Kuttab of Sultan Qaytbay, 1479.

the name of Black Maydan. This *maydan* was first illustrated at the beginning of the nineteenth century on the map in the *Description de l'Égypte* as an enclosed rectangle (approximately 220 x 100 metres) surrounded by stone walls on three sides and fed by at least one watercourse (*qastal*) that brought water from the well of Dar al-Baqar, opposite the Bustan of Sayf al-Islam.

The *basatin* and *mayadin*, however, were outside the city proper. They formed a sort of *cordon vert* in the space between the Nile and the boundaries of the city and around the Citadel (one exception was a *maydan* constructed by Baybars north of Cairo in the area of Hussayniyya). They were routinely the first victims of any urban expansion between the thirteenth and the end of the nineteenth century when the city was growing both towards the river and towards its southern satellite, Misr-Fustat. Except for the Qaramaydan, they had all long been gone when the urban expansion was redirected towards the desert to the north and east or across the Nile to the west in the twentieth century.

No large open green space existed in the urban core of medieval Cairo, and to some extent this was true of most cities of the central Islamic land between the eighth and nineteenth centuries. This is due in part to the arid climate prevalent in most Middle Eastern regions which made the maintenance and irrigation of a green space a very difficult and costly procedure. In medieval Cairo, which was situated three miles to the east of the River Nile, long aqueducts (*majari*; sing. *majra*) had to be constructed and wells had to be dug at various intervals to provide the Mamluks' *mayadin* with water. No sultan seems to have deemed it worth his patronage to spend money and effort on providing any open public space, and the people did not seem to have expected such an endowment, as they did religious or charitable institutions, and smaller civic services such as *katatib* (sing. *kuttab*, Koranic school) and *asbila* (sing. *sabil*, public drinking fountain) (fig. 15).

Another reason for this lack may lie in the conceptual distinction between private and public space in the traditional city, whereby entertainment and relaxation were kept strictly within the confines of the private domain and the public and communal spaces were devoted primarily to business interactions and worship. In practice, however, this distinction was very hard to enforce, to the chagrin of conservative commentators, all of whom noted with disapproval the scenes of debauchery that arose when people were allowed to gather in public spaces, such as *basatin* and *mayadin*, to celebrate holidays or to partake in royal ceremonies. People are reported to have indulged in all sorts of illicit activities from dancing and singing to drinking, to eating hashish, to frolicking, and sometimes even outright sex-

Fig. 16. The *majra* intake tower on the Nile riverbank built by Sultan Qansuh al-Ghawri in the early 1500s.

ual intercourse. This practice was especially abhorrent to non-Egyptian chroniclers such as Ibn al-Hajj, a fourteenth-century Moroccan jurist who lived for a while in Cairo, and was very critical of what he saw as lax morals on the part of the Egyptian people, *ulama*, and government.

MEDIEVAL SETTINGS AND FORMS

We know very little about the layout of medieval *basatin* and much less about their patterns of maintenance and use. Irrigation and drainage were among the most important problems facing their designers, and they came up with some ingenious solutions, including aqueducts, subterranean drainage canals, water tanks and *sawaqi*. The remains of the aqueduct of Ibn Tulun in the *basatin* area east of Cairo, the entire waterworks system of wells, aqueducts, and *sawaqi* around the Citadel of the Mountain and the *maydan* of Salah al-Din (formerly al-Rumayla, that is Qaramaydan), and the huge water intake tower of Sultan Qansuh al-Ghawri on the Nile Corniche today, are only the most impressive remnants of the waterways that criss-crossed medieval Cairo and fed its multiple *mayadin* and *basatin*, mansions, *asbila* and public buildings (fig. 16).

Nor are we better informed about the various functions of *basatin* and their double character as both private gardens and public parks depending on the occasion. We have vague descriptions of regular communal outings on festive days, in which rich and poor took part as spectators and sometimes actors. People lined up along the waterways or rented spaces in the tree-shaded *basatin* to observe the activities and celebrations, and take advantage of the occasion to indulge in normally frowned-upon activities, such as dancing and singing, and other diversions, which sometimes bordered on the religiously prohibited. Most notable are the festivals that preserved the memory of pre-Islamic ceremonies, such as the *nawruz* (the Persian New Year and a celebration of spring), the *kasr al-khalij* (the opening of the Nile Canal to mark the peak of the yearly flood, the life-giver to Egypt), and the *'Id al-Ghitas* (perhaps an ancient rite of the Nile modified by Christian overtones). They were given an Islamic cachet of sorts, and were occasionally sponsored by the state, especially in times of plenty.

Fig. 17. An early Mamluk representation of a *manzara* in mosaic at the Umayyad Mosque in Damascus.

On other, less formal and more private outings, rich patrons would organise *majalis* (sing. *majlis*) in their *basatin* for poets, musicians, and literati, who would gather to drink, sing and recite poetry, and indulge in *adab* debates. These *majalis* were not seen as debauched entertainment. Many great learned men enthusiastically took part in them, such as 'Imad al-Din al-Katib al-Isfahani, Salah al-Din's secretary and a trained jurist himself who left us vivid descriptions of the lively *majalis* he attended. Some of these *majalis* took place in the open air, others in tents, and still others in special structures which seem to have been adapted for the particular setting of these *basatin*. Most important among these elements were the *manzara* and the *maq'ad*, both of which first appeared as accoutrements of *basatin* and both were later to inform the development of residential architecture in Egypt.

The word *manzara* is derived from the verb *nazara*, "to look, to watch", which refers to the structure's basic function as a place from where one looks out, perhaps the equivalent of a belvedere. In Cairene *basatin*, a *manzara* appears to have been primarily a pavilion with numerous openings, small and large. But because of their presumably lightweight construction material such as wood and reed, all *manazir* mentioned in the sources have disappeared. The only clues we have of their forms are occasional representations in contemporary Mamluk miniature paintings, such as the fifteenth-century illustrated manuscripts of *Kalila wa Dimna*, the *Maqamat* of al-Hariri, and the *Iskandarnama*, or those rare mosaic representations dating from the early Mamluk period in the Citadel of Cairo, in the funerary dome of al-Zahir Baybars in Damascus, and in the scenes repaired under Baybars and Qalawun at the Umayyad mosque in Damascus (fig. 17).

The word *maq'ad* means "a place to sit" and is usually translated as loggia, but in the medieval Cairene context it appears to have denoted an upper floor or simply a raised rectangular loggia with an arcaded opening overlooking a courtyard, garden, or some other setting. If we can believe the sources, *manazir* and *maqa'id* dotted the medieval *basatin*'s waterfronts in Rawda Island and elsewhere, but it is very difficult from the available information to imagine whether they stood alone or in some prescribed formation and what, if any, kind of structures they were attached to. Moreover, the exact architectural difference between *manazir* and *maqa'id* is difficult to ascertain although they were to become very distinct in later times when they both migrated to urban residential architecture and became integral components of the Cairene courtyard house. This process seems to have started in the late fourteenth century

Fig. 18. A *mashrabiyya* in the Zahabi House in Cairo, c. 1634.

around the time when the rule passed from the Qalawunids to the Circassian Burjis under Sultan Barquq (1382-1400). Huge suburban *basatin* were slowly being replaced by smaller urban plots in the Mamluk Burji (1382-1517) and later in the Ottoman period (1517-1805). This development, no doubt related to the shrinking base of wealth for the ruling amirs with the change of the Mamluk power structure, could also have been affected by the expansion of the city towards the ponds and the Nile bank. It resulted in the interiorisation and urbanisation of the *bustan*. This in turn restored the courtyard to its former central position, a position that it had lost during the Ayyubid and early Mamluk periods when huge urban mansions, such as the palaces of Amir Alin Aq (1293), Amir Bashtak (1334-1339), and Amir Qawsun (1337) had only small, service-oriented courtyards. Their main reception halls generally turned their backs on the courtyard and looked towards the outside street or *birka* (pond) depending on their location. The situation was reversed in Burji and Ottoman residences. The major reception halls and rooms were arranged around, and opened onto, the large, planted courtyard with their very few openings to the outside heavily shielded by *mashrabiyya* (fig. 18). The new arrangement became clear from as early as the middle of the fifteenth century as shown in the plans of the few remaining palaces from the time of al-Ashraf Qaytbay (1468-1496) and Qansuh al-Ghawri (1501-1516), especially the palace of al-Razzaz (major phase of building in the late fifteenth century).

Not surprisingly, the two architectural elements, the *manzara* and *maq'ad*, made a forceful appearance in Burji urban palaces. They migrated from open-air settings to the courtyard house and became the common reception spaces in the Ottoman palaces, probably as a consequence of the transposition of the *bustan* to the residence, and its reduction to an urban garden. From the fifteenth to the nineteenth century every mid-sized Cairene house boasted a *maq'ad* with at least two arches, and larger houses sometimes had up to five arches as in the case of the *maq'ad* of Amir Mamay (1490)

Fig. 19. The *maq'ad* of the Suheimi House in Cairo, *c.* 1796.

Fig. 20. The interior of the *manzara* of the Musafirkhana in Cairo, between 1779-1888.

(fig. 19). The *manzara* adaptation to the new urban setting is less clear, since a *manzara* is architecturally very similar to a common *qaʿa*, with its raised *iwans* and central *durqaʿa*. In the Ottoman period, it appears that the term *manzara* was used exclusively to designate a first-floor *qaʿa* which opens onto a courtyard and is used solely for receiving male guests. The most famous of these *manazir* can be found in the Ottoman mansions of the seventeenth to the nineteenth centuries such as the Suheimi House, the Zahabi House, the al-Harawi House, and in the ill-fated Mus-

Fig. 21. View of the *majlis* in the Shubra Palace, designed by Pascal Coste, 1820.

afirkhana which unfortunately burned down a few years ago. They were characterised by shallow fountains with single-stream jets, usually located in the middle of their central *durqaʿas* (fig. 20).

Gardens began to be laid out in the otherwise functional courtyard that always existed in Cairene palaces and residences beginning with the ninth-century Fustat houses. They contained flowers and medicinal herbs, evergreen trees, and palm trees and vines. Their flowerbeds were sunk both for aesthetic and irrigation purposes. (A good example is in the Zahabi House, begun in 1634). The palace was given an introverted composition centring on its verdant courtyard. This could hardly have been seen from the street, and the inevitable impression many pre-modern visitors had was that Cairo was an overbuilt city that lacked green, open spaces.

NINETEENTH-CENTURY DEVELOPMENTS

The situation was partly and inconclusively improved by the new *basatin* established in the nineteenth century by Muhammad Ali, his sons, sons-in-law, and grandsons (primarily Tusun, Ibrahim, Said, and Ismail) following the draining of the seasonal ponds to the south and west of the city and the stabilisation of the riverbanks on both sides. These royal *basatin*, endowed with palaces and used both as *jardins de plaisance* and as orchards, plantations, and nurseries, were the sites of the first true westernising gestures in residential Cairene architecture (most noteworthy among them are the palaces of Shubra and Gazira; fig. 21). The first among them appear to have been the two no-longer-extant palaces, Qasr al-Rawda and al-Qasr al ʿAli (1835), that Ibrahim Pasha, Muhammad Ali's son and successor, built on land granted him by his father on Rawda Island and in Bustan al-Khashshab, on the eastern bank of the Nile. They followed on the heels of very timid attempts that appeared in Alexandria where Muhammad Ali Pasha built his first residences *à la grecque* and in the Citadel of Cairo where he built his more official Jawhara Palace and Harim Palace, completed between 1814 and 1827.

Fig. 22. Cast iron arcades remaining from the Gazira Palace in today's Marriot Hotel.

The royal *basatin* cordoned off the urban agglomeration from the west and south and spread to the areas formerly occupied by the seasonal ponds of Azbakiyya, al-Fil, al-Ratli, and Qasim-Bey, the newly formed island of Gazira, and the west bank of the Nile at Giza and Imbaba. No developments were initiated in the east where the Mamluk North Cemetery (al-Qarafa al-Kubra) and the slopes of the rocky Moqattam Hills hindered construction and where water was scarce and hard to procure. They each had a palace or a pavilion, and sometimes more than one, built by a member of the royal family.

With very few exceptions, these *basatin* did not last long. The state bankruptcy after the extravagant reigns of Said (1854-1863), and especially Ismail (1863-1879) and mounting urban pressure from the phenomenally growing capital city at the turn of the twentieth century forced their apportionment for development. They ultimately formed the framework upon which much of modern Cairo was developed including the posh quarters of Tahrir, Munira, Manial, Zamalek and Aguza. Consequently, only truncated remnants of what must have been huge parks are left in the Azbakiyya Garden; in the Maydan al-Tahrir area where the two palaces of Dubara and Ismailiyya once stood; in Garden City, which once formed part of Ibrahim Pasha's plantation and High Palace (al-Qasr al 'Ali); in the Gazira Club, Marriot Hotel, and the Fish Garden, all pieces of a much larger park attached to the Gazira Palace that Ismail completed in 1868 in time to house the Empress Eugenie whom he invited to attend the inauguration of the Suez Canal; and in the Orman Gardens (today the Giza Zoo) and the nearby University of Cairo, both standing on the grounds of the Gazira Palace, also built by Ismail (fig. 22).

In recent decades the rapid and chaotic growth of the city has accelerated the destruction of even the very small green spots left from the earlier days around some of the old villas in the same quarters that once formed parts of larger parks. Many of the left-over palatial gardens and the verdant promenades along the river banks have been given away to exclusive luxury hotels and expensive clubs and restaurants after the economic opening-up (*infitah*) of the 1980s and 1990s. Even the small patches of agricultural land on the left bank of the Nile which were forgotten amid urban incursions in the Haram (Pyramid) and al-Muhandisin areas have disappeared in the last few years under the pressures of an ever-swelling population with its unrelenting demands for more housing, more roads, and more shopping malls.

In conclusion, what are we to make of this brief history of green spaces in Cairo? Clearly, there is no particular model to be recovered as far as the layout of *basatin* or *mayadin* is concerned. The khedivial *basatin* were imported wholesale from Europe with varying degrees of success in adaptation to the local environment. (One particularly successful import were the Banyan trees brought from Bengal to line the roads circling the Gazira [present-day Zamalek] when it was made into the park for Ismail's palace). These *basatin* also depended on a system of patronage that is impossible to replicate today. But these traditional *basatin* and khedivial parks offer many architectural and horticultural elements that can be reintroduced, not out of nostalgia alone but also because they function well within the prevailing environmental and social constraints of Egypt. Thus, *maqa'id* and *manazir* can form the basis of a typology of indigenous architectural elements of landscaping and viewing. Similarly, medieval irrigation tools and techniques and native plants could be incorporated in the design of parks both as claims to an 'authentic landscape' and as tried and proven good solutions for sensible use of water and soil, for shading and greening, and for decoration.

But the most important lesson to be learned from the historical record, in my opinion, is related more to a strategy for survival than to the actual design of new parks. *Basatin* and *mayadin*, and later on small villa gardens disappeared because they offered attractive sites for the development of much more profitable real estate. Speculators and contractors as well as state agencies responsible for housing saw in them obvious targets, already plotted and irrigated though neglected, disputed, and therefore easy and cheap to acquire. They were in a way the victims of their own success. Can we devise a design strategy — in addition to the much-needed legal and zoning devices — that would insure the survival of parks in the heart of the ever-growing metropolis? That is the real challenge facing the new generation of Cairenes.

FURTHER READING:

Janet Abu-Lughod, *Cairo: 1001 Years of the City Victorious*, Princeton University Press, Princeton 1971.

Doris Behrens-Abouseif, "Gardens in Islamic Egypt", in *Der Islam* 6, 1992, pp. 302-312.

Jean-Claude Garcin, "Toponymie et topographie urbaines médiévales à Fustat et au Caire", in *Journal of the Economic and Social History of the Orient* 27, 1984, pp. 113-155.

Laila Ibrahim, "Residential Architecture in Mamluk Cairo", in *Muqarnas* 2, 1984, pp. 47-59.

Alexandre Lézine, "Les salles nobles des palais Mamelouks", in *Annales Islamologiques* 10, 1972, pp. 149-205.

Edward William Lane, *Cairo Fifty Years Ago*, ed. Stanley Lane-Poole, John Murray, London 1896.

Nasser Rabbat, *The Citadel of Cairo: A New Interpretation of Royal Mamluk Architecture*, E. J. Brill, Leiden 1995.

André Raymond, *Le Caire*, Fayard, Paris 1993.

Caroline Williams, "Islamic Cairo: Endangered Legacy", in *Middle East Journal* 39, 3, 1985, pp. 231-246.

The History and Fate of al-Darb al-Ahmar

SEIF EL RASHIDI

> *What to think of this confused labyrinth, as large, perhaps, as Paris or Rome,*
> *of its palaces and its mosques that one can count by the thousand?*
> *Without a doubt, all of this had once been splendid and marvellous,*
> *but thirty generations have passed on; everywhere the stone crumbles and the wood rots.*
> *It appears that one is travelling in a dream in a city of the past…*
>
> Gérard de Nerval, *Journey to the Orient*, 1851

I n AD 969, following the Fatimid conquest of Egypt, a new urban settlement was founded specifically to house the Fatimid court and those related to it; originally called al-Mansuriyya, its name was later changed to al-Qahira — Cairo. Although designed as a walled royal precinct, Cairo was not totally inaccessible to the public. Thriving markets catered to the population at large, most of which lived to the south-west, in Misr-Fustat, an urban settlement located close to the Nile and developed following the Arab conquest of Egypt in the seventh century around the Roman fortress of Babylon. As an extended palatial complex, Cairo, although physically separate, was socially and politically part of the earlier settlement, which even then remained the nucleus of urban agglomeration in economic, administrative, and religious terms.

Accounts of the elaborate rituals and festivals of the Fatimid court stress the importance of sites outside the walled city, even in early times. This, as well as the existence of other earlier settlements to the north, such as Matariyya, meant that there was a populated zone stretching from Misr-Fustat all the way north of the city walls, comprising distinct areas that were nevertheless interconnected.

The area now known as al-Darb al-Ahmar is located just outside the southern walls of the Fatimid palace-city and had originally been cemetery grounds for its residents. In the eleventh century, a period of drought and famine led to the impoverishment of Misr-Fustat, and the exodus of most of its population to the area around Cairo. By then, the city had already expanded, and a reconsolidation of the city walls between 1087 and 1092, during a period of civil strife, involved the enlargement of the original walled precinct to incorporate these newly developed urban areas.

Fig. 23. Al-Muayyad Bimaristan (or Hospital), *c.* 1420.

55

Fig. 24. View of the Citadel, Cairo.

As the area lying immediately outside Bab Zuwayla, Cairo's main southern gateway, al-Darb al-Ahmar was one of the first zones of urban expansion. Thus, in 1160, the Fatimid vizier al-Salih Tala'i, fearing Frankish desecration of the shrine of the prophet's grandson al-Hussein in Ascalon, built a mosque outside the Zuwayla Gate in order to house al-Hussein's relics, indicating that al-Darb al-Ahmar was no longer a truly peripheral zone.

The rise of the Ayyubids in 1171, under Salah al-Din, marked the beginning of a radical change in the urban development of Cairo: Salah al-Din constructed a citadel on a rocky spur slightly south of the walled city. Intended from the onset as the sultan's residence, it was only to become the real seat of power in 1206 under Salah al-Din's nephew, al-Kamil, thereby stripping the original Fatimid settlement of its royal status. It was the construction of the Citadel, more than anything, that shaped the urban development of al-Darb al-Ahmar, as we know it today. The transfer of the seat of power outside the city walls created a clear stretch of urban development to the south, connecting the new seat of power to the old, and giving rise to al-Darb al-Ahmar (as the area in between Fatimid Cairo and the Ayyubid citadel).

One of the most striking features of the Fatimid city had been its *qasaba*, the main north-south thoroughfare, which formed an uninterrupted route between the city gates. The *qasaba*, lined with palaces and other caliphal buildings, was the site of elaborate royal processions, cornerstones of a

Fig. 25. The site of Azhar Park before construction began.

dynasty that had developed complex courtly etiquette. During the Ayyubid period, the *qasaba* was extended southwards to reach the Citadel, thus adding a new, equally prestigious stretch to the road whose buildings were to define elite Cairene society up until the mid-nineteenth century.

The construction of the Citadel also brought about a second, equally important urban development: the extension of the city walls to create an enlarged walled city, known appropriately as al-Qahira al-Mahrusa (Cairo the Protected). The extension of the eastern city wall to the Citadel served to define the eastern edge of al-Darb al-Ahmar. It marked the boundary between the urban area of the new elite, for whom proximity to the seat of power was essential, and the peripheral activities which were equally important for the functioning of the city, but less desirable. Among these were markets for animal fodder and dumping grounds for the city's rubbish, and, a century later, cemeteries.

The location of the cemeteries followed a constant trend in the history of Cairo — established on the peripheries of the metropolis, as the city expanded, they were removed to make way for new urban development. In contrast, the dumping grounds remained a permanent feature of the eastern edge of the city — in a sort of vicious cycle, the mounds of rubbish that accumulated outside the city walls served as a barrier towards eastward urban expansion, which in turn encouraged more and more dumping. This practice continued for centuries, resulting in the creation of formidable

Fig. 26. Al-Muayyad Bimaristan
(or Hospital), portal.

mounds of debris, closely resembling natural formations, which dwarfed the city walls and eventually buried them. The Aga Khan Trust for Culture has now converted these mounds into Azhar Park, while the eastern city wall has been exposed and is currently being restored.

The persistence of the Citadel as the seat of power ensured that al-Darb al-Ahmar remained a prestigious area, and a centre of economic and political life during the Mamluk period (1250-1517). In 1250, immediately following the fall of the Ayyubid dynasty, a power struggle at the citadel led to a group of seven hundred Mamluk princes, in opposition to the then-ruler Aybak and thus fearing for their lives, deciding to flee to Syria, from where they would later regroup and return to take over power. The night-time escape took place from one of the eastern city gates, Bab al-Qarratin (burned in the process and consequently renamed Bab al-Mahruq, "the burnt gate").

As an area whose urban importance spanned many generations, most of al-Darb al-Ahmar's early residential buildings were destroyed to make way for the buildings of later patrons seeking to build houses, palaces or mosques in an area whose location remained prime. However, a few residential structures remain from medieval times, among them the Alin Aq Palace, a building whose monumental scale is still evident despite its ruined condition, and parts of a house built during the reign of Sultan Qaytbay (1468-1496), incorporated into a later residential structure called Bayt al-Razzaz.

Institutional buildings fared better: maintained by an elaborate system of endowments, *waqf*, and in the case of religious buildings, considered to be sacred spaces and therefore indestructible except by the force of time, most still stand today. The Bimaristan of al-Muayyad, a large hospital built *c.* 1420 in the vicinity of the Citadel, exemplifies the attention paid to the founding of civic institutions by members of the court.

Al-Darb al-Ahmar's steady urbanisation can best be observed through the changes in the form and size of religious buildings

Fig. 27. Aqsunqur, or the Blue, Mosque, courtyard, *c.* 1350.

constructed in the area between the thirteenth and fifteenth centuries. In response to the increasing scarcity of land in the centre of the city, mosques evolved from large, symmetrical structures with accommodating open courtyards, to much smaller buildings with ground plans cleverly adapted to fit onto awkward-shaped plots of land. By the end of the Mamluk period, mosque construction in the area was primarily a pious and prestigious act — given the sheer number of mosques that already existed, there was no real social need for new religious buildings.

Fig. 28. Aqsunqur, or the Blue, Mosque, tilework.

The construction of important architectural complexes often included the building of multi-family residential units, usually for the poorer classes. This ensured that while al-Darb al-Ahmar remained a prestigious area, it nevertheless housed a very mixed community. It was also an area where quiet residential cul-de-sacs existed alongside vibrant commercial streets and markets. Some of the latter, especially those catering to the military establishment, such as the weaponry and horse markets, had been transferred from the centre of the Fatimid City to al-Darb al-Ahmar for the sake of proximity to the citadel.

The Ottoman conquest of Egypt in 1517 marked a new phase for al-Darb al-Ahmar. The rulers of Egypt were now Ottoman governors, posted to Egypt for a limited period of time, and thus with political aspirations in Istanbul rather than Cairo. As such, while the seat of power remained at the Citadel, the transformation of Cairo from the capital of an empire to an Ottoman province meant that the sponsorship of the large-scale complexes that had characterised al-Darb al-Ahmar decreased considerably. Architectural patrons found new, more resourceful ways of leaving their mark upon the city. The appropriation, and subsequent 'Ottomanisation' of the fourteenth-century Aqsunqur (or Blue) Mosque by an Ottoman official, Ibrahim Agha Mustahfazan in 1650, is a case in point. Instead of constructing a new mosque, the patron simply added blue Turkish tiles, a distinctly Ottoman feature, to a well-located Mamluk building on al-Darb al-Ahmar Street, thereby symbolically transforming it into an Ottoman building — his own.

While the founding of monumental religious buildings declined, the high value given to charitable work ensured that the patronage of smaller-scale projects continued. The Ottoman answer to

Fig. 29. A 19th-century mansion.

Fig. 30. Early 20th-century residential
building, to become the future
Darb al-Ahmar community centre.

the expansive Mamluk foundations were *sabil-kuttabs* (water fountains surmounted by Koranic schools), which were relatively inexpensive to build, required tiny plots of land, and served a social need. In parallel, the building of residential structures in al-Darb al-Ahmar proliferated to meet the demands of an expanding population. Thus, Ibrahim Agha Mustahfazan, the same patron who appropriated a Mamluk mosque for reasons of economy, had no qualms about constructing a series of residential and commercial buildings on al-Darb al-Ahmar Street — a decision probably grounded in an understanding of the considerable value of such property in light of its excellent location.

Despite new political allegiances, the architecture of Ottoman Cairo remained by and large true to a local tradition which had developed over centuries to meet the specific conditions of a dense urban fabric. By the eighteenth century, open spaces within the city walls were few and far between. Even the city gate, which in 1250 had permitted the flight of the dissenting Mamluk princes, had been blocked by residential construction.

The aftermath of a French invasion of Egypt in 1798 led to the rise of Muhammad Ali, an Albanian general in the Ottoman Army, as *wali* (governor) — giving him virtual autonomy though nominally a vassal of the Ottoman Court in Istanbul. This resurgence of local power spearheaded by a dedicated reformer, coupled perhaps with an openness towards new ideas following three years of French presence in Egypt, heralded a cultural revival for al-Darb al-Ahmar. Important members of Muhammad Ali's army were granted plots of land in the area, which led to the construction of palatial mansions and palaces. These were often a synthesis between local spatial tradition, the architecture of the Balkans and Turkey, which was familiar to Muhammad Ali and his entourage, and the decorative vocabulary popular in Europe at the time.

This cultural revival was short-lived, however; in the 1860s Muhammad Ali's grandson, Khedive Ismail, visited Paris and, amazed by the development of the city since his days as a student there, returned to Egypt with visions for a new, European-style capital. Ismail moved the seat of power from the Citadel to Abdin Palace, constructed in his newly created Ismailiyya quarter west of the historic city, thus effectively ending al-Darb al-Ahmar's seven-hundred-year-old role as a centre of political, cultural and economic activity.

The effects were not immediately apparent, yet a building boom in the 1880s must have marked the influx of bourgeois merchants eager to live in the area — a move due in part to al-Darb al-Ahmar's still-illustrious reputation, and facilitated by the gradual exodus of the city's political elite to the new Ismailiyya quarter. Al-Darb al-Ahmar still retained a sense of economic vitality, however, and even the most grandiose houses of the late nineteenth century had shops built along their main façades. Despite widespread eclecticism, architectural standards remained high; attention to space, proportion, and architectural detail was evident, even in the more modest buildings. In keeping with local historic urban trends, the grandest houses were generally located on main thoroughfares or adjacent to popular shrines, especially those associated with members of the prophet's family such as Fatma al-Nabawiyya. Poorer families tended to live in the narrow alleyways abutting the eastern city wall.

The first few decades of the twentieth century saw al-Darb al-Ahmar attempting to emulate the new quarters of Cairo. Sporadic urban development schemes involved the subdivision of large estates, into regular grid-like blocks, totally alien to the area's traditional urban fabric. Yet, fortunately, urban projects of this type remained rare. In the 1950s and 1960s the rise of large-scale industrialisation meant that areas such as al-Darb al-Ahmar, whose commercial activity was based on small-scale enterprises and workshops, were no longer seen as the basis of the city's economy. While many local industries did in fact continue to function, the new trend was for mass production in huge factories located in newly developed industrial areas.

New construction techniques, using reinforced concrete, began to replace traditional building materials, and 'modernist' urban design policies came into effect. While innovation had always been an important factor in al-Darb al-Ahmar's development, earlier modernisation attempts had still maintained strong links to the past. The new mindset, however, saw little value in tradition, and the impact of this was profound.

THE FATE OF AL-DARB AL-AHMAR

The last century has been a paradoxical century as far as al-Darb al-Ahmar's development is concerned. On the one hand, diligent efforts to conserve historic buildings by the Comité de Conservation des Monuments de l'Art Arabe (an Egyptian government body founded by khedivial de-

Fig. 31. Demolition for a street widening scheme.

Fig. 32. 20th-century pseudo 'revivalism'.

cree in 1882), ensured the preservation of the area's historic buildings, many of which had fallen into a state of disrepair. Encroachments on derelict property (resulting from a demand for housing or work space) were common, and the idea of clearing these encroachments from prominent historic buildings, erroneously considered as isolated monuments, developed. Such a policy, which at the beginning of the twentieth century saved many valuable historic buildings from disappearance, was codified into an article in the Egyptian Antiquities Law, with devastating results. It gave rise to a misguided idea that all listed buildings should be free-standing, prompting widespread demolition of buildings abutting so-called 'monuments'; an idea especially inappropriate in a city whose entire architectural tradition developed in response to high urban density, and whose most ingenious buildings were designed as part of a closely-knit urban fabric.

The negative consequences of a conservation policy that failed to see the larger urban picture were exacerbated by planning policies that overlooked the specificities of historic areas — a detrimental combination. In general, over the last century, planning schemes were developed by government officials poorly acquainted with the character of historic areas like al-Darb al-Ahmar, and unaware of their value as unique urban environments. Plans to widen existing streets, usually developed by arbitrarily drawing lines across a map of the area, with little thought given towards the social and urban consequences of such decisions, were common. Such schemes, developed with the intention of improving accessibility, have contributed to the destruction of al-Darb al-Ahmar's urban fabric, and if allowed to continue will completely obliterate its urban character, turning a valuable historic environment into a text-book example of 1960s planning ideology.

Fortunately, in recent years, awareness towards the value of historic areas has increased. However, the discrepancy between the intent and the result of policies affecting the development of al-Darb al-Ahmar is startling. While building codes stipulate that new construction must be sympathetic to the architectural traditions of historic Cairo, 'architectural traditions' have been interpreted to

Fig. 33. Bab Zuwayla Street, by Robertson and Beato, *c.* 1860s.

Fig. 34. Bab Zuwayla Street, 1987.

Fig. 35. "Rue du Carré", by Zangaki, *c.* 1880.

Fig. 36. View of al-Darb al-Ahmar Street
showing Umm al-Sultan Shaaban Mosque, 1986.

Fig. 37. Street view, Cairo, by C. G. Wheelhouse, 1849-1850.

Fig. 38. Street view looking south down al-Darb al-Ahmar Street, showing Aqsunqur Mosque and Khayrbek, 1987.

Fig. 39. Street view in Cairo, by Francis Frith, 1856-1859.

Fig. 40. Southern end of al-Darb al-Ahmar Street, showing the mosque of Aytmish al-Bagasi, 1986.

mean building façades incorporating arches and 'Islamic'-looking stuccowork. No real attempt has been made to truly understand what in fact local architectural traditions are, nor to develop a building code that is sensitive to the urban conditions of areas like al-Darb al-Ahmar.

Equally worrisome is the tendency to value historic areas only for their potential as a tourist venue. While sustainable tourist development can stimulate al-Darb al-Ahmar's economy, the type of tourist development generally envisioned for historic Cairo is to replace viable local industries with souvenir shops and bazaars. Such an idea is driven by the desire to turn what remains of the medieval city into an Orientalist painting come to life — an unrealistic, socially destructive, and economically unsound proposition.

Nevertheless, the attractiveness of such a radical idea is understandable given the seemingly hopeless state of affairs in areas like al-Darb al-Ahmar today. Gradual impoverishment, declining infrastructure accelerating building deterioration, and the inadequacy of essential services such as waste collection and drainage systems are among the area's chronic problems.

Yet, all of these conditions belie the fact that al-Darb al-Ahmar remains an extremely vibrant, commercially productive area of Cairo. It benefits from a socially cohesive population of long-term residents, many of whom are involved in the area's numerous industries and workshops, focusing predominantly on furniture production, shoe making and inlay-work. With appropriate guidance many such industries, especially carpentry, have proven capable of producing high quality products, much demanded today in an age when the shortcomings of cheap mass production have become apparent. Despite fifty years of decline, al-Darb al-Ahmar's built environment has numerous redeeming qualities: its closely-knit urban fabric has helped maintain a strong sense of community identity, and its turn-of-the-century buildings, with their courtyards, light wells and large windows have the potential of creating markedly more attractive, healthier conditions than new, cramped apartment buildings. Further, the predominance of two- and three-storey buildings ensures that although highly urban, al-Darb al-Ahmar is not overpopulated.

For all its potential, al-Darb al-Ahmar's current state may make regeneration appear overly optimistic. The revitalisation process is in fact a long and challenging one, requiring concerted efforts, institutional support, and a great deal of perseverance. To many outsiders the prospects seem bleak. Yet, Cairo in 1842, while being described by Gérard de Nerval as a "city of the past", was in fact at the dawn of a golden age. Tremendous technological advancement, cultural development, and intellectual enlightenment were to transform a comfortably Ottoman city which seemed to have complacently accepted that it was past its prime. There is no question that al-Darb al-Ahmar has seen better times. But the mechanism for sustainable regeneration and long-term revitalisation has been set in place, and the future looks promising.

PRESENT

A COMPREHENSIVE APPROACH

The articles in this section deal with the complete range of interventions carried out by the Historic Cities Support Programme (HCSP) of the Aga Khan Trust for Culture (AKTC) in the eastern sector of historic Cairo, which began with the construction of Azhar Park in 1997. The first contribution by Stefano Bianca places the various activities in the context of the overall philosophy and approach of the HCSP, and describes interdependences and synergies amongst the main project components. It is followed by three articles describing in greater detail the three major elements: the park and its planned facilities, by Cameron Rashti; the restoration of the Ayyubid wall, by Francesco Siravo and Franco Matero; and finally the combination of physical and socio-economic rehabilitation projects in the Darb al-Ahmar district, adjacent to the park and the wall.

A New Path to Urban Rehabilitation in Cairo

STEFANO BIANCA, DIRECTOR, HISTORIC CITIES SUPPORT PROGRAMME

Exposed as they are to ever increasing pressures of modern urban development and to creeping globalised uniformity, the historic cities of the Islamic world represent a rich cultural legacy worth preserving as a reference and source of inspiration for future generations. Unlike most of their Western counterparts, many of them managed to survive as authentic living cities, in spite of physical decline and economic depression. Their skilfully adorned monuments, whether made of stone, brick or timber, carry the imprint of timeless spiritual messages which still speak to present users. The cohesive patterns of their historic urban fabric embody meaningful modes of social interaction and tangible environmental qualities, which transmit the experience of past generations and are still able to shape and support contemporary community life; for the values inherent to their spatial configurations transcend short-lived changes and fashions.

Such contextual values, sadly absent in most of our planned modern towns, constitute the cultural essence of historic cities. To use an analogy from literature, the qualitative rapport between single components has the power to transform a series of words into significant information or, even better, to make the difference between 'prose' and 'poetry'. This is why a city can become a collective work of art, or rather a living cultural experience, perpetuated by means of social rituals and local myths and tales. Cairo, in particular, is engraved in the cultural memory of Muslim visitors, readers, and listeners. Since medieval times, prominent travellers such as Nasir-i-Khosraw, Ibn Jubayr and Ibn Battuta have praised its splendours.[1] The endless flow of stories contained in *The Thousand and One Nights* features Cairo, together with Baghdad, as the most recurrent backdrop for all sorts of experiences and adventures. More recently, Naguib Mahfouz, in his novels, has immortalised the popular life in old Cairo, as he witnessed it in the first half of the twentieth century.[2]

The accumulated architectural legacy of historic Islamic cities, then, is not of merely material character, but encompasses much wider dimensions of human existence and aspirations. Physical restoration alone can therefore never come to grips with the essential task, which is to keep historic cities alive as a matrix of perpetuated cultural productivity and achievement. That is why more comprehensive approaches are needed which may best be summarised by the term 'rehabilitation'. The intended connotation is that urban rehabilitation aims not only at the restoration of the outer shell, but also at reviving the inner driving forces, which need to be revitalised in order to enable a

Fig. 41. Panorama of Cairo by Pascal Sebah from around 1890, with al-Darb al-Ahmar in the foreground.

historic city to recover its inherent inner strength, to make the best use of its inbuilt resources and potentials, and eventually to progress in accordance with its own rhythms and constraints.

THE COMPLEXITY OF URBAN CONSERVATION

Conservation of historic cities is collateral to, and yet fundamentally different from, conservation of single monuments. While archaeological sites and unique monuments can occasionally be 'frozen' in a given or chosen state of evolution, historic cities as a whole cannot be kept in a museal state – with the rare exception of small urban ensembles conserved for tourist purposes. As a rule, however, historic cities are required to cope with the changing needs of their inhabitants in order to flourish and to be properly sustained. The real challenge is not how to preserve them, but how to establish a living, that is, an ongoing and evolving, cultural tradition which leads organically from the past into the future, while respecting most significant historic and environmental characteristics of a given urban fabric. This implies continuous maintenance, repair, and adaption (rather than demolition) of the traditional housing stock which provides the flesh, as it were, around the historic landmarks. Social facilities, public services, and public open spaces become other key components of such a contextual approach, since they are closely interlocked with housing, with commercial activities, and with major monuments still used by local communities.

Fig. 42. The transforming historic city of Cairo in the foreground, earth mounds of the Azhar Park site in the middle, and Moqattam in the distance.

The complexity of urban rehabilitation, understood as a multifaceted cultural, social, technical, economic and institutional task, calls for equally wide-ranging measures which need to be applied

judiciously to the delicate grain of the physical and social fabric of historic cities. Coordinated investments by the government and by residents, land-owners, and other stakeholders are required to ensure maintenance and, occasionally, careful substitution of obsolete single elements of the built environment. This presupposes the availability not only of a modicum of funding but also of the specific technical and social skills which used to be part of the traditional know-how.

Unfortunately, in most surviving historic cities in Islamic countries – and Cairo is no exception – funding sources and local expertise have become equally rare. Both the public and the private sector suffer from inherent weaknesses, are not used to cooperating efficiently, and tend to keep their limited investments for the further development of modern urban districts. Imported modern Western planning procedures tend to disaggregate previously integrated urban and social structures, thus dissolving the contextual values which constituted the strength of the historic urban fabric.[3] While modern, Western-type city administrations exist (and often tend to block the traditional self-management of local communities which used to function in the old times), they rarely have the tools to deal with the intricate and complex problems in the old city. Here, focused grass-roots involvement, qualified plot-by-plot decisions and permanent feed-back are required, rather than simplistic top-bottom implementation of abstract planning schemes which are too remote from the realities on the ground.

Yet the most important single factor responsible for the decline of historic cities in the Islamic world of today may well be of a psychological nature. It consists of prevailing negative prejudices and attitudes towards the depressed image of historic districts – some of them reflecting Western concepts of Modernism now outdated in their own countries of origin. With the progressive emigration of the former bourgeoisie from the old city into modern urban extensions (as has happened since the middle of the twentieth century), the social profile of historic cities has changed. A new population, often originating from the countryside, has been urbanised by adapting to the mould of the traditional urban fabric, which, in fact, is much closer to the structure of traditional villages than to that of modern urban developments. In doing so, the new residents have tended to constitute new social networks and economic sub-systems, but can find little or no support as long as the historic city is wrongly considered as a sort of 'slum' awaiting demolition and modern wholesale redevelopment.

THE NEED FOR AN INTEGRATED APPROACH

Any intervention in historic cities, particularly in the developing world, must therefore aim at reversing this poor image by creatively uncovering new, previously unsuspected opportunities. Restoration and reuse of historic landmarks or public open spaces as focal points of civic pride and identity are one step towards achieving this, but they have to go hand-in-hand with the revitalisation of the resources and capacities of local communities from within. Broad-based and well-focused socio-economic development projects are needed in order to raise living standards, provide employment, support existing small enterprises and deal with health, education, and women's affairs. Most importantly, the prevailing mood of general disinvestment and lack of trust — resulting from the threat of eventual demolition and displacement of residents — must be overcome by appropriate confidence-building initiatives. Only then will it be possible to tap and unlock the dormant assets of the old city — which reside in its convenient central location, in its potential environmental qualities, and, most of all, in the available social capital constituted by people's sense of initiative and solidarity.

Taking into account the complexity of the subject, the art of urban rehabilitation (or 'urban husbandry' as it has once been defined[4]) is therefore predicated on the involvement of a wide range of professional disciplines and corresponding interventions. Their mutual interaction is essential for

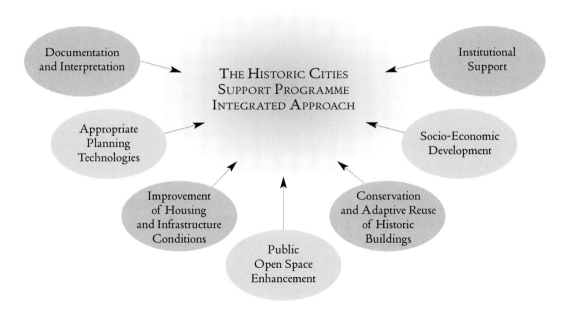

achieving an integrated approach to the various layers of problems in historic cities. The following list is an attempt to sketch out the scope to be covered.

Documentation and Interpretation. The morphology of the historic urban form, in most cases 'organically' grown over many centuries, must be recorded, analysed, and creatively interpreted to provide a suitable framework not only for conservation, but also for careful repair and substitution of individual components, whenever needed. Detailed historic and structural analyses, sometimes including archaeological research, are also required to understand the structure and the historic layers of significant monuments. In parallel, the urban fabric has to be surveyed plot by plot with regard to land use, social stratification, physical condition, and so on.

Appropriate Planning Technologies. Sustainable ways of introducing modern infrastructure must be investigated, and existing tools and techniques must be adapted in order to provide an optimum level of viability without disrupting the essential features of the historic urban form. This often calls for trade-offs, particularly when it comes to vehicular traffic. For uncontrolled vehicular accessibility can annihilate the human scale and environmental qualities of centrally located historic nuclei and cause far-reaching damage in their physical and social fabric. Alternative options to be explored are peripheral car parking combined with limited service access and public transportation reaching the pedestrian city centre.

Improvement of Housing and Infrastructure Conditions. Introducing or improving water supply, sewerage, and electricity networks is essential, but requires the corresponding networks to be adjusted to the constraints of the given urban form and the particular housing typology. The crucial issue here is that urban conservation has to integrate many modern planning and engineering disciplines without allowing conventional practices and procedures (derived from a different context) to dictate the form of intervention in the historic fabric. Rehabilitation of the traditional housing stock must be pursued directly (through technical assistance, small grants, and special credit lines), as well as indirectly, that is, through improvement of infrastructure, social facilities, and environmental quality.

Public Open Space Enhancement. Often public open spaces — whether streets, squares, or barren land — are neglected because they are seen as residual spaces towards which no one feels responsible. Re-establishing a sense of ownership and care by involving the local community in corresponding upgrading projects is a tool to foster civic pride and solidarity. Moreover, improvements in public open spaces often provide an important leverage by motivating adjacent house owners or tenants to upgrade their own premises.

Fig. 43. In the northern areas of Pakistan, projects include the restoration of several forts (such as Baltit and Shigar) and other landmark buildings in conjunction with rehabilitation of traditional settlements.

Fig. 44. In Zanzibar, the HCSP has completed the restoration of the former 'Old Dispensary', one of many empty landmark buildings on the waterfront now being put to new uses.

Fig. 45. In Samarkand, Uzbekistan, the HCSP has assisted the Municipality in preparing a new master plan for the Timurid city. Several private houses and a Mahalla centre were restored with active cooperation by residents.

Fig. 46. In Mostar, Bosnia, projects concentrate on the rehabilitation of the historic neighbourhoods adjacent to the famous Old Bridge and on the restoration of a number of key monuments destroyed during the civil war.

Fig. 47. A detailed planning and urban design scheme is being developed around Aleppo Citadel, Syria.

Fig. 48. Rehabilitation and upgrading of the Timur Shah Mausoleum, an important landmark set in the midst of the old markets and adjacent to a former garden and the Kabul riverbanks, Afghanistan.

Conservation and Adaptive Reuse of Historic Buildings. When funding is short, it may not always be possible to conserve or restore the architectural heritage in full. Priority must be given to projects that can foster a sense of ownership and solidarity in the local community, and that can become catalysts for corollary urban conservation and renewal processes. The best way to achieve this is to combine the restoration with an appropriate type of adaptive reuse which is socially relevant to the community and generates an income basis capable of ensuring the long-term maintenance of the restored building.

Socio-Economic Development. Raising existing living standards is essential in order to back up parallel conservation and rehabilitation projects and to ensure that local communities stand behind the overall rehabilitation effort. The most urgent needs of the population living or working in the project area have to be surveyed and assessed. Projects in health, education, employment, and small enterprise development have to be set up in order to boost income, generate opportunities, and enable residents to actively participate in a continuous rehabilitation process. Incidentally, conservation projects offer many opportunities for training in specialised conservation skills and for the creation of new economic dynamics. Most importantly, the pride, solidarity, and sense of ownership of local communities can be boosted through their active involvement.

Institutional Support Systems. An appropriate local institutional system has to be built up (or strengthened) in order to coordinate, drive and sustain the rehabilitation efforts, drawing both on internal resources and external contributions and incentives. Local associations, non-governmental organisations (NGOs), and local government have to work closely together. Central government institutions need to encourage this effort, particularly with regard to overriding legal and planning frameworks, funding priorities, and financial mechanisms. However, no overriding planning policies will ever work if local communities are not backing such initiatives at their own level of action.

THE HISTORIC CITIES SUPPORT PROGRAMME AND ITS CAIRO ACTIVITIES

The approach sketched out above is a distillation of the field experience accumulated by the Historic Cities Support Programme (HCSP) — a division of the Geneva-based Aga Khan Trust for Culture (AKTC), established in 1992 to implement the initiatives of His Highness the Aga Khan in the field of conservation and urban rehabilitation. Since its inception, HCSP has built up experience in a variety of geographical regions of the Islamic world, in both urban and rural settings.

Instances of interventions have included, so far: the restoration of historical forts and palaces in the valleys of Hunza and Baltistan (Northern Pakistan), in conjunction with the rehabilitation of traditional villages and environmental ensembles; the conservation plan for the Old Stone Town in Zanzibar combined with the improvement of its old housing stock, as well as the restoration of key monuments and the upgrading of the waterfront; a plan for the revitalisation of the Timurid city of Samarkand; restoration and reconstruction projects in the war-struck historic nucleus of Mostar (Bosnia). In addition, major conservation and urban rehabilitation projects are now being implemented in Aleppo and Kabul. While many of these projects were initially tackled from the conservation and adaptive reuse end, further evolution led to the progressive integration of associated activities, such as housing improvement, urban planning, landscaping, social initiatives, small enterprise development and micro-credits, thus generating a new type of holistic area development project. The duration of projects and their expansion have largely depended on the response of local communities and support received from local authorities and other donors. The overriding principle has always been that technical and financial aid should stimulate revitalisation within local communities, rather than making them dependent on external support.[5]

Intervening in the historic city of Cairo was perhaps the biggest challenge of the Programme so far. Not only is the wealth of monuments in this Islamic metropolis overwhelming, it is also matched by towering problems linked to poor socio-economic conditions, deficient services and infrastructure, rising ground-water table, lack of public open spaces, and poor maintenance of the traditional housing stock often no longer inhabited by the owners. To make things worse, the pressures of a sixteen to eighteen million metropolis on the historic centre are enormous in terms of vehicular traffic impact, large-scale economic activities, tourism, and so on. Moreover, the intricacies of Egyptian bureaucracy, notorious since Pharaonic times, pose certain problems due to a highly centralised system with little decision-making power being delegated to local administrative units. The division of governmental authority into various sectorial domains (Traffic, Housing, Antiquities, Religious Domains, and so on) makes it difficult to overcome fragmentation of tasks and functions in the field. The role of NGOs, although agreed to in theory, has not been fully implemented. During the past decades, several well-intentioned planning projects for the historic city initiated by UNESCO, the UNDP, and the Egyptian Government have failed (or were only partially realised). This confirms the difficulty of implementing a project in conventional ways, that is, through mere top-bottom planning strategies, whereas conditions for the reverse approach are not yet in place.

The current HCSP activities in the Darb al-Ahmar district can be seen as an attempt to bridge this gap – by closely cooperating with the Cairo Governorate, the Supreme Council of Antiquities and the Awqaf Department (Religious Endowments), while at the same time mobilising a maximum of community participation and involvement. Without aiming at an over-ambitious 'general' solution for historic Cairo, it provides a pragmatic model for an action area intervention which is both holistic and focused on well-articulated spaces and corresponding social constituencies.

Reflecting the progressive evolution of the Programme, the objectives of the HCSP project in Cairo in the early years (1992-1995) were limited to a landscaping project on the Darassa Hills, thus converting a vast derelict site at the heart of the historic metropolis into a thirty-hectare urban park. Alone, the Azhar Park project would already have had a major impact on the city of Cairo. But during its implementation the total scope of work took on much more complex dimensions, combining and integrating a number of additional activities. The conservation of the newly uncovered twelfth-century Ayyubid city wall (on the western slope of the park) became a natural follow-up to the general park intervention. The conservation of the wall

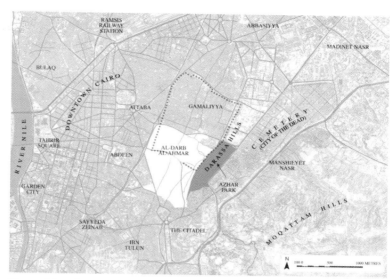

Fig. 49. Map of central Cairo. The dotted line indicates the position of the Fatimid city.

was, however, not feasible without simultaneously tackling the abutting fabric of the Darb al-Ahmar district, which in turn led to extended programmes for the rehabilitation of historic housing clusters, the improvement of public open spaces, and a range of socio-economic development projects in the realm of health, education, community participation, small enterprise development, and so on. Built up step by step, this extended scope of work will continue for several years, beyond the completion of the initial park project, inaugurated in spring 2004. Its total impact will rely on the fact that the synergies between single project components make it become much more than the sum of its parts.

Accordingly, the benefits to be derived for the city of Cairo are manifold: Azhar Park itself provides a major public facility on a metropolitan scale and complements other *grands projets* undertaken by the Egyptian Government, such as:

- the recent construction of the Azhar Tunnel (which will eventually allow the re-connection of the two halves of the Fatimid city, hitherto divided by an elevated express road cutting through it);

- the forthcoming pedestrianisation and beautification of the large square between al-Azhar Mosque and al-Hussein Mosque, that is, the major place of assembly in the historic city;

- the 'Massive Intervention' aimed at restoring the series of major Islamic monuments along the old Fatimid spine of al-Muizz Street (see also the chapter by Nairy Hampikian).

Acting as a new pole of attraction for visitors, the park will pull important pedestrian streams from Azhar Square and al-Muizz Street into its boundaries, thereby galvanising the intermediate districts. Thus, it will be acting as a catalyst for the revitalisation of the whole adjacent Darb al-Ahmar district — a trend which is reinforced and extended by the historic wall restoration and by the array of physical and socio-economic rehabilitation projects across the wall. What is more, the new park will help change the perception and the 'image' of the complete old city, by literally allowing it to be seen from a new and extremely attractive perspective.

SCOPE OF WORK AND INTERACTION BETWEEN PROJECT COMPONENTS

The thirty-hectare Azhar Park project on the vacant dumping site of the Darassa Hills was first proposed by His Highness the Aga Khan to the City of Cairo in 1984. Implementation was delayed because the site had to be cleared from storage facilities and because USAID had to use the site for the construction of three large water tanks ensuring the drinking water supply to the city of Cairo. Indeed, the site offers a unique resource, miraculously preserved throughout centuries of urban development. It is surrounded by the most significant historic landmarks of Islamic Cairo, all of which are major destinations for visitors to the city. To the west are the Fatimid city and its extension, al-Darb al-Ahmar, with their wealth of mosques, *madrasas* (religious schools) and mausolea, signalled by a long series of minarets. To the south is the Sultan Hasan Mosque and its surroundings, as well as the Ayyubid Citadel. To the east is the Mamluk City of the Dead, with its many social welfare complexes sponsored by Mamluk sultans and dignitaries — a former necropolis which has developed into a dense urban entity of its own with an estimated two to three hundred thousand inhabitants. The hilly topography of the site, formed by debris accumulated since the fifteenth-century, provides elevated vantage points that dominate the city and offer a spectacular 360° panorama over the townscape of historic Cairo — a potential which has been fully exploited by the site plan.

The aim of the project was to provide an exceptional facility not only for the residents of the historic city but for all citizens of Cairo. The park therefore has both a popular dimension in terms of wide-spread leisure areas inviting people to meet, to rest and to picnic on the ground, and a more sophisticated dimension in terms of a prestigious hilltop restaurant and a lakeside café. The latter will set high-quality standards for the whole complex and add two prominent new landmarks to the Cairo townscape. The design of the park projects typical geometrical elements of traditional Islamic gardens onto the topography of the site without subjecting it to rigid transformations. Thus the formal 'spine' and the associated terraces and geometrical gardens are complemented by soft-shaped hills and a small lake. A network of informal pathways surrounds the more formal garden areas and leads through all levels and corners of the site. Together, the various components of the park design will provide the visitor with a unique and rich visual experience not available in any other area of Cairo (for more details, see the chapter by Cameron Rashti).

During the massive re-grading of the western park slope descending towards al-Darb al-Ahmar, the formerly buried Ayyubid city wall from the late twelfth-century AD, built under Sultan Salah al-Din along the western edge of the historic city, was re-discovered and, in part, excavated. One section had been covered by a road and temporary market structures and had to be excavated *in toto*. This wall, with its gates, towers, and interior chambers and galleries, is in itself one of the most important archaeological discoveries of the past decades relating to the Islamic period in Egypt. Over 1300 metres long, it will form a distinctive third element between the park and al-Darb al-Ahmar, providing an interesting enclosure and backdrop for the park, as well as a monument which can be visited from within, by acceding to the various gates, towers, and galleries. The historic wall physically separates the park from al-Darb al-Ahmar and the historic city, but also acts as an attractive visual and functional connection, offering opportunities to visitors to enter the city from the park, and vice versa.

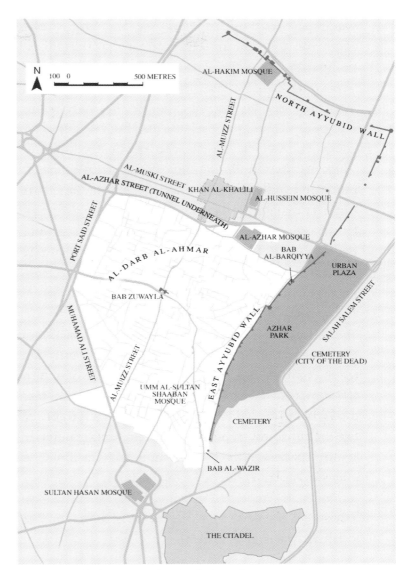

Fig. 50. Map of Islamic Cairo showing the immediate surroundings of the AKCS-E's projects in historic Cairo.

While constituting an architectural feature in its own right, the city wall could not be dissociated from the adjacent Darb al-Ahmar district, neither conceptually nor physically. Over the centuries, the houses and monuments buttressing the wall on the city side became an integral part of Cairo's urban and social history. Selective removal of encroaching elements was undertaken by the project as part of the restoration process (see the chapter by Francesco Siravo and Frank Matero). Yet a wholesale demolition of the historic housing stock attached to the city wall — as foreshadowed in a twenty-year-old decree by the Supreme Council of Antiquities — was discarded, since it would have contradicted today's prevailing international conservation philosophy and practice. Moreover, such radical clearance might have introduced undesirable and dangerous development pressures.

Currently, selective case-by-case approvals for restoration and rehabilitation of individual buildings along the wall are being obtained from the authorities, without lifting the current freeze on new construction which prevents speculative redevelopment in this sensitive area. The goal is to take advantage of the stimulus resulting from the upgrading of the park and at the same time impose clear building regulations and redevelopment models, in order to achieve a balanced rehabilitation process on this critical edge of the city facing the park. The most prominent ruined building restored under this 'gentlemen's agreement' with the authorities was the Shoughlan Street School, a hundred-year-old apartment building which later served as a school and is now being converted into a community centre. Its pivotal location makes it a symbol of the connection between the park, the wall, and al-Darb al-Ahmar.

Al-Darb al-Ahmar as a whole will indeed benefit from the dramatic reversal of environmental conditions brought about through the park construction. From a former backyard, used for centuries as a dumping ground, the site has now been turned into a highly attractive forecourt to the historic city of Cairo. Thus the community has overcome its former marginalisation, revived historic gates in the old city wall and new additional transition points (such as the Shoughlan Street School) will provide welcome connections between the park and al-Darb al-Ahmar — both for residents who want to use community sports facilities in the park and for visitors who want to cross over or to visit al-Darb al-Ahmar as part of their tour through Islamic Cairo. New itineraries for culturally interested visitors will connect the local Darb al-Ahmar economy to the tourist market — a privilege which has so far been monopolised by the Khan al-Khalili markets in the northern district of historic Cairo.

However, considering the volatility and the potentially destructive impact of the tourist industry, the main efforts for the rehabilitation of al-Darb al-Ahmar are directed at a broad-based internal revitalisation of the local community and its built environment. To this end, a variety of sub-projects have been initiated which closely associate physical improvements in the domain of housing and public open spaces with a number of socio-economic development projects, such as training and skill enhancement programmes (some of them related to current physical restoration and rehabilitation activities), small enterprise promotion including micro-credit programmes, health clinics, women's and children's education, and so on. Most of these programmes are using or will eventually use spaces in restored historic buildings (for more details, see the chapter by Francesco Siravo). Public participation and NGO enhancement are essential aspects of this endeavour, and have already resulted in increased community pride and commitment.

Within this context, conservation projects on the Khayrbek complex and Umm al-Sultan Shaaban Mosque were initiated, including the restoration of partly collapsed minarets in order to complement the skyline of the historic city as seen from the park site. The ancient *madrasas* and *sabil-kuttabs* (fountains with children's schools on top of them), as well as the remains of an ancient Mamluk palace, all attached to these buildings, offered a welcome potential for community-relevant reuse programmes.

Fig. 51. The Khayrbek complex located between the Darb al-Ahmar spine and Azhar Park.

All in all, and unlike the park, the Darb al-Ahmar rehabilitation programme is not geared towards a previously defined end-product, but represents a *process* which was launched three years ago and will continue for at least another four years, responding to the feed-back received from the initial activities; it is expected that it will enable the local community to take a greater share of responsibility in the management of its built environment. The key-stone of the combined physical and social development strategies may well be a future Community Development Agency with strong local participation. To make it self-sustainable, such an institution must be enabled to raise income, drawing on the added value of restored and rehabilitated buildings entrusted to it.

While the AKTC is acting as the lead agency in this comprehensive rehabilitation process, it was fortunate to find other donors, such as the Egyptian Swiss Development Fund, the Ford Foundation, and the World Monuments Fund — all of whom have endorsed and supported this combined conservation and social development programme for years.

CAPTURING FRINGE BENEFITS

Apart from the park project, the historic wall restoration and the Darb al-Ahmar rehabilitation programme, the AKTC decided to become involved, together with the Cairo Governorate, in two further projects which are being planned and implemented in order to consolidate the fringes of Azhar Park and al-Darb al-Ahmar.

The first project is the 'Urban Plaza' complex now being constructed on the north-eastern edge of the park, adjacent to the busy al-Azhar Street. This fringe area, close to the Khan al-Khalili markets and benefiting from excellent vehicular accessibility, has an obvious commercial potential, while it is too noisy and too detached from the upper plateau to be part of the park proper. A commercial building with shops, offices and an integrated multi-storey car park is being developed,

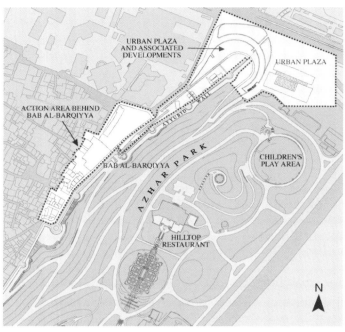

Fig. 52. Map showing planned projects
on the north-eastern fringe of Azhar Park.

the plan of which was closely coordinated with the park design in terms of entrances, terraces and shared facilities.

All the net income from the future operation of this complex will be used to sustain the future operation, maintenance, and enhancement of the park and its neighbourhood. It thus provides a further source of income for the park and al-Darb al-Ahmar in addition to entry tickets. This method of ensuring self-sustainability is based on a traditional concept of Muslim societies, that is, the *waqf* model, whereby income-generating facilities are constituted as an endowment to support the maintenance of religious and public buildings. The same idea is behind the inclusion of commercial facilities within the park, such as the Hilltop Restaurant and the Lakeside Café.

The second fringe project concerns a strip of completely ruined houses on the west side of the newly excavated Ayyubid wall, along a former street leading into al-Darb al-Ahmar which has been lowered by four to five metres in order to expose the historic wall. A complete action area programme has been designed to provide an alternate service road into al-Darb al-Ahmar and to convert the former road along the wall into a pedestrian zone linked to Bab al-Barqiyya — a revived and restored old city gate now leading into the park. The ruined houses along this strip facing the wall and the park are irretrievable and represent prime redevelopment opportunities benefiting from the added value of the AKTC interventions on the park. A programme is currently being prepared for comprehensive and adapted redevelopment of the whole strip of houses with apartments in the upper floors and commercial facilities at street level.

The financial benefits obtained from this urban renewal operation will flow back into the Darb al-Ahmar programmes and the project can eventually constitute a model for similar operations in prime locations, which may later be handled by the future Darb al-Ahmar Development Agency. This venture may pave the way for new, much needed modes of public-private sector cooperation which will work in the interest of a well-balanced development of the historic city. Once repeated in other sectors of the historic city, this procedure could establish an internal cross-subsidising mechanism, whereby the economic potential of easily accessible, prime real estate on the fringe of

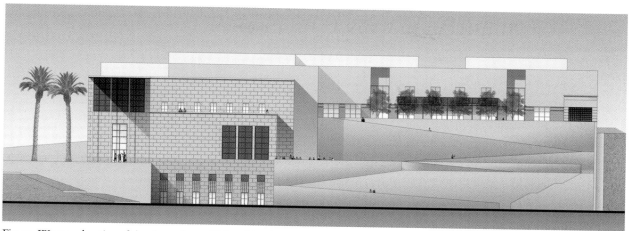

Fig. 53. Western elevation of the planned new 'Urban Plaza', with the projecting wing of the future Museum of Historic Cairo facing the northern section of the Ayyubid Wall (for northern elevation see pl. 31).

the historic city can be used to support improvement of more remote and less privileged areas. The model of the park intervention would thus have shown how the enhancement and revalorisation of a sensitive part of the urban system can act as a financial engine for a comprehensive, self-supported urban rehabilitation process by capitalising on previously dormant assets and making sure their added value is recycled internally, rather than being absorbed by external investors.

[1]Ibn Battuta described Cairo as the "mother of cities, boundless in a multitude of buildings, peerless in beauty and splendour, the halting place of feeble and mighty, whose throngs surge as the waves of the sea and can scarce be contained in her for all her size and capacity". From *Travels in Africa and Asia*, published by H. A. R. Gibb, London 1929.

[2]For the flavour of old Cairo around a hundred years ago, see also Albert Adès/Albert Josipovici, *Le Livre de Goha le Simple*, Calmann-Levy, first published in 1919.

[3]For more details see Stefano Bianca, *Urban Form in the Arab World - Past and Present*, Thames and Hudson, London/New York 2000.

[4]See Roberta Brandes Gratz, *The Living City - Thinking Small in a Big Way*, Simon and Schuster, New York 1989.

[5]A comprehensive presentation of the first twelve years of HCSP activities will be found in the forthcoming book *Towards the Rehabilitation of Historic Islamic Cities*, edited by Stefano Bianca, Prestel, Munich/New York 2005.

1. An aerial view of the project site shows the topography of Azhar Park
after master grading (2000). On the edge of the site is the uncovered, 12th-century Ayyubid city wall
and, to the right, the Darb al-Ahmar district. In the distance, two major landmarks can be seen:
to the left, Salah al-Din's Citadel and, to the right, the complex of the Sultan Hasan Mosque.

DARB AL-AHMAR

To Bab Zuwayla

32

Aslam Neighbourhood
Action Area

Aslam
Mosque

Al-Darb al-Ahmar Street

Fatma al-Nabaweyya
Mosque

33   34

Umm al-Sultan Shaaban
Mosque

30

Bab al-Wazir
Action Area   31

23

22

AYYUBID WALL

Lakeside
Café

5

7

29

4

28

Khayrbek
Complex   1

27   2   6

To Sultan   3
Hasan Mosque
and the Citadel   21

Tarabay al-Sharif
Mausoleum   Cemetery

AZHAR PARK
LANDMARKS AND FACILITIES

1. Neighbourhood recreation field
2. Park administration office
3. Citadel esplanade
4. Picnic meadow
5. Lakeside Café
6. Park orchard
7. Sunken garden
8. Trianon Café
9. Palm processional walk
10. South lookout point
11. Main park gate at Salah Salem Street
12. Visitor parking
13. Al-Geneina amphitheatre
14. Formal garden
15. Hilltop Restaurant
16. North lookout point
17. Children's play area
18. Museum of Historic Cairo
19. Urban plaza
20. Visitor parking and underground garage

AYYUBID WALL RESTORATION PROGRAMME
MAJOR RESTORATION LOCATIONS

21. Conservation project
    and community gate at Tarabay al-Sharif
22. Visitor circuit and community park gate
    between Towers 4 and 5
23. Archaeological presentation
    and community park gate at Bab al-Mahruq
24. Planned Ayyubid Wall interpretation centre
    at Burg al-Mahruq
25. Development of a pedestrian zone
    and restoration at Bab al-Barqiyya gate
26. Planned archaeological visitor centre
    in the north triangle

Labels on map:

Al-Azhar Mosque

To al-Hussein Mosque
and Khan al-Khalili Area

Al-Azhar
University

Al-Azhar Street

Burg al-Zafar
Action Area

36

Al-Hussein
Hospital

35

13 24 25 26

18

ZHAR PARK

Hilltop
Restaurant

10

14 15 16

Urban
Plaza

11

12

17

19

20

Salah Salem Street

'City of the Dead'

0 20 50 150 m

N

DARB AL-AHMAR NEIGHBOURHOOD ONGOING PHYSICAL INTERVENTION
AND SOCIAL DEVELOPMENT PROJECT SITES

27. Development of open space
and housing rehabilitation at Bab al-Wazir

28. Conservation project at Khayrbek Complex

29. Darb al-Ahmar Planning Authority office

30. Conservation project
at Umm al-Sultan Shaaban Mosque

31. Restoration of the former Shoughlan Street School
into a community centre

Completed Darb al-Ahmar
housing rehabilitation projects

Monument conservation projects

32. Vocational training facilities
and carpentry workshop

33. Open space development and housing rehabilitation
at Aslam Square

34. Conservation project at Aslam Mosque

35. Infrastructure and open space improvements
of Burg al-Zafar Street

36. Darb al-Ahmar micro-credit and loan centre

● Social development programme locations
and adaptive reuse schemes

←- Community gates between Darb al-Ahmar and Azhar Park

3.

4.

3. A late 19th-century panorama of al-Darb al-Ahmar taken by Pascal Sebah.
The image shows a highly urban residential fabric, comprising large mansions
as well as smaller houses, built right up to the eastern city wall.

4. A late 19th-century view of the so-called 'Darassa Hills',
the mounds of debris that have now been transformed into Azhar Park.

5. An early 20th-century view of what is now
the southern extent of Azhar Park, showing
the almost-buried Ayyubid city wall,
with the Khayrbek and Aqsunqur Mosques
in the foreground (left and right, respectively).

6. A view of the Umm al-Sultan Shaaban Mosque
(*c.* 1369) taken by H. Béchard in 1884, just before
the pavilion of its minaret collapsed due
to an earthquake. The minaret is being reconstructed
by the AKTC as part of a larger project to restore
the mosque complex. The image also shows a wealth
of late Ottoman residential architecture.

Following pages
7. An early 19th-century lithograph by David Roberts
showing what is now the southern boundary of Azhar
Park. In the foreground of the image are the Khayrbek
and Aqsunqur Mosques (left and right, respectively),
the former currently being restored by the AKTC.
The eastern Ayyubid city wall is also clearly visible.

Cairo looking West

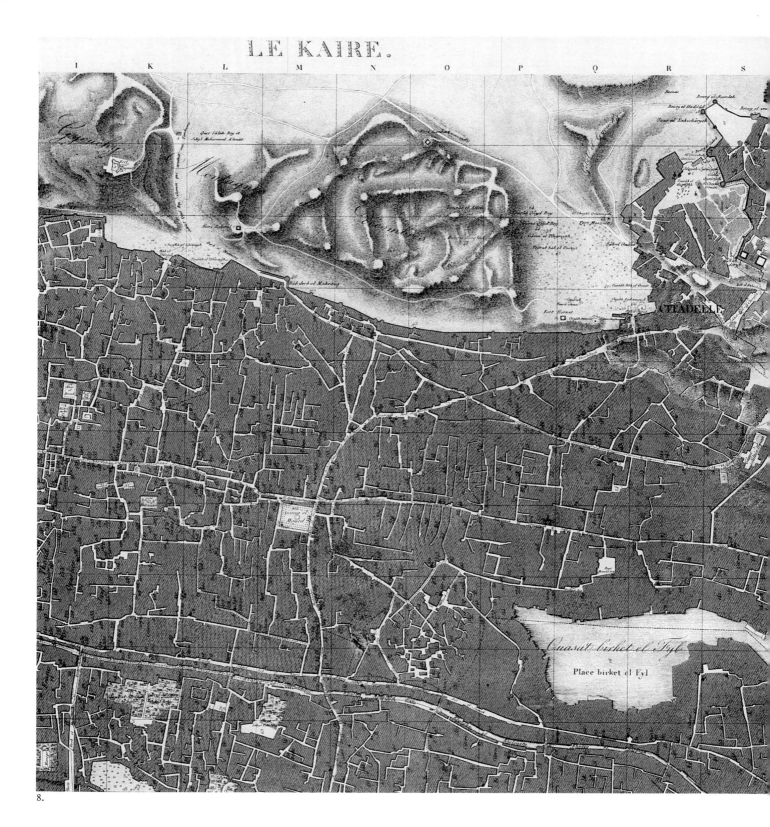

8.

8. Detail of a map of Cairo from the *Description de l'Egypte* produced in 1802,
following Napoleon's expedition to Egypt (1798-1801). This detail shows
al-Darb al-Ahmar, even then a dense neighbourhood built right up
to the city wall, and the Darrasa Hills, now the site of Azhar Park.

9.

10.

9. Looking to the south over the park site, with the Citadel in the background.

10. The future park site in 1992, before work commenced, looking to the south. In the distance to the left is the Citadel of Salah al-Din and, in the centre, the minarets of the Sultan Hasan Mosque complex.

11. A picture of the site also taken in 1992, looking towards the north-east. In the background is the City of the Dead, with the mausolea of many Mamluk sultans and dignitaries, highlighted by domes and minarets.

.

12.

13.

14.

12. The southernmost water tank in 1994, during the final stage of construction.
Further southwards, on the left, a view of the Citadel of Salah al-Din
with the late Ottoman-style Muhammad Ali Mosque on a spur of the Moqattam plateau.

13. View of the southern section of the site in the early 1990s,
when it was occupied as a storage place by a major contractor.

14. Work on the southernmost water tank shows the scale of construction involved.

15.

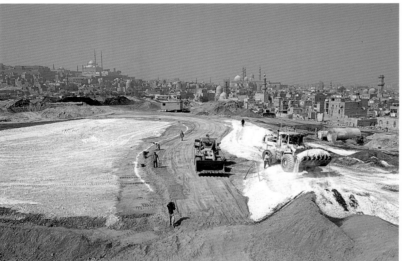

16.

17.

18.

15, 16. The nature of the site of the park required extensive grading and improvement of the soil quality in order to permit planting.

17. An aerial view of the southern water tank in 1999 (seen from the south), being integrated into the emerging new park topography. At the bottom, in the centre, a prototype of typical pavements, pergolas and water features of the future park main spine.

18. An aerial view of Azhar Park taken during the work in 2000. The eastern edge of al-Darb al-Ahmar and the periphery of the Bab al-Wazir cemetery can be seen in the foreground (on the left and right sides of the park, respectively).

19. Master grading and consolidation of the critical
western slope of the future Azhar Park
descending towards the uncovered Ayyubid wall.
In the background, the silhouette of the magnificent
Sultan Hasan Mosque complex.

20-22. The off-site nursery uses sophisticated pump
and irrigation methods to propagate plants for the park.

Following double pages
23. A view of the site with the completed formal garden on top
of the second (central) water reservoir and with the central spine
of the garden in the background pointing towards the Citadel.

24. The threefold improvement of al-Darb al-Ahmar's
physical condition: by regrading and planting the western slope
of the new park; by restoring the reclaimed Ayyubid wall
and its two gates; and by rehabilitating the houses
along the historic wall.

25. The master plan of Azhar Park displaying the various landscaping approaches used, each of which responds to the characteristics of the site. The 'spine' of the plan is the formal axis descending southwards from the northern hill (right) and pointing towards the Citadel.
It features a sequence of formal gardens, the most elaborate of which is on the top of the central water reservoir. The spine then turns westwards into the southern lower plain of the site, which leads to the Lakeside Café, offering a spectacular view of the old city.

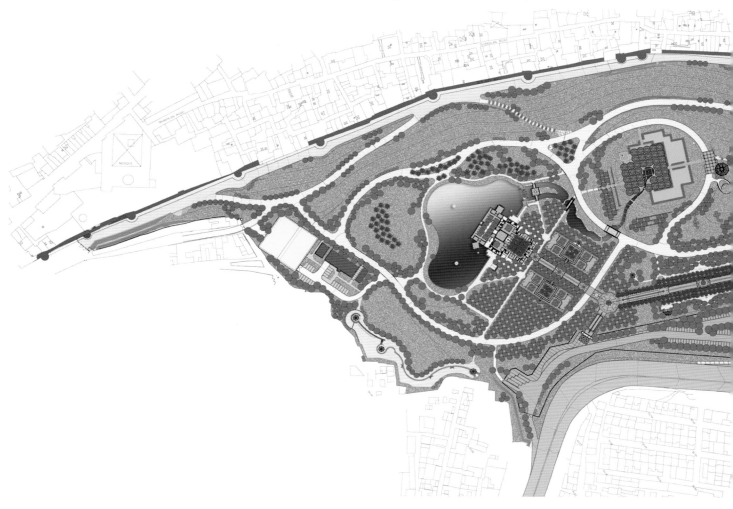

26. Lakeside Café.

27. Southern viewing platform.

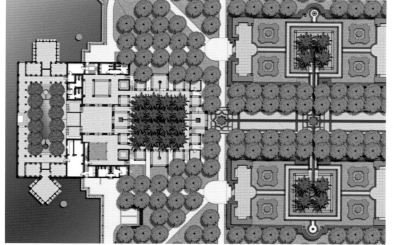

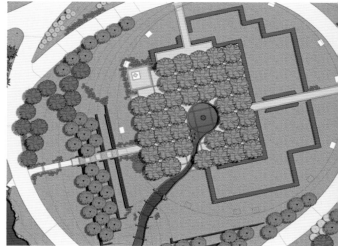

Entry gate and plaza.

29. Formal garden.

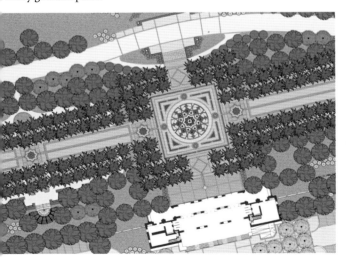

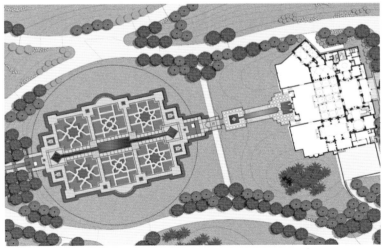

30.

30. The eastern sector of the park, looking southwards to the Citadel and the Sultan Hasan Mosque.

31. Preliminary design for the 'Urban Plaza' complex (designed by Serge Santelli) on the north side of the park, showing the entrance to the commercial compound and the future Museum of Historic Cairo.

32.

The Hilltop Restaurant,
designed by Rami El Dahan
and Soheir Farid, is inspired by
the architecture of historic Cairo.

32. The restaurant portico
and the viewing terrace overlooking
the central spine of the park.

33, 34. Two pictures
of the Hilltop Restaurant
nearing completion.

35. Overall view of the Hilltop
Restaurant from the south-west.

33.

34.

36, 37. Left page, the interior courtyard of the Hilltop Restaurant (with its central fountain), from where the various sections of the building can be accessed. Right, the play of light and shadow resulting from the timber screens in the pierced roof structure.

38. Rendering of the restaurant's southern façade by Rami El Dahan and Soheir Farid.

37.

39.

39. The Lakeside Café (designed by Serge Santelli)
projecting into the artificial lake on the southern plane of the park.

40. Construction of the Lakeside Café with the domes
and minarets of historic Cairo in the background.

40.

41.

42.

41. Computer rendering
of the Lakeside Café at night.

42. Perspective drawing
of the Lakeside Café by Serge Santelli.

43. The interior terraces
of the Lakeside Café, before reaching
the platform on the water's edge.

44.

44. View of the eastern edge of Darb al-Ahmar from the slope of the park, with a restored section of the Ayyubid wall and the restored residential building now serving as a community centre (compare with pl. 82, during works).

45. View of the southernmost section of the Ayyubid wall during master grading of the park, and before restoration.

45.

46.

47.

48.

46. The most prominent tower of the Ayyubid wall, Burg al-Mahruq, as it was in 1994, almost totally buried by debris.

47. Centuries of dumping Cairo's waste outside the eastern city wall led to the burial of the structure under piles of rubble. The wall in 1994, prior to being cleared from rubbish.

48. Aerial view of Burg al-Mahruq and the adjacent urban fabric, after the former was cleared from debris. The road to the left of the tower was constructed on top of the ramparts of the Ayyubid wall and has now been removed, exposing a section of the wall that had been buried for centuries.

Following pages
49. Some sections of the Ayyubid wall, such as this one to the south
of al-Mahruq Tower, required extensive conservation work.
The extension of houses abutting the wall in the last century
led to the loss of some of the wall's rubble core
and even its facing stone in parts.

.

2.

50. Conservation treatment of the Ayyubid wall:
repointing the mortar of the crenellations;
the Darb al-Ahmar district in the background.

51. Al-Mahruq Tower, a monumental three-storey
circular tower constructed at what was probably
the north-eastern corner of the Fatimid city,
marks the junction between the two distinct phases
of the wall's construction.

52. Using the JOS system to clean the original facing
stone of the eastern Ayyubid city wall.

53.

54.

53. Archaeological excavations near al-Mahruq Tower.

54. The ground-storey vaults of the Alin Aq Palace,
a building constructed alongside the Ayyubid wall
in the early 14th century, now being restored.

55.

55, 56. Archaeological work revealed
the remains of an Ottoman residential
structure constructed on top of one
of the towers of the Ayyubid wall.

57. Urban expansion in the last century
led to the destruction of some sections
of the Ayyubid wall to accommodate
residential buildings. A conservation policy
was developed that would reinstate
the integrity of the wall while retaining
all sections of the adjacent buildings
that did not encroach on the wall itself.

56.

58. Rooftop view of the Aslam neighbourhood in al-Darb al-Ahmar illustrating the dense existing housing fabric, much of which is in poor condition and in need of upgrading.

59. Al-Darb al-Ahmar is located between the famous al-Azhar Mosque (left) and the hills of Azhar Park, visible in the background. Direct pedestrian links exist between the park and the historic spine of Fatimid Cairo, with its many bazaars and old neighbourhoods.

60. Al-Darb al-Ahmar boasts thriving workshops, many of which produce traditional handmade items, such as these lanterns.

61.

61. The historic character of al-Darb al-Ahmar
is best represented in areas where a range of religious
and domestic historic buildings still exist alongside
each other, such as here, around the mosque of Khayrbek.

62. Restoration work on the minaret of Khayrbek.

63. Reconstructing the top of the minaret
of Umm al-Sultan Shaaban Mosque, a process requiring
a high level of skill, especially in stonemasonry.

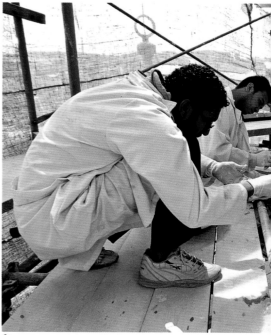

62.

63.

64.

65.

64. The reconstruction of the Umm al-Sultan Shaaban minaret
also involved the restoration of damaged sections of the existing portion
of the structure — such as the stalactite cornice — a characteristic feature
of Mamluk minarets.

65. The mosque of Umm al-Sultan Shaaban, as seen from the minaret.
The ribbed stone domes and open courtyard are typical
of 14th-century Cairene religious architecture.

66. The mosque of Khayrbek, in the course of the reconstruction
of its minaret. As with any major historic metropolis,
Cairo is renowned for the sheer number of monumental historic buildings.
In the background are the mosques of Sultan Hasan and al-Rifa'i
(left and right, respectively).

68.

67. The interior of Khayrbek Mosque. The Cairene building tradition used stone extensively. By the 16th century, when this mosque was built, the use of sophisticated stone vaulting was common.

68. Historic Cairo's skyline is punctuated by countless domes and minarets: the reconstruction of the Khayrbek minaret as seen within the larger context of preserving the cityscape of the historic metropolis.

69. Conservation work involved the training of stonemasons to work on historic buildings, a skill much needed in Cairo today.

70. The Citadel, with its Muhammad Ali Mosque, forms the termination point for historic al-Darb al-Ahmar Street, the main spine of the neighbourhood.

71. Participatory discussions with shopkeepers in front of a local vegetable market model, an area under consideration for future improvement.

72. One of the events in the programme 'Women Working Together', aimed at offering women a forum for discussion of shared gender issues.

71.

72.

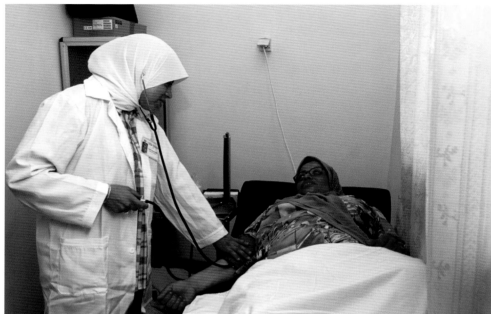

73. The Family Health Development Centre
provides professional clinical care
and referral services for local residents
at an affordable value.

74. Asaad Alley, as seen prior to rehabilitation,
exemplifies modern immigration patterns
from the countryside, where rural-oriented
residents have imposed a new set
of cultural values on the urban fabric
(see also plate 88).

73.

74.

75. Rooftops are often heaped with rubbish.
Current solid waste management systems have been unable to cope with the demands for disposal, and residents resort to using all available spaces for garbage. The AKTC is raising awareness and forming partnerships between the community and waste disposal organisations to deal with rubbish removal.

77.

78.

79.

76. The small Aslam Square in front of Aslam Mosque, adjacent to Bab al-Mahruq, one of the historic principal gates along the eastern side of the Ayyubid wall. With the opening of Azhar Park, seen under construction in the background, this old connection, long ago blocked, will be re-established (see also page 192).

77. Local businesses have benefited from the increased business generated by AKTC rehabilitation work. At the same time, many, such as this street tea seller, are eligible to complement that short-term income with longer perspective micro-credit for small enterprise loans that can allow for expansion into proper shop spaces.

78. Most local workshops operate on a small scale and are labour intensive. Few, such as these mother-of-pearl boxmakers employed in wholesale manufacturing for the nearby tourist market of Khan al-Khalili, have the capital required to invest in improving the quality and quantity of their products.

79. Part of the public open space enhancement programme targets reviving small neighbourhood nodes. Besides enduring inappropriate activities, these spaces typically suffer from a semblance of buildings clad with inappropriate materials.

80. Restoration work on the former
Shoughlan Street School included a complete
cleaning and refinishing of the original balconies.

81. All woodwork for the new school building
was fabricated in the Darb al-Ahmar Carpentry
Training Workshop staffed by local craftsmen.

82. Seen before its completion, restoration
of the former Shoughlan Street School
into a community and visitor centre
represents the first major historic building
finished by the AKTC. The building,
with the Ayyubid wall and Sultan Hasan Mosque
in the background, is ideally located near
Azhar Park.

83. The north elevation of the former
Shoughlan Steet School showing the original
appearance and colour scheme of the façade.
Originally built as a family residence in 1911,
the building follows grander European-inspired
models from the 19th century.

84. A computer rendered model of the front
façade of No. 16 Haret al-Sa'ayda,
one of the houses currently under rehabilitation
in the framework of the Darb al-Ahmar
housing programme launched by the AKTC.

80.

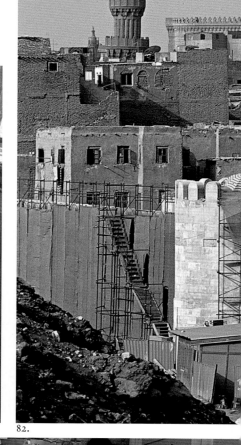

82.

81.

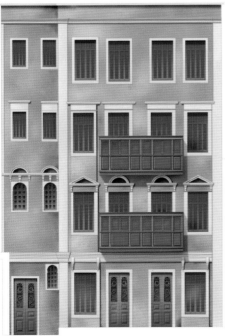

83.

84.

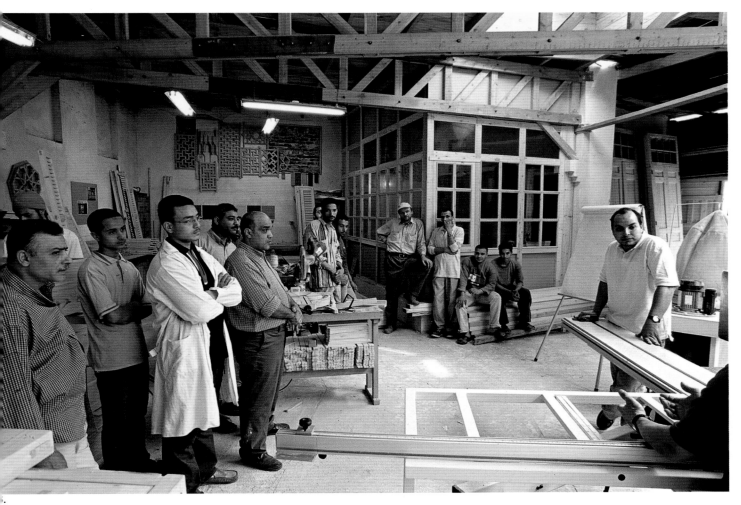

85. A wood conservation workshop was set up on site at Khayrbek to restore the numerous *mashrabiyya* screens found throughout the complex.

86. The training component of the socio-development programme includes the Darb al-Ahmar Carpentry Training Workshop, where local craftsmen have the opportunity to improve their skills and assist in the physical rehabilitation of their neighbourhood.

87. On-the-job training and apprenticeship programmes for local carpenters provide the opportunity to acquire practical skills.

88.

88. Housing improvement projects along Asaad Alley, abutting the Ayyubid wall (see also plate 74).

89. The AKTC housing rehabilitation programme in Darb Shoughlan close to the the school building.

90, 91. Two interior views of apartments in the Darb Shoughlan Street house, now inhabited by local residents.

92. Exterior view of restored houses in Darb Shoughlan Street.

89.

90.

91.

93. An interior stairwell of a Darb Shoughlan Street house after restoration.

The Development of Azhar Park

CAMERON RASHTI

Azhar Park, being currently completed by the Aga Khan Trust for Culture (AKTC) in central Cairo, furnishes rare insight, in its development process, into the impetus behind urban land development and the precarious position of parks within the otherwise relentless drive of urban development. The origins of parks, whether humble or grand in scale and design, can spring from single acts of vision and, by good design and implementation, result in the enhancement of a special tract of land. Land becomes developed when it has significant value and that value can be generated by its inherent quality or natural attraction, its location, or both. Even highly unattractive land can take on special value in certain circumstances, although, first, the social or economic case needs to become compelling for the process to start.

In more recent periods, major parks in inner cities have tended to depend on a high degree of coordination by the developing authority and some degree of serendipity in gaining access to a large, under-utilised space. In the increasingly strongly commoditised world of real estate (the market translation of the three-dimensional space of the landscape designer), the case for open space is one which is often hard to construct and harder to defend. When the criteria for judging competing potential uses of central city space are predominantly economic ones, the less-intensive, passive, reflective, and civic functions of a public park can be difficult, in these narrow terms, to promote as a priority, if not a necessity for a measure of urban balance.

Which makes it even more significant that in historic Cairo, less than four kilometres from the Nile and one kilometre from the Citadel, and abutting the eastern historic wall of the Ayyubid era, a tract of thirty-one hectares has remained essentially untouched for more than ten centuries by the residents surrounding the site, other than for the purpose of tipping loads of debris and rubble from the historic city over its eastern edge. The integrity of the site can perhaps be said to have been defended by these man-made deposits, which gradually reached such levels and heights that the more than one kilometre of the historic wall along its edge was submerged on the outside face by the undulations and hills of loose fill, up to forty-five metres in depth.

The increasingly prohibitive cost of removing the debris or finding uses for the artificial hills which could support no heavy structures without deep piling, must have excluded this tract earlier from the normal pressures of urban development. Initially, the historic walls set firm and irrefutable limits to the city's breadth and width. Fortifications on the town's perimeter were meant to protect and insulate those inside from the outside domain, to designate (protected) internal urban space from (unprotected) external rural space. As in many other medieval settlements, the void outside had for residents physical and mental attributes, only eventually worn down in later periods. An example of how stretches of the outlying city spaces can be reunited with the inner city settlement in their post-medieval phase is illustrated by the development of Azhar Park.

THE PARK'S PHYSICAL SETTING

The long-time isolation of the park site from the inner city of Cairo is better understood when viewed in a larger geographical and geological context. The city of Cairo, which has been expanding since its original founding, itself sits largely on an alluvial plain overlying approximately three hundred metres of unconsolidated sediment, transported over the millennia by the Nile. Historic Cairo was founded in the relatively narrow floodplain valley between the Nile and the neighbouring limestone escarpment of the Moqattam Hills, which rise to nearly 150 metres above the otherwise flat plain and form a natural barrier eastwards of the river.

Between the alluvial plains and the Moqattam Hills rests an intermediate zone, a structural plain of sandstone, quartzite and calcareous clay. Characterised by a diverse topography, this area features diverse landforms, including hills, ridges, remains of petrified forests, and shifting sand masses. The park site falls at the eastern border of the alluvial plain, overlooked by the nearby escarpments. The extraordinary levels of sediment have played a pivotal part in the physical development and evolution of the city and do so today where certain sites near the central city pose complex problems for the support and stability of the increasingly intensive and high-rise developments — the typical response to the high cost of land. As Cairo continues to expand along its eastern and southern edges, the city increasingly extends beyond the edge of the alluvial plain and its historic site, into this intermediary plain.

THE HISTORICAL TRANSFORMATION OF THE SITE

Since the founding of Cairo, the cyclical collapse and demolition of man-made structures have added vast amounts of debris to the overall quantum of fill the city rests upon. Large areas of historic Cairo, itself, sit on fill from earlier periods. The large-scale deposit of such fill in physically discrete zones at the edges of the expanding city seems to have been an early practice. The cycle of building decay and demolition and subsequent removal as fill to adjacent heaps east of the built city, in the vicinity of the Citadel, is noted as having intensified, by one account,[1] during the period following the end of the Mamluk era (1517).

A seventeenth-century French travelogue mentions that the heights of debris nearly hid the high walls surrounding the old city of Cairo. During the later Ottoman era, urban growth is described as having been vigorous on the western side of Cairo whilst decay was underway on the east. The opportunities created by the shifting riverbank of the Nile on the west and the geological deterrents on the east have contributed to this pattern. Maps prepared by the French expedition at the start of the nineteenth century graphically confirm large and well-established tracts of man-made hills immediately east of the Ayyubid wall and north of the Citadel and Bab al-Wazir cemetery.

Fig. 54. Historical photograph taken from the east with the Citadel in the foreground and the Darassa Hills and al-Darb al-Ahmar behind.

Reflections of this area are still visible today, in Azhar Park's topography. The park site, known also as the Darassa Hills, lies east of the historic city, and is characterised by northwards running hills, where layers from twenty to forty metres of fill have been found. Unique geological and man-made environmental pressures have jointly shaped over millennia, in the one case, and over centuries, in the other, the essential physical parameters, which ultimately were to become a park site.

THE RATIONALE FOR THE SITE'S DEVELOPMENT AS A PARK

While excluded from the historic city, the proximity and size of the park site have in recent years posed a dilemma to would-be occupants. The disadvantages of its geo-technical properties have been significant enough to create a quasi 'frontier' to urban growth, while its proximity to the historic core and offer of large open space has made it a natural zone for transformation, and the opportunities to transform Cairo's edges have not gone unnoticed in the last few decades.

The inspired proposal in 1990 to transform the rugged site into a municipal park can be singled out as the prime reason for its current integrity. The resultant use of it to contain a water reservoir as well as a park added complexity, but further underlined the civic function associated with the site, reinforcing its place in the public domain.

Parks have historically been ideal forms of buffer zones between competing urban uses as well as transitional devices in separating or differentiating various intensive districts. The surrounding inter-urban routes of al-Azhar Street and Salah Salem Street, which have, over time, become vital transport links, and the discontinuity between al-Darb al-Ahmar and the City of the Dead

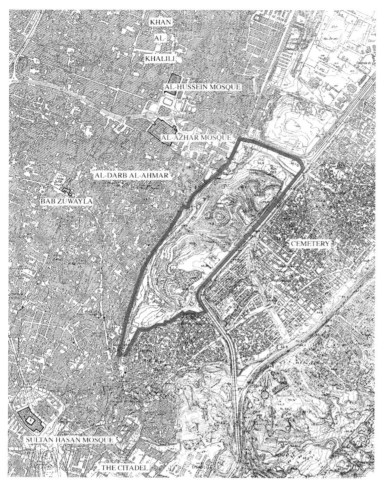

Fig. 55. Map of historic Cairo: the Azhar Park site demarcated with a heavy solid line.

in the east-west direction, and al-Azhar and the Citadel to its south, have skirted the site, turning it into a buffer zone with highly contrasting edges and vistas. The housing built on top of sections of the historic wall on its west and signs of squatter activity signalled a situation that had reached a head in terms of urban pressures needing resolution in one form or another.

The initiative to develop a park on this large but hemmed in site turns a corner in the evolution of this district, allowing the city to respect its past (the limits of the old city, the more than 1300-metre-long historic wall, and the barren expanse of the site) while providing significant open space in which the pedestrian resident/visitor can move through a three-dimensional space in the absence of the ubiquitous car, providing him with the chance to escape the predominant general urban experience. Surrounded on the north, east and part of the west by roadways, the site's park space declares a local victory of nature and pedestrian movement over the vehicle.

THE PARK MASTER PLAN

At its earlier stages, Sasaki Associates was enlisted to establish with the AKTC the guiding principles for the park's master planning process. In the mid-1990s, this included the careful insertion of a park circulatory system and feature spaces around and above the constructed water reservoir. Due to its size, centrality and proximity to historic Cairo, the park site was assigned a value by its planners, which called for its treatment as a metropolitan park in scale.

Al-Darb al-Ahmar's need for green space was a clear priority from the start. The educational or informational value of a multi-purpose park, which could be a large gateway to historic Cairo and a platform from which to overlook the monumental skyline of the city, was a further objective. Parks

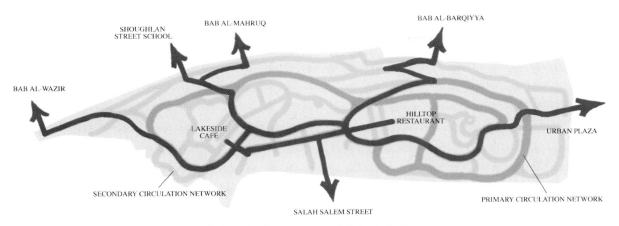

Fig. 56. Azhar Park circulatory system and links with adjacent streets and al-Darb al-Ahmar.

should contain walkways and amenities, but they are clearly intended to provide plentiful areas of green space. While small parks can thrive on a narrow range of plant life, Azhar Park was viewed as a space which would encompass a wide diversity of plant form serving as a central theme itself.

ADVANCING THE PROJECT DURING A FIRST WAVE OF DEVELOPMENT (1992-1996)
While the concept master plan had reached a clear level of definition as early as 1996, the project's advance was delayed by a requisition from the General Organisation of Greater Cairo (GOGCWS) to the Governorate of Cairo to use the same site for the construction of a municipal water reservoir complex, consisting of three large, circular reservoirs (each 80 m diameter) and a pump station to serve the adjacent district. In a comparatively short period, the site shifted from its historic derelict status to one of strategic importance with respect to the district infrastructure. In a sense, in modern terms, the real estate pressure on the site had begun.

A multi-year programme of excavation, piling and grading works was set in motion to construct the reservoir system between 1991 and 1996. The superimposition of this water reservoir system on the site inevitably created an additional set of constraints in terms of safeguarding the investment value of the infrastructure and the necessity to provide maintenance access to the reservoir tanks and distribution lines (including a 1400 mm diameter transmission line), which run the length of the park. A set of design guidelines, prepared by the GOGCWS consultant team, established criteria for areas of interface between the park design and the reservoir system. As the AKTC team resumed design in the mid-1990s, it was clear that the park design would need to nimbly incorporate the reservoir tank tops into a general master plan.

RESUMING THE DESIGN OF THE PARK
By 1998, a number of preliminary environmental strategies for overcoming the site's geo-technical and soil problems had been advanced and tested, an off-site nursery established to commence propa-

gation of a wide range of plants, and a landscape architectural team, Sites International, appointed. As lead design consultant, Sites International took on the central organising role in the development of the final master planning and schematic design.

The resultant scheme — developed over 1998-1999 — tackled head-on the problem of creating a natural, organic landscaped area with an array of amenities next to a dense, urban community and medieval monuments. Linkages through gates in the wall with the community were sought and, by means of extensive excavation along the historic wall, the park topography was brought in cascading slopes down to a new 'Historic Wall Promenade', which forms a principal walkway at the base of the wall and western slopes, interconnected to all parts of the park. Flatter areas were studied for more intensive pedestrian-water-viewing relationships, and the large reservoir tank tops were incorporated into the design as special gardens at higher altitudes.

THE MASTER PLAN'S RESPONSE TO THE SITE CHALLENGES
In the further development of the master planning of the park, site analysis capitalised on the opportunities offered by the site, deriving from its neglect over the centuries as a result of its exclusion from the living urban fabric of Old Cairo. The historic wall, a massive defence wall system, exceeding 1300 metres along the eastern perimeter of the city, represented an absolute edge on the east of the original Fatimid city. It was later extended but essentially respected in an outer line built by the Ayyubids. It provided, at one stroke, both a limit to sprawl and a magnificent testimony to the abilities of military engineering and masonry skills of the twelfth century.

Following a major programme of debris removal and master grading by the AKTC, involving the excavation and off-site disposal of more than one million cubic metres of fill, the experience of the site has been radically changed. Excavation of debris to depths of seven to eight metres along the eastern face of this wall and the discovery and exposure of a buried 300-metre extension of the wall along the north has re-established visually the original scale and importance of the wall system, in turn raising renewed interest in the archaeological richness of this part of Cairo. Uncovering the wall reinforced the importance of utilising the park project not only as general park space but also as a platform to view panoramically, and re-interpret, the built heritage of historic Cairo. Large areas of the park sit over twenty metres above the Darb al-Ahmar district, while the peaks of the park hills exceed it by around forty metres.

Master grading of the western half of the site from the high fixed points of hills and reservoir tank tops to the lowest point of the historic wall has relieved the original slopes. The western slopes remain radical from the viewpoint of landscape treatment, and design solutions have necessitated, accordingly, attention to slope stability, techniques of planting, irrigation, and drainage in this relatively steep and narrow zone flanking the wall.

THE GEO-TECHNICAL CHALLENGE: 1997-1999

Extensive soil physical property tests, initiated in the concept phase, led to the classification of site fill as being very silty and compressible, with an extremely low level of absorbency of water. While variable across the site, the fill had been laid over the years without proper compaction. Under light loads, the fill naturally undergoes moderate settlement, if it does not become wet; upon wetting, the fill compresses under its own weight. Geo-technical studies conducted early in the project made it evident that anything heavier than light structures would need piling support.

A number of strategies to overcome the inherent problems in the site soils in supporting hardscaped and planted areas were developed. While major buildings would clearly require piling or raft foundation support, a technique involving the partial excavation and replacement of soil in compacted layers of 'structural fill', to depths of two to three metres, is sufficient for support of hardscape areas. To further minimise chances of settlement due to infiltration of water from planted zones, an impervious barrier has been provided below the compacted layer.

This, in turn, further justified the removal of one to two metres of the top layer of existing fill for replacement with a similar barrier and improved soils. Isolation of the irrigated top zone, combined with systems of controlled irrigation and below-grade drainage, will enable the planted area to operate independently of the ancient layers of fill below. Wetting agents and mixtures of imported sand and agricultural soil will further improve the physical soil properties.

THE CHALLENGE OF PLANTATION ON THE SCALE OF THE PARK

Most of Egypt and Cairo fall within an extremely arid climate belt, which continues westwards across the North African desert. It is the river, the sustenance of much of Egypt and Cairo, that allows the Nile valley to avoid the harshness otherwise implicit in extremely arid climes. The realities of high temperatures, low humidity, scant rainfall and desert winds at certain seasons set possible if stringent criteria for planting systems.

A plentiful and reliable source of irrigation water is of critical importance to man-made gardens in any arid climate. The existence of a pipeline supplying river water from the Nile within adjacent Salah Salem Street, on the east of the site, was indispensable. Realising the growing pressures on available water supplies in the region, irrigation system efficiency and the goal of moderating total consumption by selective usage of xerophytic plants have been set as high priorities.

Despite these climatic extremes, Egypt boasts a wide range of native plants and trees, including dry landscape and desert species. The project has, in a sense, coincided with a phase of significant research and development projects involving desert reclamation, the introduction of new irrigation application techniques, and the expansion of commercial farming in Egypt, culminating over recent decades. While landscape architecture is still struggling for its rightful position as a speciality distinct from horticultural engineering in Egypt, the level of public and private interest in, and involvement with, horticultural issues is significant and growing.

The park project presented a special horticultural case in which highly unusual man-made environmental conditions were found to be superimposed over the normal constraints and challenges found on arid climate sites. Initial testing of existing soil and mixtures with various additives over several months demonstrated, in the early investigative phases, that a reasonable range of plant types could survive with conditioning of the soil medium. In order to support other than solely xerophytic plant types, which can survive in drought-like conditions and tolerate highly saline soil conditions, a programme of soil improvement including additives (sand, agricultural soils, gypsum), nutrients, and salt flushing by initial irrigation was proposed and tested on site. Planting prototypes were established on both flat and highly sloped areas to test these options. Feedback from both horticultural and prototype planted areas has been an essential part of the design methodology.

With approximately two-thirds of the site scheduled to be covered by planting of various types, sources of sufficient plant stock for 210,000 to 220,000 square metres became a significant issue. Despite the presence of some commercial nurseries, a decision was taken to establish a limited on-site nursery for the above-described horticultural testing and a larger, off-site nursery for propagation of the main stock. In an important example of cooperation, the American University of Cairo made available to the project a plot of fifty *feddans* in their desert agricultural research centre in South Tahrir over a multi-year period for cultivation as a park nursery. The park's landscape will vary from dry, succulent plants on the western slopes to lush, grassy meadows with shade trees, to formal gardens, and finally to *bustan*-like orchard space. The variety of species, particularly native Egyptian plants, will aim at establishing a new benchmark for park spaces in the region.

THE PARK'S FINAL DESIGN

Due to size and centrality, Azhar Park is expected to fulfil a vital function in expanding park and green space available to the public in Greater Cairo, the population of which stood close to seventeen million in 2002. It is anticipated that the park will attract visitors from other regions as well. Total annual visitation is projected to reach as many as 1.5 million persons in the initial years. The park design, of necessity, has needed to keep this large potential user group in perspective.

The design of the park also sought to make maximum and skilful use of the site's location, elevated topography, and unique vistas overlooking historic Cairo. Generously dimensioned pedestrian paths follow the contours in most areas, allowing comfortable circuits of the entire park site. An important exception to the curvilinear path system occurs along the main promenade, off the eastern entry gate. Here a formal and linear promenade runs along a straight, but descending, course from a restaurant on the northern hill, through the centre of the central tank-top, and continues 250 metres southwards on axis with the Citadel complex to the south. This processional path measures eight metres wide and is flanked on both sides by a double row of royal palms and parallel side paths, with pockets for seating.

At an *étoile* at the southern extreme of this path, the main promenade turns in a south-western direction, passing through a compartmentalised, formal garden and thence to a lakeside pavilion café overlooking a large lake. The outer zones of the plain feature an orchard (*bustan*), which will provide shade, a stimulating variety of flowering and fruit trees, and further room to stroll. The main promenade and series of formal gardens are anchored at each end by the hilltop restaurant and lakeside pavilions, which provide internal landmarks for the park. Water features provide an additional and traditional theme from Islamic gardens, tying this central pathway together along its entire length. Water fountains, pools, and carefully confined water channels are dispersed and lead, ultimately, to the freer form of the lake in the south meadow. Lighting has been introduced into the park with maximum use of low-level, custom-built bollards and restriction of pole-type light fixtures to the parking and eastern edge. Along the main spine, custom marble light towers are integrated, as with all seating, into the main spine's design motifs.

The terrain in the western half of the park consists predominantly of steep and continuous slopes, running from the summits to the foot of the historic wall. A continuous pathway has been carved into the hillside at approximately mid-height between the walkway along the historic wall and the summits of the hills and provides lateral access at points to the eastern half. The western hillside will be cloaked with flowering and succulent plants with luxuriant tones. Views from the many vantage points along the west, across these slopes and the restored historic wall to Old Cairo, beyond, with its beguiling constellation of monuments and minarets, will be captivating for residents and visitors to Cairo alike.

The sensitive and purposeful integration of the recently constructed reservoir tank tops into the surrounding park plan has been an important design priority from the start. The park design calls for a seating area under trees on the south tank top, with views out over the city. The central tank top, in line with the main promenade, will contain a formal garden symmetrically sub-divided into a rich geometric design of landscaped zones. Here, associations with historical models of Islamic gardens are evoked in the form of symmetrical layout, inner and outer zones, the defining medium of pools and fountains, and important axes. The northern tank top, easily accessed from the main park as well as al-Azhar Street from the north, is scheduled to serve as a play area for various age groups and in close vicinity to an intimately-scaled amphitheatre.

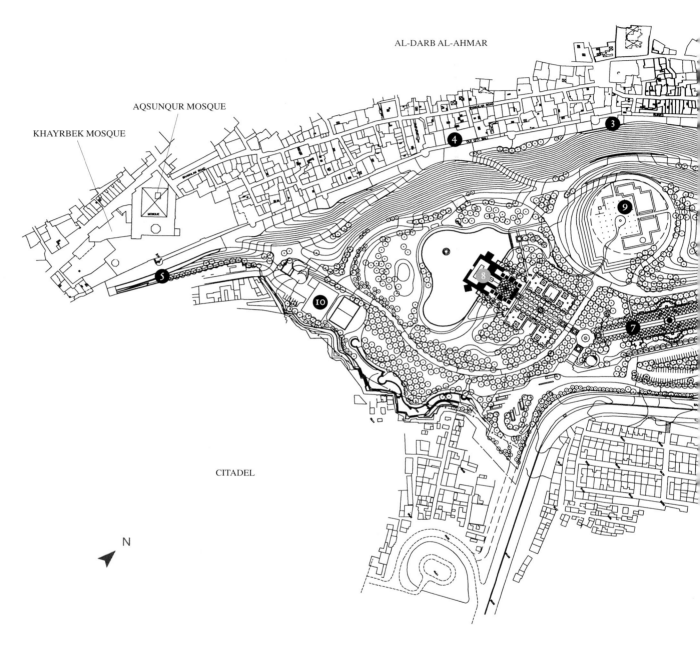

AL-DARB AL-AHMAR

AQSUNQUR MOSQUE

KHAYRBEK MOSQUE

CITADEL

N

Fig. 57. Azhar Park Master Plan.

1. Main entrance from Salah Salem Street.

2. Side entrance through rediscovered city gate in the Ayyubid wall (Bab al-Barqiyya).

3. Connection with al-Darb al-Ahmar via old city gate and Aslam Square.

4. Proposed community centre and park administration in the rehabilitated Shoughlan Street School. This location will connect the park and the old city, visitors being led through the internal chambers of the Ayyubid wall.

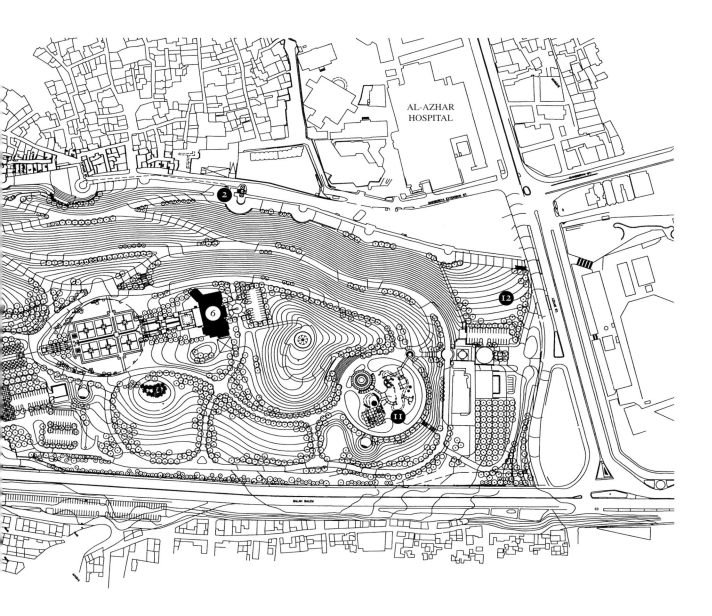

5. Connection towards the Bab al-Wazir area, the Citadel and the Sultan Hasan complex, as well as a way of entering the courtyard behind Khayrbek Mosque.

6. Hilltop Restaurant with sweeping views of Cairo's major landmarks.

7. Main spine on the plateau connecting both the restaurant facility and the Lakeside Café.

8. Lakeside Café with courtyards and orchards in the Islamic tradition.

9. Viewing platform and gardens on the southern tank top, offering a panorama of historic Cairo.

10. Community sports complex, for residents of al-Darb al-Ahmar and local youth clubs.

11. Children's playground on the northern tank top.

12. Preferred site of 'Urban Plaza' now under study.

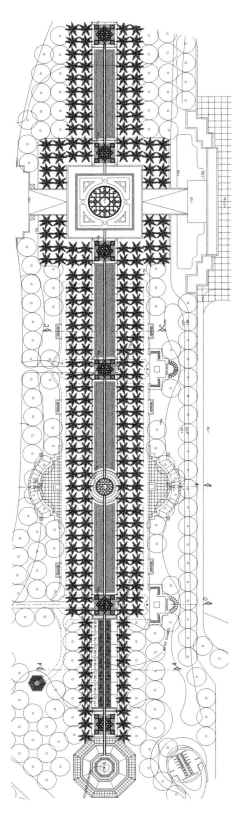

During the course of the park's design, significant time and attention was devoted, on the part of the AKTC, to exploring the potential for a sound, creative, and interpretative relationship between the architectural design treatment of key architectural features in the park — in particular, the lakeside pavilion café, hilltop restaurant, and various plazas — with the architecture of historic Cairo. This inquiry was taken to the level of a design competition for the restaurant facility, the outcome of which has led to the appointment of design architects for each facility, working in close co-ordination with the park architect. As an intrinsic part of the competition brief, the designs of these structures are each informed, in varying ways, by the careful survey of earlier examples of Fatimid and Mamluk architecture. These exercises led to the agreement by the Trust to construct two food-and-beverage facilities within the park, described in further detail below.

THE HILLTOP RESTAURANT

Originally conceived as a secluded, five-star restaurant set on the higher hills within the park, the design has evolved to that of a two-storey facility featuring a full restaurant, outdoor terrace, lobby, and, upstairs, a tearoom and *manzara* café. The total facility will consist of 1300 square metres on the ground floor and 500 square metres on the first. Access will be via the park main entrance (see drawings) and along an internal access drive. A zone for parking (twenty-four cars) will be provided opposite the restaurant entrance; valet parking will be able to park surplus cars in the main parking bays off the park entrance.

The building, designed by architects Rami El Dahan and Soheir Farid, provides a traditional shell for the various dining zones within an interpretation of historic Cairene architecture. The restaurant plan is based on a symmetrical

Fig. 58. Plan of the park's main spine from the entry plaza to the *étoile*.

160

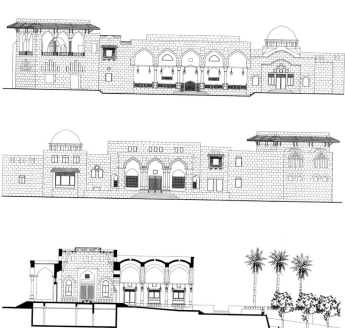

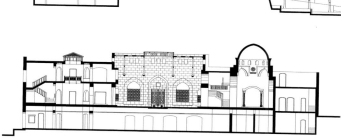

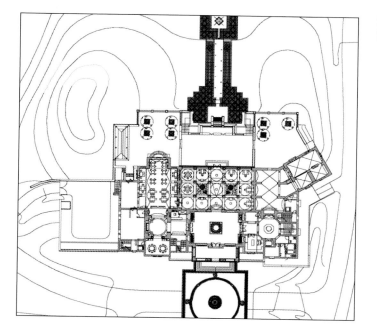

Figs. 59, 60. Hilltop Restaurant.
Four principal elevations; ground-floor plan.

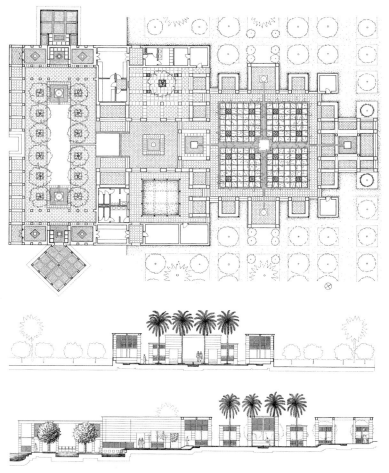

layout whose central axis passes through an entrance palm court, an entry portico, or *takhtaboush*, before arriving at a terraced garden overlooking the main axis of the park. Along this axis, vistas of the park's main promenade and the Citadel complex, beyond, can be seen.

THE LAKESIDE CAFÉ

The conceptual design of the Lakeside Café, prepared by architect Serge Santelli, is based on a highly geometric array of pavilions set around the sides of a palm court, on the east side. On its western end, the café encloses a poolside terrace on three sides with the open edge overlooking the lake in the south meadow. While providing ample shade and fascinating courtyard areas, the Lakeside Café can be considered an indoor-outdoor space. The lakeside zone is further defined by two square pavilions at each end of the poolside terrace, enclosed with wood screen walls, with in-

Fig. 61. Lakeside Café. Ground-floor plan and elevations below.

tricate detail referring to traditional *mashrabiyya* panels. In contrast to its hilltop counterpart, the Lakeside Café will offer light salads, snacks, and pastries together with a tea and coffee service, depending, naturally, on the time of day.

In the eastern portion, seating is provided under the various twelve shade pavilions, which provide shaded seating area on the sides of the palm court. Further service spaces are provided in the intermediate zone where one enters the Lakeside Café. The Palm Court is intended to serve general park visitors who wish to relax informally during their visit to the park.

THE PARK'S SUSTAINABILITY AND EVOLUTION

Park space marked by walkways, pools, hills, greenery and amenities constitute a park's identity at its inception, but parks are unlike buildings and more like living urban districts, begging for the life and animation of users. Also unlike buildings, park softscape in particular — its biomass and plant profile — do not stand still but, rather, mature over time as its plant life takes root and prospers. Parks

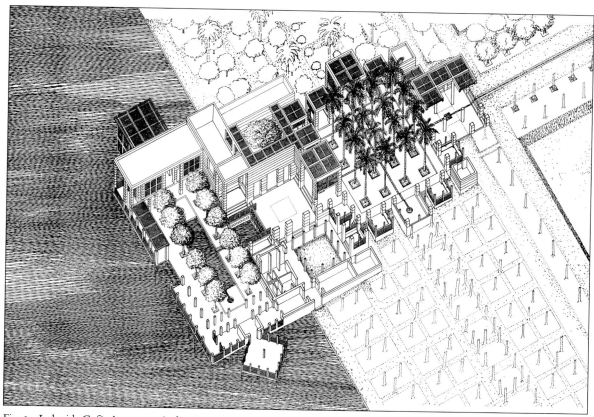

Fig. 62. Lakeside Café. Axonometric drawing with cutaway view of the interior.

really do need protection and the watching eye of a supervising entity. This fact has been recognised by the Governorate of Cairo and the Aga Khan Trust for Culture, and a Park Authority Board has been introduced as a special layer of trusteeship in the park's long-term maintenance.

Over time, well maintained parks take on significant but less tangible values, and this is expected to be the case for Azhar Park as well. Successful parks inspire residents, provide joy to viewers, and foster civil society in the important realm of leisure and connection to nature and one's environment. They become the settings for novels, films and festivities and often the containers for memories of a society. This is surely the role that Azhar Park aspires to over time.

[1]See Janet Abu-Lughod, *Cairo: 1001 Years of the City Victorious*, Princeton University Press, Princeton 1971, p. 52.

The Restoration of the Ayyubid City Wall

FRANCESCO SIRAVO AND FRANK MATERO

The historic urban wall below the Darassa Hills is the south-eastern segment of Cairo's Ayyubid fortifications, which were partially exposed during the works carried out by the Aga Khan Trust for Culture (AKTC) in the creation of the new Azhar Park. The wall measures over 1300 metres in length, running north from al-Wazir Gate to al-Azhar Street, and forms the boundary between the Darb al-Ahmar district of historic Cairo and the new park.

Built as part of the city's fortifications in the twelfth and thirteenth centuries by Salah al-Din and his successor, this portion of the city wall was Cairo's eastern boundary for centuries. Over time, the wall's role changed: although it continued to be a defining element for the city, it long ago ceased to serve as a defensive structure. This shift in function meant that the city gradually spread to the very edge of the wall, following an accretive process common to historic cities everywhere.

Fig. 63. The Ayyubid wall in the 1920s.

From the fifteenth century, the area just outside the wall began to be used as a dumping ground and the wall was gradually buried under the debris, where in fact it remained protected from the ravages of time and weather. Today, following the interventions to create the park, the outer face of the historic wall is once again exposed to view and to the elements, while, on the city side, private development pressures as well as institutional requirements raise complex urban development issues. Current interventions must consider not only the preservation of the wall, but also how best to intervene in the surrounding urban context. Thus, comprehensive planning and design policies are needed both with regard to the residential fabric abutting the wall as well as the points of access and the pedestrian promenade along the western edge of the new park.

HISTORICAL BACKGROUND

Construction of the Ayyubid wall was begun in 1176 by Salah al-Din, a Kurd of the Ayyubid clan who came to Cairo from Syria and overthrew the Fatimid caliphate in 1171. Salah al-Din's fortifications were built to contain Cairo, his citadel and the pre-Fatimid settlements (Fustat, al-

Fig. 64. An old photograph showing the Comité's reconstruction of Towers 3 and 4.

Askar and al-Qata'i) within a single system. These new fortifications were far more ambitious and sophisticated than the earlier Fatimid walls, which had been limited to enclosing the palace area and were more ceremonial than defensive. Although Salah al-Din's best known architectural achievement in Egypt is the Citadel he built on a spur of the Moqattam Hills, his idea of a single wall surrounding the much expanded metropolis would also prove a long-lasting legacy.

The new project incorporated rebuilt portions of the Fatimid fortifications and added extensive new sections. Salah al-Din pushed the northern city wall west to the Nile, and the eastern wall south to the Citadel, from where it continued south-west around Misr-Fustat, the settlement developed by the Arab conquerors who invaded Egypt in the seventh century.[1] The new city walls were built entirely of stone and made use of new advanced defensive techniques imported from Syria, with bent entrances and arrow slits reaching to the floor.

The east wall seems to have remained important for some two centuries after its construction. Aslam al-Silahdar, a Mamluk prince and sword bearer to the sultan in the mid-fourteenth century, built a mosque just inside Bab al-Mahruq, an indication that the eastern gateways still functioned. This would also seem to signify that the prestige of this part of the city was still such that a prominent member of the court would choose this location for a monumental religious complex in his name.

Fig. 65. Tower 9 before the removal of debris and subsequent excavation.

Soon after, as the threat posed by crusader armies and other invaders declined so did the importance of maintaining the defensive walls. The result was that, where urban growth was vigorous, the city walls were rapidly obliterated by subsequent construction, as was the case on the western side of Cairo. However, on the eastern side, where urban expansion virtually stopped, the walls continued to mark the limits of the old city. It was already during the late Mamluk and early Ottoman periods, that the area outside these walls became a dumping ground, a practice that continued unabated during the following centuries.

A description by the French traveller Jean de Thévenot mentions, as early as 1658, the height of the debris, which nearly hid the high walls of the city:

> [these walls] are at present all covered in ruins which are so high that I have passed over some places where they wholly hide the walls, and are much above them; and in these places one would think that there were no wall [...] and though it would be very easy to clear the rubbish, and, by repairing what is wanting, make the walls appear beautiful and high, yet the Turks make no reparations; but suffer all to decay...[2]

A century and a half later, the maps drawn during the Napoleonic era show that buildings in al-Darb al-Ahmar were generally built right up to the edge of the city at the time of the French occupation around 1800. Many buildings actually abutted the Ayyubid wall and additional rooms were constructed into and indeed on top of the one-time fortifications, an accretive process common in many Middle-Eastern and European cities where the old defensive systems had lost their significance.

During the nineteenth century an increasing number of travellers came to Egypt, who sketched and photographed what they saw. In 1839, the artist David Roberts drew the southernmost portion of the walls, which appear partially buried and with numerous houses constructed along the city side.[3] A series of panoramas taken by French photographer Pascal Sebah[4] in 1880 provide one of the most valuable visual documents of the eastern Ayyubid wall, showing that much of the original stonework, including the crenellations, still existed at that time.

In 1882, the government established the Comité de Conservation des Monuments de l'Art Arabe to preserve Egypt's Islamic and Christian architectural heritage. In 1902, the Comité employed Edouard Matasek, an architect, to document the city walls with a view to restoring them at a later stage. Matasek produced elevations, sections and sketches of the east wall towers, but does not seem to have drawn the wall itself.

Although the Comité repaired the city walls from time to time during the first half of the twentieth century, it was not until 1950 that they undertook a major campaign. This consisted of a reconstruction of the two towers no longer standing (towers 3 and 4) along with extensive replacement of the missing facing stonework in several areas of the flank wall. This work was documented with photographs taken before, during and after the interventions.

For the next almost fifty years no further repairs or restoration was undertaken. The Ayyubid wall remained, as it had been for centuries, the eastern boundary of the densely built up Darb al-

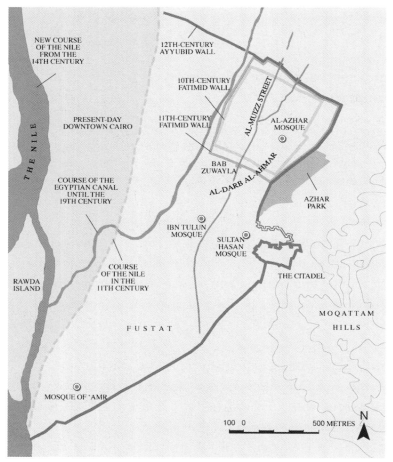

Fig. 66. Map showing the location of the earlier Fatimid walls
and the later Ayyubid fortifications built by Salah al-Din.

Ahmar district of historic Cairo. The continued dumping of rubbish meant that the mounds of debris, now known as the Darassa Hills, had buried the outer face of the wall all the way up to the level of the crenellations. It was only after AKTC began moving earth for the future Azhar Park that the accumulated debris was removed. The re-grading brought to light not only the buried section of the wall known through early photographs and historic maps, but also the northern section, unrecorded even on Napoleon's map of 1798, and probably buried since Mamluk times.

PRINCIPLES OF CONSERVATION

The restoration works carried out by the AKTC started in 1999 with a comprehensive study and the launching of pilot interventions on limited sections of the wall, and gradually extended to increasingly greater portions of the monument.[5] Currently, approximately 450 metres of the historic wall are under restoration, while an additional 300 metres are due to be completed by the end of 2004. The principles underlying the interventions can be summarised as follows:

- to research and document all evidence, including physical, archival and historical information, before, during and after intervention;
- to respect the cumulative age-value of the structure by recognising the stratification of human activity and displaying the passage of time and the different materials and techniques, as well as the changing cultural beliefs and values;
- to safeguard authenticity as a cultural value associated with the original actions of the making or re-making of the object or site, recognised as the embodiment of authorship or the record of a time and place;
- to avoid harm to the monument, either by minimising physical interference to re-establish structural and aesthetic legibility and meaning, or by intervening in ways that will allow other options and further treatment in the future.

These tenets are rooted in internationally recognised and accepted standards of conservation, namely the Athens Charter (1931) and the Venice Charter (1964). The Venice Charter in particular emphasises the importance of context, the discouragement of reconstruction except in cases of anastylosis (the re-assembling of collapsed elements), and the integration of modern scientific technology where appropriate and useful. More recent charters, such as the Burra Charter of 1981, established by ICOMOS Australia, point out that the ultimate aim of conservation is to retain or recover the cultural significance of a place and provide for its security, maintenance and future survival.

In line with these general principles, the intervention guidelines applied by the AKTC team to the conservation of the historic wall express a preference for the retention or compatible repair of the original fabric over reconstruction. The AKTC's recommendations for intervention on the surrounding urban fabric advocate respect for the changes accrued over time in order to preserve the

AL-MAHRUQ TOWER
(SECTION A TO B)

A   B

GROUND FLOOR   FIRST FLOOR

Fig. 67. Drawing of al-Mahruq Tower (from Creswell).

integrity, scale, and significance of the wall in its current configuration and context. Ultimately, the proposed interventions promote continuity rather than transformation. The long-term goal is to integrate and harmonise the remnants of a valuable past with present realities and future needs in ways that are compatible and sustainable.

PHYSICAL ASSESSMENT AND CONSERVATION ACTIONS

The first step in the conservation process was a comprehensive study of the wall's physical condition followed by a detailed assessment of each part of the monument that would be subject to intervention. The general study documented the wall's overall condition, including an analysis of the masonry and identification of areas of significant deterioration, distinguishing between the loss of facing stonework and the total loss of the wall. It also documented the presence and extent of previous repairs. The subsequent detailed condition survey provided a fuller quantitative analysis, complemented with a qualitative assessment of the causes and effects of deterioration. Severity of loss, for example, was classified according to the extent and depth, as well as whether the

Fig. 68. Panorama of Cairo by Pascal Sebah, 1870s.

Fig. 69. Panorama of Cairo looking west from the central section of the Ayyubid wall, 2003.

Fig. 70. General view of Cairo by Junghaendel, c. 1890.

Fig. 71. Panorama of Cairo showing the Aqsunqur and Khayrbek Mosques, and the southern end of the Ayyubid wall, 2003.

process was still active or inactive. In addition, samples were taken for laboratory testing to ascertain the exact nature of the materials and their conditions and problems.

Together, the field survey, graphic documentation and laboratory work yielded a comprehensive record of the construction of the wall and its present state of conservation, as well as the diagnostic tools needed to formulate an intervention programme. Recommended measures included archaeological investigation, emergency stabilisation, masonry treatments (including cleaning, removal of salt and biological growth, grouting, consolidation of deteriorating stone and selective stone replacement) as well as limited reconstruction where needed to maintain the structural stability or visual continuity of the wall. The resulting policies and guidelines for masonry intervention were designed to achieve maximum retention of the original historic fabric while ensuring the visual and functional continuity of the wall as an urban element.

In particular, the following intervention guidelines for masonry works are being followed in response to the different conditions found along the historic wall:

- *where the original Ayyubid masonry is still in place*, fallen stones are re-instated by anastylosis (as in the case of the fallen crenellations), and missing or structurally unsound veneer stones are replaced using similar stones, dimensions and coursing as in the original Ayyubid construction;

Fig. 72. A view of al-Barqiyya Gate.

- *where the original Ayyubid wall veneer stonework is mixed with subsequent repair stonework*, the missing stones are replaced in the manner of the repair, except where the number of missing stones is extensive and the repaired area is in very poor condition; in this latter case, the replacement stonework is carried out in the original Ayyubid manner;

- *where the wall is in a ruinous state*, with only the masonry core and no surviving veneer stonework, the ruin is stabilised;

- *where the Ayyubid wall has totally disappeared*, reintegration is effected by building a visually and structurally compatible new wall rather than through a hypothetical reconstruction of the original structure.

The survey, assessment, and conservation treatments along the approximately 450 metres designated for completion during Phase I are being carried out with the help of professionals and conservators recruited by the Trust and its local company, the Aga Khan Cultural Services-Egypt (AKCS-E). These activities also include a training component for Egyptian professionals, junior staff of the Antiquities Department and local craftsmen, and will continue after the opening of the park as an ongoing process of restoration, repair and long-term maintenance.

INTERVENING ON THE ADJOINING URBAN FABRIC

In addition to documenting the condition of the monument itself, the general survey analysed the wall's relationship with the adjoining urban fabric. Over the centuries, the houses and monuments built up against the wall on the city side became an integral part of Cairo's urban and social history. While selective removal of encroaching elements may be necessary, wholesale demolition of the historic housing stock attached to the city wall would contradict international conservation philosophy and practice. Demolition would also be likely to introduce undesirable development pressures. Therefore, the project team made a careful plot-by-plot study of the fabric along the his-

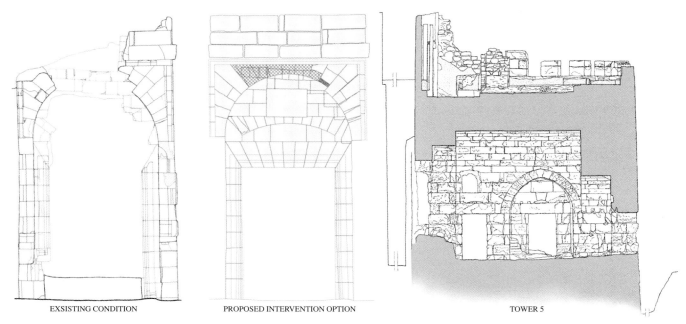

EXSISTING CONDITION   PROPOSED INTERVENTION OPTION   TOWER 5

Fig. 73. Elevations showing the existing condition   Fig. 74. Section through Tower 5.
and reconstruction of al-Barqiyya Gate.

toric wall, defining appropriate modes of intervention for each building within the larger framework of the Darb al-Ahmar conservation and rehabilitation plan.

The extent and configuration of the abutting houses was recorded by the team and assessed with regard to use, condition, date of construction, architectural integrity, and significance. In addition, in a series of typical sections, the team documented the physical connection between the wall and the adjacent buildings, and, in particular, whether these structures are built up against, on top of, or into the wall at the lower levels. Special attention was given to recording all cases where adjoining buildings pose a specific threat to the structural integrity of the wall, as a result of damaging industrial activities or water seepage from plumbing installations.

These various analyses were complemented by an in-depth investigation of the social and housing conditions in the strip of urban fabric along the wall, and became the basis for the interventions currently under way. The latter include the removal of incongruous, detrimental or structurally unsound additions and accretions, the retention and rehabilitation of selected historic buildings, and the improvement of housing conditions in order to avoid the displacement of residents. In parallel, the AKTC planning team is working to introduce new building regulations to selectively modify the current antiquities legislation so that buildings or structures within immediate proximity of a monument are not automatically cleared, thus allowing for the preservation of the surrounding historic context. Altogether, the plans and ongoing interventions advocate the con-

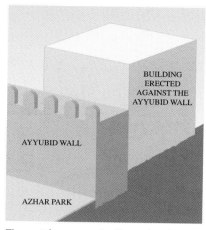 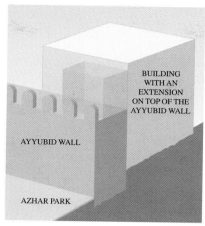 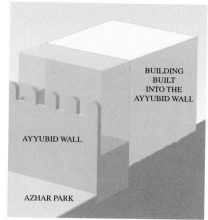

Fig. 75. Three examples illustrating the types of encroachment encountered along the Ayyubid wall.

servation and harmonious integration of the Ayyubid wall within the traditional urban fabric and contemporary life of al-Darb al-Ahmar.

THE WALL AS A CULTURAL RESOURCE AND VISITOR DESTINATION

Together, conservation of the original wall structure and preservation of the living city fabric in and around it should be seen as the best antidotes against further decay as well as the destructive commercialisation that comes with excessive numbers of visitors and uncontrolled tourism. Certain risks to the wall and al-Darb al-Ahmar can be foreseen following the opening of the park in 2004. Too often cultural resources around the world have become mere commercial commodities to be consumed by mass tourism. The result is that genuine historic places are compromised and emptied of meaning and the local residents become overly dependent on an unpredictable tourism service economy.

Contrary to the above scenario, the historic wall can and should be turned into a resource and an opportunity to deepen the public's appreciation and understanding of the city's cultural heritage and the traditional social fabric associated with it. In pursuing this alternative, some questions become immediately relevant in planning for the future role of this important landmark: how can a forgotten and long-buried monument be re-introduced into a rapidly evolving new context without losing its significance? How can it be re-invented as a living component of today's historic Cairo? And, more generally, how can tourism generated by Azhar Park be reconciled with the traditional life of the Darb al-Ahmar community? Answering these questions is not just an academic exercise, but must be part of a pragmatic search for new meanings, functions, and activities around and within the wall. In particular, future actions to ensure that the historic wall maintains its original significance and is properly re-integrated into its contemporary context are anchored in four concepts, listed below.

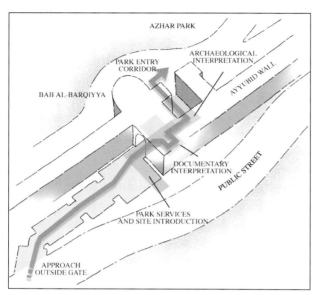

Fig. 76. Proposed interpretive programme
and visitor circulation for al-Barqiyya Gate.

Designing pedestrian access and circulation along the western side of the park to enhance the perception of the historic wall as a dynamic edge and meeting point, rather than as a barrier between the community and the park. The proposed access and circulation system identifies the locations of the former city gates as the natural and historically appropriate connections between the park and al-Darb al-Ahmar. Three gates or entrances are being revived: al-Barqiyya, close to the main traffic artery of al-Azhar Street, to serve as the main access from the north-western edge of the park; al-Mahruq, the vanished gate that is currently the subject of an archaeological excavation, to create a mid-point entry; and al-Wazir at the south-western corner of the park, to provide access close to the main religious sites and historic monuments along the southern stretch of al-Darb al-Ahmar Street. In addition, two more connections are proposed in conjunction with the visitors' exhibits and circuits at Shoughlan Street and al-Mahruq Tower. All of these links are conceived as meeting points to foster visitor and community interaction and sustain carefully planned venues into the daily life of al-Darb al-Ahmar.

Establishing didactic programmes and experiences in order to enhance appreciation of the wall as a monument and as an important urban feature of historic Cairo, to explain its changing role in the development of the city, and to introduce visitors to the life of the community that inhabits the adjoining district. Planned initiatives include visitors' circuits and exhibits through the Shoughlan Street School and along the ramparts and interior galleries between towers 4 and 5, and in al-Mahruq Tower, featuring the presentation of the archaeological, historical, military, cultural, and social aspects related to past and contemporary uses of the wall. In addition, a major archaeological park is also being planned for the northernmost area, between towers 14 and 15, where there is a unique opportunity to explore the archaeological remains along the city side of the wall, which has been buried since Mamluk times. Finally, the establishment of a space for exhibitions and other cultural activities is planned in the Khayrbek complex next to the southern edge of the historic wall. This facility will offer a focal point for the community and provide visitors with a better understanding of the local culture and traditions.

Introducing activities that are relevant to promoting a deeper understanding of the cultural heritage among visitors and residents and the development of local skills and abilities to preserve and protect historic Cairo. The wall offers great opportunities in this respect, both as an arena to demonstrate the aims and methods applied to its discovery and conservation, and as an ongoing training ground where local craftsmen, national bodies, and international institutions can come together to explore and identify appropriate restoration techniques. These experiences will also promote the creation of a manpower base specialised in traditional building crafts, modern restoration techniques and small enterprise development, all of which are needed throughout historic Cairo. Conservation can thus be linked to programmes that foster economic development and future employment opportunities for the local community.

Ensuring the future management and long-term sustainability of the wall through the establishment of permanent repair and maintenance programmes and the monitoring of future changes and transformations. In order to be successful in the particular context of the historic wall, sustainability must be considered as a dynamic process of public participation, achieved through dialogue and consensus, that ultimately leads to better stewardship of the monument. Future programmes must therefore ensure that the long-term benefits are understood and enjoyed also by the surrounding community, as it is one of the principal stakeholders in ensuring the continued life and appropriate use of the structure. In future, a refuse collection system, open space maintenance, repair of the wall, and rehabilitation of the surrounding buildings, should not be implemented against the will of the community, but with its direct involvement and participation.

This shift in perceiving the historic wall as an abstract, isolated monument to its re-invention as part of a larger urban programme, together with the gradual implementation of the plans and activities described above, can turn this obsolete structure, buried for centuries and removed from the city's mainstream development, into a cultural asset and vital component of the rehabilitation of historic Cairo. The challenge ahead lies in safeguarding the remains and true significance of the historic Ayyubid wall, while shaping its new role in the years to come.

[1]Neil D. MacKenzie, *Ayyubid Cairo: A Topological Study*, The American University in Cairo Press, Cairo 1992.
[2]Jean de Thévenot (1633-1667), [Relation d'un voyage fait au Levant.] *The Travels of Monsieur de Thévenot into the Levant. In Three Parts, viz. into I. Turkey. II. Persia. III. The East-Indies.* Newly done out of French. Printed by H. Clark, for H. Faithorne, J. Adamson, C. Skegnes, and T. Newborough, London 1687, folio. Translated by Archibald Lovell.
[3]David Roberts (1796-1864), *The Holy Land, Syria, Idumea, Arabia, Egypt & Nubia*, Day & Son, London 1855-1856.
[4]Pascal Sebah (1823-1886). On the life and work of Pascal Sebah see also *From Sebah & Joiallier to Foto Sebah: Orientalism in Photography*, YKY, Istanbul 1999.
[5]Aga Khan Trust for Culture, "The Eastern Ayyubid Wall of Cairo. Study Findings and Recommended Conservation Programme", HCSP Technical Brief No. 4, Cairo, n.p. 2001.

Urban Rehabilitation and Community Development in al-Darb al-Ahmar

FRANCESCO SIRAVO

The work on the park and the historic wall along the critical western edge of the Darassa site raised the issue of how best to harness the dynamics unleashed by the park project onto the adjacent urban area of al-Darb al-Ahmar, a densely built-up district of historic Cairo. The area lies south of the prestigious al-Azhar Mosque and the popular Khan al-Khalili, historic Cairo's principal tourist bazaar, and is bound by al-Azhar Street, the Darassa Hills and al-Darb al-Ahmar Street. Today, the area is the focus of much public interest, and is on the verge of major changes induced by a number of large-scale projects, including the recent completion of the Azhar Street tunnel, the planned pedestrian square between al-Azhar and al-Hussein, the development of new parking and commercial facilities on the 'Urban Plaza' site, and, lastly, the creation of the new Azhar Park on top of the Darassa Hills, a strategic location between the Fatimid city, the Mamluk cemeteries and the Citadel. These developments will dramatically improve the image and importance of al-Darb al-Ahmar over the next several years and call for a carefully studied urban plan of action to guide future interventions in the district.

RISKS AND OPPORTUNITIES

A vital residential district with many artisans, small enterprises and a strong social cohesion, al-Darb al-Ahmar suffers today from poverty, inadequate infrastructure and a lack of community services. Although endowed with sixty-five registered monuments and several hundred historic buildings, its residential building stock is in very poor condition due to the area's low family incomes and an economic base that often lags behind other parts of Cairo. The deterioration of the buildings is exacerbated by the imposition of unrealistic rent controls, counter-productive planning constraints and limited access to credit. The common perception of al-Darb al-Ahmar as a haven of crime and drug-related activity generates easy support for plans calling for radical clearance and 'sanitising' of the district, thus posing yet another threat to the survival of the historic urban fabric.

Contrary to common perceptions, the Aga Khan Trust for Culture's survey shows that most adults are gainfully employed and that crime in the district is negligible. Furthermore, over sixty percent of the people have lived in the area for thirty years or more, and almost twenty percent have been there for more than fifty years. Length of residence was found to be the result not of necessity, but

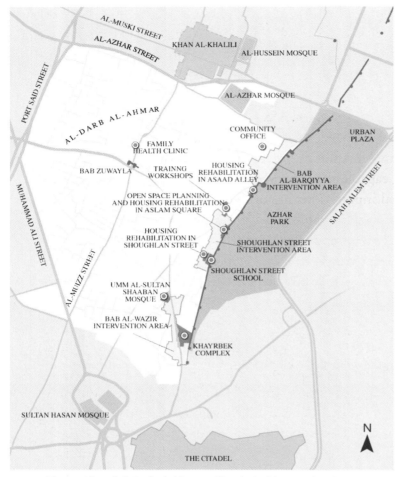

Fig. 77. Map of al-Darb al-Ahmar with principal intervention sites.

of choice. Most inhabitants feel comfortable and safe in their neighbourhoods. They cite the proximity of family and mosques, as well as the support of their neighbours, as reasons to stay in the area, thus highlighting the very traditional values and sense of community that are said to be lacking. Most importantly, residents view al-Darb al-Ahmar as their permanent home and are ready to invest their own resources to improve their living conditions. The survey thus demonstrates that the essential pre-conditions needed to implement a housing rehabilitation and economic revitalisation programme exist, and that such a programme can be firmly based on the district's social setting and local resources.

With its pedestrian scale, distinctive monuments, historic buildings and active community al-Darb al-Ahmar has the potential of becoming a vibrant residential and commercial area, as it was in the past, as well as an alternative destination for visitors to Islamic Cairo. The Azhar Park initiative further enhances the district's prospects and provides a strong impetus for parallel rehabilitation efforts in the area.

But these new opportunities cannot be separated from a number of inherent risks. On the one hand, the new Azhar Park, which is to become metropolitan Cairo's major green space, will no doubt represent a powerful attraction and a catalyst for change in the old city. It will transform the character of the area as a whole, and it is likely to spur increased public and private investment in the area. On the other hand, speculative pressures could soon determine a pattern of uncontrolled development in the area, leading to the expulsion of both current residents and their enterprises and activities, and so paving the way for a total substitution of the traditional urban fabric. These opportunities and risks must be anticipated, carefully managed and properly channelled through a conscious planning effort.

To this effect, beginning in 1996, the Aga Khan Trust for Culture (AKTC) and its local subsidiary, the Aga Khan Cultural Services-Egypt (AKCS-E), expanded the scope of its activities in the area and embarked on a comprehensive urban rehabilitation programme for al-Darb al-Ahmar.[1] The AKTC's long-term strategy focuses on the physical upgrading of the building stock and the socio-economic development of the community, two complementary objectives aimed at the general re-vitalisation of the entire district. This strategy is consistent with the AKTC's belief that synergy be-tween physical improvement schemes and community development is essential for launching a genuine process of urban rehabilitation, capable of producing results that can become sustainable and eventually independent of external inputs. This important synergy is recognised by the AKTC's funding partners, the Egyptian Swiss Fund for Development, the Ford Foundation and the World Monuments Fund, who have generously participated in the combined socio-economic and physical rehabilitation of al-Darb al-Ahmar.

The AKTC's long-term strategy focuses on an integrated programme of physical and economic re-vitalisation in an effort to reverse the pattern of decay and improve living, leisure and working con-ditions. This strategy sees preservation as part of a comprehensive rehabilitation process; it envi-sions a future for the district in which a stable residential core is enlivened and sustained by a ca-pillary system of small workshops and retail activities, supported by essential infrastructure and community facilities, and made more attractive by well-maintained open spaces and monuments. To realise this vision, conditions must be established to sustain and encourage a stable and self-suf-ficient population. In turn, this requires improving the economic climate, addressing community development issues and physically upgrading the area. More specifically, actions must be aimed at creating and facilitating access to sustainable employment opportunities for unemployed young

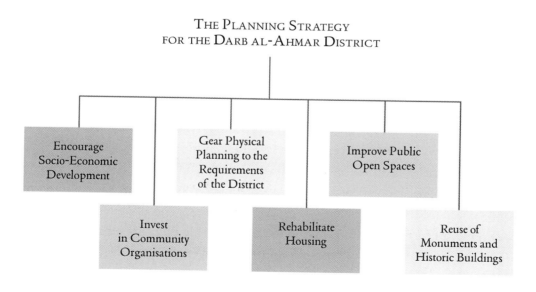

THE PLANNING STRATEGY
FOR THE DARB AL-AHMAR DISTRICT

Encourage Socio-Economic Development

Gear Physical Planning to the Requirements of the District

Improve Public Open Spaces

Invest in Community Organisations

Rehabilitate Housing

Reuse of Monuments and Historic Buildings

people, providing health and educational facilities, particularly for women and children, and, above all, strengthening civic groups and local institutions that will steer and sustain future actions in the district. Such socially relevant activities can and must go hand in hand with physical rehabilitation projects, such as restoring and reusing key historic structures and providing for their maintenance, upgrading open spaces and the urban environment and ensuring their upkeep, and rehabilitating and improving the existing housing stock. Both the social and the physical aspects are indeed interdependent and can foster significant synergies.

Implementation of such interrelated activities is being sought through a series of pilot projects in specific locations within al-Darb al-Ahmar, strategically located along the historic wall bordering the new park, the corridor that is at relatively higher risk of uncontrolled transformation. The pilot projects take advantage of special opportunities identified during the course of the survey, focusing on individual monuments and historic buildings, on significant public open spaces, and on residential clusters, as described below. These projects offer an opportunity to investigate key conservation and development issues and help identify policies and solutions for physical improvements that can then be applied throughout the district. Whether individual monuments, public spaces or residential areas, these should be viewed not only as rehabilitation projects but also as catalysts towards future social and economic revitalisation.

Fig. 78. Dressing stone at the Umm al-Sultan Shaaban worksite.

ENCOURAGING SOCIO-ECONOMIC DEVELOPMENT

As is the case with any depressed historic area, the priorities in al-Darb al-Ahmar are first and foremost social and economic. The widely held view that only substantial government intervention and public capital can produce results in these spheres overlooks the fact that relatively simple initiatives can have a significant impact. Such a 'minimalist' approach is being followed by the AKTC/AKCS-E's management and staff in al-Darb al-Ahmar with encouraging results. Their experience has been that in order to generate employment it is not necessary to create new jobs. A more efficient strategy is to connect people with existing employment opportunities. With this in mind, a job placement and counselling service was established in the Project's office in the neighbourhood, leading to the placement of dozens of people. Acquiring on-the-job experience has also proven the best and most direct way for the unemployed young to prepare for and eventually find a job. Project staff formed agreements with a number of existing workshops in the area to train young people. Quite often these have led to longer-term employment opportunities.

Training is in fact crucial in introducing appropriate know-how, developing independent capabilities and re-establishing vanishing crafts and skills, especially those related to traditional construction so highly relevant to the future maintenance of Cairo's historic areas, al-Darb al-Ahmar in particular. All of the AKTC restoration projects in the district include a training component and employ as much as possible local craftsmen and labour, complemented when necessary by external trainers. Also in this case, direct apprenticeships on AKTC restoration sites have led to the development of skills and employment prospects for residents of the district.

Finally, the availability of micro-credit for al-Darb al-Ahmar residents has had a very promising impact on the area, enabling people to engage in what they do best. With limited loans, and through the establishment of a lending and credit-recovery programme, the Project has been able to help businesses and individuals, especially women, to start income-generating activities and improve their trades. Approximately 270 loans, averaging LE2,500, have been disbursed to date, and an expansion of the micro-credit programme is envisaged for the next four-year cycle of project activities.

INVESTING IN COMMUNITY ORGANISATIONS

The Project also recognises the key importance of promoting community awareness and self-governance as a means of making people more aware of their cultural traditions and restoring civic pride. Self-governance in residential areas was a distinctive feature of traditional Muslim cities and can be at least partly restored by enabling people to share their problems and identify solutions, and by creating the confidence needed to act on their own behalf rather than passively wait for outside intervention. To this effect, the project has promoted the creation of the Darb al-Ahmar Business Association and the Family Health Development Centre, two locally based organisations charged with the delivery of services to the community in the all-important sectors of health and business development. In addition, it has provided support for a number of existing non-governmental organisations (NGO's) in the area who are seen as key partners in raising community awareness and channelling local resources towards the future revitalization of the district.

In the longer term, the AKTC and its partners envision the establishment of a Community Development Agency based in the area. This body will operate as a self-sustaining community-managed private-sector initiative working to mobilise community resources within the framework of locally identified problems, needs and priorities. It will combine the mobilisation of resources, technical coordination, community affairs and institution-building with physical upgrading and environmental improvement activities. It will do so while building up the community and encouraging the development of new entities capable of providing leadership, technical support and assistance in mobilising and managing resources. A case in point is the successful pilot activities promoted by the 'Women Working Together' group, established within the framework of the Project

Fig. 79. A dilapidated house in al-Darb al-Ahmar.

to encourage and support educational and income-generating activities among women residents of the area. Building upon these promising initiatives, the new Darb al-Ahmar agency, once fully operational, will offer the critical support needed to help residents become more self-reliant and the community to take greater responsibility for maintaining and developing the district's social and physical environment.

GEARING PHYSICAL PLANNING TO THE REQUIREMENTS OF THE DISTRICT

At the institutional level, the AKTC Project provides support in reorganising the planning and building process within the district in order to include a conservation agenda as well as those issues that residents perceive as a priority, including long-standing stumbling blocks. More particularly, the AKTC has been working with national and local institutions to ensure that the district and its historic fabric are treated differently than contemporary city fabric, with finer-grain surveying and planning, special attention to the context and closer monitoring of building activities. Gearing the planning process to the requirements of a historic area must be effected from the outset, starting with plot-by-plot physical surveys and in-depth socio-economic investigations. Only detailed preparatory work can provide the basis for comprehensive physical planning that responds to the particular conditions of an historic area.

While working with local institutions is essential, an equally important level of action is to facilitate a greater involvement of local community interests in planning decisions and in addressing the complex, long-standing issues that have created a climate of uncertainty over tenure, thus discouraging residents from investing in the area. The paramount concern in this respect is the revision of building codes and building regulations for the district, the lifting of obsolete planning constraints, and the resolution of the tenure issue for properties along the Ayyubid wall under restoration. To this effect, the AKTC has obtained from the Egyptian Supreme Council of Antiquities (SCA) a partial waiver of the demolition order condemning the traditional houses in proximity of the historic wall. Alternatives to demolition are now being put into effect to allow the residents to continue to live in the area and the monument to be preserved together with its living urban context.

Eventually, a revision of the current planning and institutional framework will be necessary to preserve the physical fabric, maintain the present inhabitants, and achieve balanced development throughout the area. Declaring al-Darb al-Ahmar a conservation area subject to special planning provisions and establishing a dedicated task force charged with its continued planning and management are seen as essential steps in demonstrating public commitment to the revitalisation of the district and creating the confidence needed to mobilise resources within the area.

REHABILITATING HOUSING

Detailed surveys carried out in 1999 along the eastern boundary of al-Darb al-Ahmar show the worsening conditions of the residential fabric due to limited access to housing finance and insecure tenure. Tenure is a particularly serious issue in al-Darb al-Ahmar, where over thirty percent of the historic fabric is subject to demolition orders. Those forced to abandon their houses or shops cannot find affordable alternatives in the same area, and are forced to seek alternatives in the peripheral areas of Cairo, where public services and infrastructure are limited or non-existent, and social and community ties difficult to re-establish. If the present pattern of abandonment and disinvestment per-

Fig. 80. A residential street in the intervention area.

sists, it can only pave the way for further deterioration and the eventual demise of irreplaceable social, economic, and cultural assets. It will also deprive the district of the critical mass of inhabitants needed to sustain the area's social and economic life.

Housing rehabilitation can play a crucial role in the future improvement of al-Darb al-Ahmar and should be seen as the best long-term antidote to the district's decline. In the long-term, the realisation of better living conditions for individuals and families is the driving force needed to establish cleaner and more stable neighbourhoods, and a primer that can set in motion a positive chain reaction to preserve and revitalise al-Darb al-Ahmar.

For these reasons, the AKTC, as part of its larger revitalisation effort, is giving priority to the identification of policies and programmes that will ameliorate housing in the area. A dual strategy is being pursued, to facilitate the gradual rehabilitation of existing residential units on one hand, and to promote the redevelopment of ruined buildings, vacant plots and blighted areas into new housing on the other.

In 1998, the AKTC initiated a pilot study of 125 plots and buildings in al-Darb al-Ahmar's Aslam neighbourhood to find out what kinds of housing improvements are needed and how best to intervene. At the same time, the study was used to ascertain residents' interest in remaining in the dis-

Figs. 81, 82. Existing condition and proposed elevation of No. 16 Haret al-Sa'ayda after rehabilitation.

trict and their willingness to contribute to the rehabilitation of their homes. The results of the study showed not only that the overwhelming majority of residents wishes to remain in the area, but also that a substantial portion of the rehabilitation costs could be met by the residents themselves, without having to depend on very limited public resources. In this respect, creating the conditions to upgrade occupied buildings and helping people to afford to continue living in their homes not only reduces the threat of abandonment, but also saves the government the considerable social and economic expense associated with relocating entire households to other parts of the city. In addition, the study developed a series of models for both rehabilitated and newly constructed housing that take into account residents' lifestyles, income levels and tenure status. The study also included technical solutions and innovative institutional and financing schemes to facilitate implementation.[2]

Based on the results of the initial study, the AKTC launched, in 2002, a pilot rehabilitation housing credit scheme near the historic wall, comprising approximately fifty residential buildings. Project staff discusses priorities with the residents, identifies a building programme, carries out rehabilitation work, or, alternatively, makes funds available directly to approved contractors, and ensures repayment of loans to replenish the revolving fund. The scheme is now being implemented and is receiving considerable local interest, following the completion of rehabilitation works for the first group of houses and the return of the residents to their renovated apartments.

The rehabilitation of existing houses is the AKTC's primary focus, but rehabilitation must be complemented and reinforced by new developments in order to meet the need for more housing, which is in short supply throughout al-Darb al-Ahmar. The many plots of vacant land in the area offer ample opportunity: in 1997, a physical survey identified close to 320 vacant ruins and unimproved plots out of a total of two thousand – sixteen percent of area properties. At least part of this available land can be returned to full residential use by encouraging private development, particularly where clusters of ruins and vacant land offer the possibility of building multiple housing units and realising operational economies. In these cases, incentives could be provided with low-interest loans administered through special arrangements with lending institutions and owners (or tenants). Project staff can act as facilitators between the two, providing technical assistance programmes for low- and moderate-income households. Such schemes already exist for new development, but have never been applied in historic areas. Their adaptation would present special challenges, but also open up new opportunities for high-profile exemplary initiatives.

The AKTC is currently exploring one such opportunity in the area immediately north of al-Mahruq Tower, in conjunction with the recent lowering of the road built over the historic wall. Here, the high percentage of ruins combined with easy pedestrian access present excellent prospects for a comprehensive housing redevelopment scheme. In shaping the proposal, special attention will be devoted to creating a promising mix of commercial activities and housing, and to identifying design solutions that are compatible with the surrounding historic context.

IMPROVING PUBLIC OPEN SPACES

Public open spaces are poorly maintained and deteriorating throughout al-Darb al-Ahmar due to a lack of planning and investment in public infrastructure. Their deterioration may also be attributed to the fact that it is unclear what purpose they are to serve and who is to be responsible for their maintenance. In future, a clear understanding of how these spaces are to be utilised within the community, and how they can be brought back to full use, will be essential if they are to serve civic purposes effectively and be maintained over time.

Towards this end, the AKTC has carried out detailed surveys in al-Darb al-Ahmar's neighbourhoods and discussed with residents ways in which the current uses can be discontinued, when harmful, or maintained and improved, when desirable. The AKTC's plans target not only major and highly visible spaces, but also commercial streets and

Fig. 83. Discussing an open space clean-up project in the intervention area.

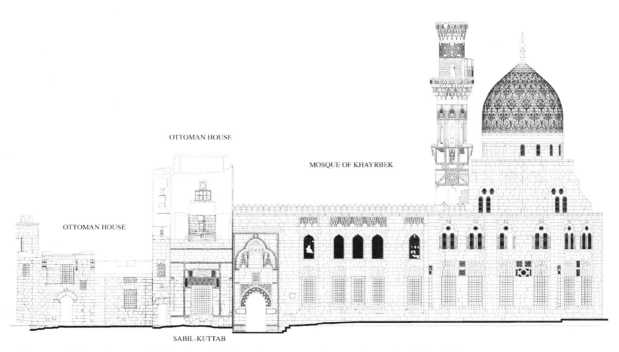

OTTOMAN HOUSE

OTTOMAN HOUSE

MOSQUE OF KHAYRBEK

TOMB OF KHAYRBEK

SABIL-KUTTAB

Fig. 84. Bab al-Wazir Street elevation from the edge of Aqsunqur Mosque to the tomb of Khayrbek.

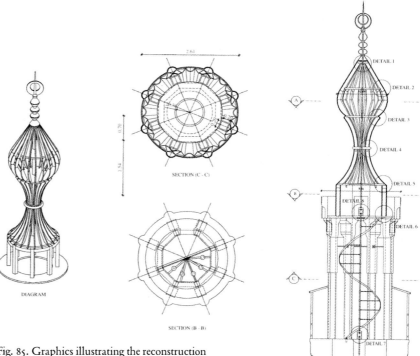

DIAGRAM

SECTION (C - C)

SECTION (B - B)

DETAIL 1
DETAIL 2
DETAIL 3
DETAIL 4
DETAIL 5
DETAIL 8
DETAIL 6
DETAIL 7

Fig. 85. Graphics illustrating the reconstruction of the Khayrbek minaret.

Figs. 86-88. Aspects of the ongoing conservation work in Khayrbek Mosque.

small neighbourhood squares that play an important role in the quality and appearance of public spaces in the district. Proposed interventions, to be carried out with the involvement of the district authorities and the development of self-help initiatives, focus on a variety of these spaces.

Commercial streetscapes. Possible improvements range from basic space planning to accommodate conflicting activities, to upgrading street paving, public lighting and signage, as well as façades and storefronts. While these improvements by themselves do not generate economic activity, they can do much to attract and enhance commerce.

Important public squares and public concourse areas. These often require comprehensive re-organisation and space planning. Improvements in these highly visible spaces can do much to enhance the image of the area and attract visitors.

Fig. 89. Historic image showing the Umm al-Sultan Shaaban minaret before its collapse.

Small neighbourhood squares. These are found throughout the inner blocks of al-Darb al-Ahmar, often associated with tombs of saints and community mosques. These spaces can be targeted for simple low-cost improvements that are designed to encourage informal contact and community life.

Aslam Square is an example of a small neighbourhood square selected for improvement by the AKTC team. Interest in this area stems from its proximity to Bab al-Mahruq, one of the historic principal gates along the eastern side of the Ayyubid city wall, later blocked. In the past, the gate was connected to Aslam Square and, from here, to the important thoroughfare leading to the Fatimid gate, Bab Zuwayla. With the creation of the new Azhar Park, this old connection will be re-established and Aslam Square gradually equipped to serve both as a pedestrian link and as a forum for commercial activity and social interaction in the closely-knit Aslam neighbourhood.

Archaeological excavations have started near the al-Mahruq Gate as a first step to re-opening the old connection with Aslam Square. Future actions foresee the involvement of local residents in an improvement scheme for the square that includes elimination of informal vehicular parking and the upgrading of public utilities, paving and lighting. The scheme will be complemented by a façade improvement programme for the residential and commercial buildings facing the square, as well as selective restoration of Aslam Mosque.

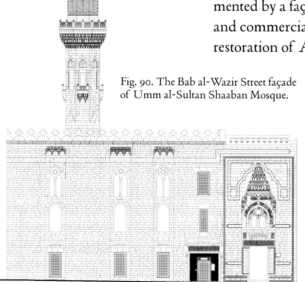

Fig. 90. The Bab al-Wazir Street façade of Umm al-Sultan Shaaban Mosque.

Another open space improvement project actively pursued within the framework of the Project is the rehabilitation of Tablita Market, located on the main pedestrian road linking the heart of the Fatimid city with Azhar Park. Here, the proliferation of street vendors, poor management and severely deteriorated environmental conditions are threatening the very existence of the market, with dire consequences for the local economy. In an attempt to resolve

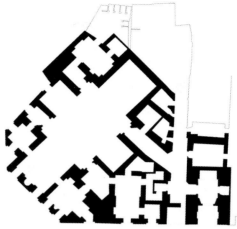

Fig. 91. The ongoing reconstruction of the Umm al-Sultan Shaaban minaret.

Fig. 92. Ground plan of Umm al-Sultan Shaaban.

the deadlock and provide a suitable architectural solution for this sensitive vacant space, the AKTC's team prepared plans that call for an enclosed new market hall to contain and reorganise the vendors. The design was developed in close cooperation with representatives of the market vendors and in consultation with the Cairo Governorate.

REUSING MONUMENTS AND HISTORIC BUILDINGS

The restoration and adaptive reuse of monuments and historic buildings complete the pilot programmes initiated by the AKTC. Monuments are in fact plentiful in the district, which contains some of medieval Cairo's finest and most admired historic structures. There are sixty-five monuments registered by the SCA in the area, as well as several hundred unregistered but architecturally significant buildings that determine the quality of al-Darb al-Ahmar's urban context. Their long-term preservation is crucial to maintaining the architectural character and quality of the area. Future development strategies should therefore promote the stabilisation and long-term maintenance of these structures, and their integration in the district's social, recreational and educational life.

The AKTC has targeted three representative projects to fulfil these strategic objectives through practical, direct actions: restoration of the Khayrbek complex (composed of several associated buildings), restoration of Umm al-Sultan Shaaban Mosque, and the rehabilitation and adaptive reuse of the former Shoughlan Street School.

The Khayrbek complex is named after Khayrbek, Egypt's first governor after the Ottoman conquest, and was built in stages during the Mamluk and early Ottoman periods. The stabilisation and partial restoration of the complex includes the thirteenth-century palace of Alin Aq, Khayrbek Mosque and the *sabil-kuttab*, two partially ruined Ottoman houses and the surrounding open space. The AKTC plans to re-establish the extraordinary urban value of this ensemble, which lies at the southern end of the new Azhar Park, in close proximity to Aqsunqur, or the Blue, Mosque. The combined programme includes restoration works (Ayyubid city wall, Khayrbek Mosque and the *sabil-kuttab*), stabilisation of ruins (Alin Aq Palace), adaptive reuse (the Ottoman houses) and environmental and landscape improvements. The complex will eventually offer a setting for recreational and cultural events and provide a focal point for the community as well as visitors to the district.[3]

The mosque and madrasa of Umm al-Sultan Shaaban, built in 1369, is one of the principal monuments along Bab al-Wazir Street, the processional route that crosses al-Darb al-Ahmar and connects the Citadel to the historic city. The complex, built by Sultan Shaaban for his mother Khawand Baraka, is one of the finest examples of Mamluk architecture in Cairo. It comprises a mosque, a two-storey *madrasa* and two domed tomb chambers located on either side of the *qibla iwan*. The minaret, the focal point of the structure, is highly visible from both sides of the street, even though its uppermost portion is missing as a result of an earthquake in 1884. The work currently under way includes reconstruction of the missing section of the minaret and restoration of the southern and western façades, interior of the mosque, ablution area, the roof and domes, as well as rehabilitation of the *madrasa*. The latter will house the community activities initiated by the AKCS-E, in particular the literacy, employment, social and economic development programmes. The interior will be equipped to serve as meeting rooms, offices and classrooms. In addition, the rear courtyard will be used as an outdoor open area for occasional community events.[4]

The former Shoughlan Street School, an early twentieth-century residential building located along the historic wall, later converted into a school, represents the first major historic building project completed by the AKTC in the area. The project makes use of the former school's close proximity to the historic wall and the future park, as well as its potential, given its location and size, to serve the community. This led to the idea of reusing this large structure as a combined community facility, visitor centre and AKCS-E office space. An orientation and exhibition space and a rooftop area with views of the park and the Citadel will accommodate visitors, while recreational as well as family, educational and community services are to be housed in other parts of the building. This programme will introduce much needed services in a context that sorely lacks public facilities. The conversion of the structure also includes provisions for the future reuse of the building as a guest-house to generate revenue for the operation of the planned Community Development Agency.[5]

Fig. 93. Cross section of the Shoughlan Street School.

The Khayrbek and Umm al-Sultan Shaaban projects are being undertaken through special agreements between the AKTC and the SCA. These agreements have provided occasions to work with the various offices of the national authority concerned to develop and implement innovative and realistic solutions towards preserving Cairo's monuments. The solutions planned range from identifying appropriate restoration techniques to finding compatible new uses. In particular, for the first time in Cairo, the AKTC has been given permission to partially adapt historic monuments to serve social and community uses, a step that will facilitate their maintenance and their integration in the life of the district. The AKTC's efforts have thus established an important and innovative precedent that can go beyond al-Darb al-Ahmar and be applied to the preservation and reuse of historic structures elsewhere in Cairo.

Being able to rehabilitate the many underused, often decaying historic structures, particularly those in public ownership, should also be seen as an opportunity to revive dormant assets, introduce much needed facilities and services in the area, and promote the preservation and adaptive reuse of old buildings. In this respect, the reuse of the former Shoughlan Street School as a community and visitor centre will show that old buildings need not necessarily be associated with poverty and neglect, and that they can still play a useful role in contemporary life.

FUTURE PROSPECTS

The action plans and pilot interventions in al-Darb al-Ahmar seek practical and sustainable alternatives to the current dilemma confronting officials and planners in historic Cairo — alternatives that can provide valuable examples for other historic districts and cities. Often, the only perceived options are either to accept the current decay as inevitable, or to embark upon a costly and socially disruptive policy of radical transformation. Continuation of the present inertia and disinvestment would no doubt condemn the area to ever

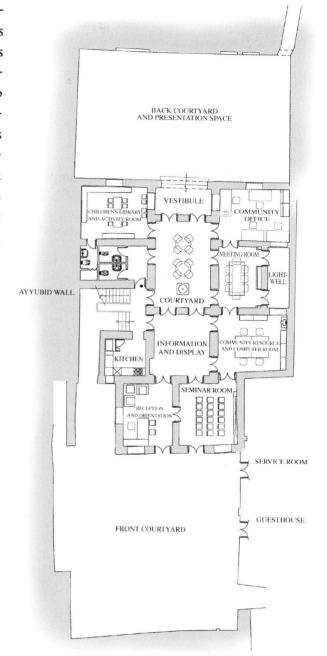

Fig. 94. Ground plan of the Shoughlan Street School.

191

Fig. 95. Rendering showing how the area between Aslam Square and the historic wall can be improved without demolition, and how new links between the park and al-Darb al-Ahmar can be provided (see also plate 76).

lower standards of living and the continued deterioration of public services and infrastructure. On the other hand, radical redevelopment fuelled by the urban projects already under way in and around al-Darb al-Ahmar could arouse strong speculative pressures and start a reaction of uncontrolled change.

Contrary to these two scenarios, the alternative being pursued in al-Darb al-Ahmar by the AKTC builds on the direct involvement of residents, community groups, and local institutions towards a gradual rehabilitation of the existing residential and commercial property and a phased improvement of the urban environment. With strong institutional support and active management of the residents' capacity for direct intervention, the social fabric can become the engine driving the rehabilitation efforts. Paramount is the conviction that, in the long run, community involvement is the best means of achieving lasting results. This alternative is both achievable and wise: it is far less costly over time than either abandonment or radical intervention; it actively engages the existing social setting and it does not disrupt or alienate the people concerned; furthermore, it keeps the historic fabric of the district alive, thus preserving a significant portion of historic Cairo for future generations.

Ultimately, institutional coordination and community involvement within a gradual process of economic improvement and physical rehabilitation must be viewed as the necessary ingredients for taking on the manifold conservation and revitalisation needs of historic Cairo. Too often, this task has remained an abstract notion predicated on grand and difficult-to-implement schemes, rather than being pursued through practical rehabilitation efforts based on actual needs and realistic programmes for action.

The results of the AKTC's ongoing activities will be important beyond the Darb al-Ahmar setting, since they offer a living model of old city rehabilitation that may be applied in identifying both general policies and practical solutions throughout historic Cairo, and indeed many other historic cities in the Islamic world.

[1] Aga Khan Trust for Culture, "A Demonstration Project for al-Darb al-Ahmar. An Agenda for Revitalisation: Conservation and Development Proposals for a Historic District of Cairo", Final Report, Cairo: n.p. 1997. See also Aga Khan Trust for Culture, "The Darb al-Ahmar Project. Urban Rehabilitation and Community Development in Historic Cairo", HCSP Technical Brief No. 5, Cairo: n.p. 2001.
[2] Aga Khan Trust for Culture, "Conservation Planning in the Aslam Mosque Neighbourhood. The Status of Activities of Urban Revitalisation in Historic Cairo's al-Darb al-Ahmar", HCSP Technical Brief No. 2, Cairo: n.p. 1999.

[3] Aga Khan Trust for Culture, "The Complex of Khayrbek: History and Proposed Interventions", HCSP Information Brief, Cairo: n.p. 1999.
[4] Aga Khan Trust for Culture, "The Mosque of Umm al-Sultan Shaaban: Background and History", HCSP Information Brief, Cairo: n.p. 1999.
[5] Aga Khan Trust for Culture, "Reintegrating Historic Buildings into the Life of the Neighbourhood: The Adaptive Reuse of the Former Darb Shoughlan School", HCSP Technical Brief No. 3, Cairo: n.p. 1999.

FUTURE

THE WAY FORWARD

The interventions of the Aga Khan Trust for Culture (AKTC) through the creation
of Azhar Park, the restoration of the Ayyubid wall and the rehabilitation of al-Darb al-Ahmar
go a long way to establishing links between the past, the present and the future of Cairo.
Robert Ivy comments on the contemporary architecture and design of the new park,
Nairy Hampikian explains why Cairo's historic areas are now at a crucial juncture
and Nawal El Messiri underlines how the perception of public gardens in the city is changing.
The different periods of Cairo's history meet here and open the way
to what Philip Jodidio calls "the city of the future".

The Role of Contemporary Architecture

ROBERT IVY

The transformation of Azhar Park from arid hillside to green oasis overshadows discussions of any individual architecture placed within its bounds. The metamorphosis of this prominent open space, offering release within the compressed confines of one of the world's densest cities, will attract attention on a large scale, as urban intervention, as master plan, and as social amenity. Yet several buildings situated within the park, primarily two restaurants and an entrance structure, created by two teams of architects, demand critical attention, embodying human intention in their design and construction and bringing focus to the planning efforts of the entirety.

While relatively small in relation to the park or to its surrounding cityscape, their architecture, visibility, and prominence convey semiotic messages, important signs and signals to onlookers and the community. In the midst of idealised parkland, these structures strung along the hilltop of a reclaimed landfill assert human values, including the potential for change and the vital role of leisure in revitalising human energy. Additionally, by approaching historic precedent in differing ways, they extend the debate on the role of modernity within a rapidly evolving, historically rich setting.

In an earlier essay on the city of Cairo, critic Michael Sorkin summed up the challenge both architectural teams would face when he said: "The issue for architects is [...] how to create environments that speak to both the aspirations and traditions of an extremely complex culture without prejudice for either old or new". The question Sorkin outlines (without foreknowledge of the park architecture), and the Azhar architects confronted in their designs, consists of architecture's stance towards the past in constructing a contemporary identity.

Historically, cultural identity rose in importance concurrently with the rise of nationalism in the nineteenth and twentieth centuries. In recent decades, the

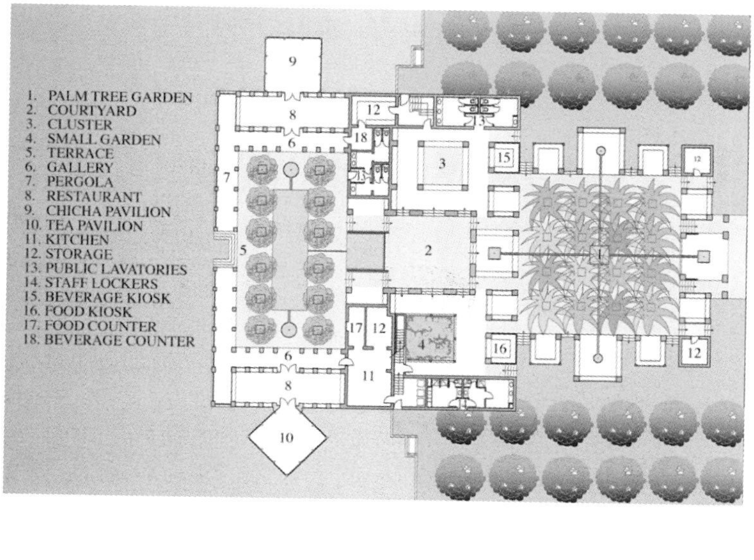

Fig. 96. General plan of the Lakeside Café by Serge Santelli.

1. PALM TREE GARDEN
2. COURTYARD
3. CLUSTER
4. SMALL GARDEN
5. TERRACE
6. GALLERY
7. PERGOLA
8. RESTAURANT
9. CHICHA PAVILION
10. TEA PAVILION
11. KITCHEN
12. STORAGE
13. PUBLIC LAVATORIES
14. STAFF LOCKERS
15. BEVERAGE KIOSK
16. FOOD KIOSK
17. FOOD COUNTER
18. BEVERAGE COUNTER

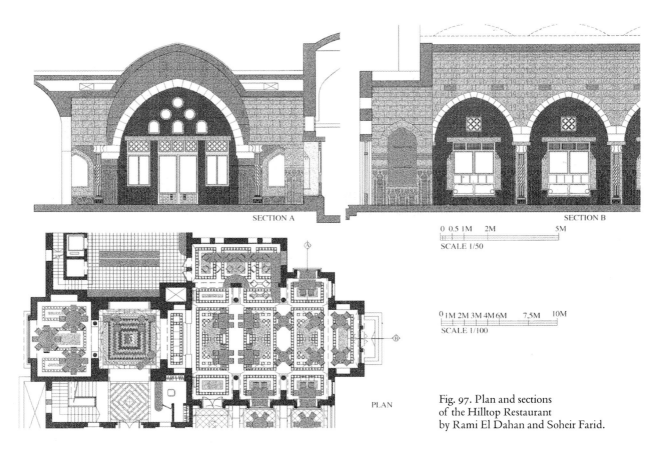

SECTION A

SECTION B

0 0.5 1M   2M   5M
SCALE 1/50

0 1M 2M 3M 4M 6M   7,5M   10M
SCALE 1/100

PLAN

Fig. 97. Plan and sections
of the Hilltop Restaurant
by Rami El Dahan and Soheir Farid.

difficulties of asserting individual personality have become compounded by the universal corporate hegemony in the late twentieth century, in which certain streets in Manila appear indistinguishable from those in contemporary Cairo, with their array of tall buildings in steel and glass. In the presence of this international sameness in commercial and institutional construction, what might serve as sources of meaning or of inspiration for placemaking? In seeking architectural responses to sameness, much of the critical discussion has focused on cultural absolutes, such as the term 'authenticity', a term that proves difficult to define.

What constitutes an 'authentic' architectural response? Zeynip Celik suggests that the answer proves subtler than the authentic "ethnic, social, and cultural differences" might suggest. According to Celik, the globalisation of economic development and widespread dissemination of education and information render such terms as authenticity and purity obsolete. At one extreme, theme park or so-called entertainment architecture trivialises the terms by reducing history to façadism, in which appearance or perception constitutes the underlying reality. By contrast, developments in digital media have resulted in structures without precedent or apparent contextual referents — architecture as sculptural expressionism.

Yet despite the complications inherent in determining appropriate theoretical underpinnings for architectural development today, architects such as those at Azhar Park have continually returned to history and to human memory, in some cases recalling familiar elements of scale, proportion, and rhythm, and in others transforming familiar forms and patterns into new designs. For the two primary projects within the park itself, the Hilltop Restaurant and the Lakeside Café, each team took a different, clearly defined approach.

For Rami El Dahan and Soheir Farid, the commission to design the Hilltop Restaurant began with a competition. The planning of the park itself by Sasaki Associates and Sites International set the park's overall organisation, including its principal axes and focal points, and located its specific architectural features. Dahan and Farid were invited as one of seven teams to compete for the design of the restaurant in 1999. Following an August presentation to the AKTC that year, their proposal emerged as winner.

For the architects (both personal and business partners), the Azhar Hilltop Restaurant represents a continuing working relationship that began when the two worked with the late Hasan Fathy, Egypt's most prominent architect of the twentieth century. Fathy, widely published in professional and consumer media, espoused a return to local traditions in building, including forms, materials, and methods of construction. His architecture, which was aimed at improving the lot of the indigenous Egyptian population, while forging a new identity based on qualities arising from the Egyptian culture, relied on environmentally sensitive, load-bearing masonry structures which featured, noticeably, vaults and domes, set above simple masonry square or rectangular walls.

By extending planning to include entire communities, such as New Gourna, and encouraging local craftsmanship in the construction process, Fathy envisioned architecture as the generator of a complete system — one that engaged physical improvement from historic models with economic well being. By multiplying individual units into clusters of structures, Fathy composed urban settings that were uniquely Egyptian, grafting vernacular forms with contemporary planning principles.

Emerging from their work with Fathy, who died in 1989, Dahan and Farid commenced their formal practice in 1984/1985. Since that time, their own work has included the design of new resort towns and plans for twenty-five hotels, including projects nominated for the Aga Khan Award for Architecture.

While to the casual observer, the Hilltop Restaurant Dahan and Farid designed for Azhar Park recalls historic elements from Cairene architecture, the architects are adamant that the project avoids the traps of replication or historicism. "It is not an imitation of anything else," they assert. Instead,

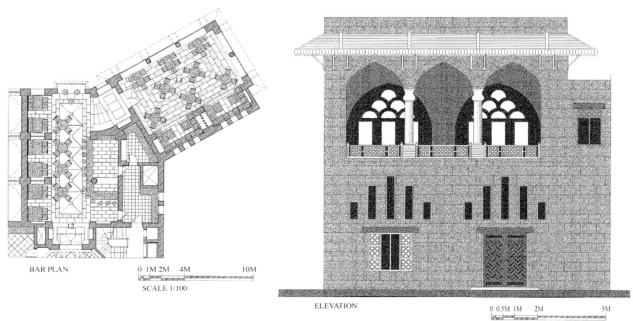

BAR PLAN

0 1M 2M 4M 10M

SCALE 1/100

ELEVATION

0 0.5M 1M 2M 5M

SCALE 1/50

Fig. 98. Plan and elevation of the Hilltop Restaurant by Rami El Dahan and Soheir Farid.

the pair has employed elements from history, adapting "old techniques for new needs and functions" intentionally, employing familiar architectural elements like a vocabulary, but changing them according to contemporary usage and requirements.

The restaurant occupies high ground, prominently sited as an individual structure within the park. Unlike the dense neighbouring city, this three-dimensional building stands alone, a structure with implied formal connections to early Cairo, resembling more a large villa than an urban commercial structure. The restaurant functions as a critical component to the park's success, since the donor intended the park to sustain itself economically.

In plan, the restaurant maintains the strong axis that proceeds from the vehicular access to its hilltop location, dropping into gardens that follow along a watercourse, past the Lakeside Café, and out towards the citadel. All architectural elements reinforce the axis and its view out towards the gardens, including the covered portico, or *takhtaboush*, on the south elevation, a seating area overlooking the gardens surmounted by domes. Exterior massing places forms of varying height and weight in asymmetrical equilibrium.

Programmatically, the project includes restaurant, exhibition gallery, and tearoom spaces, with public and private dining areas. The plan proceeds axially from the vehicular drop-off point through an entry portico, to a multi-domed shaded seating area. On one side of the primary axis lies the bulk of the restaurant; on the other, the art gallery, bar, and cafeteria. A hierarchy of spaces, from large to small, characterises the interiors. A *durqa'a* entrance, comparable to the large hall found in historic Arab palaces, serves as the restaurant's main entrance, topped by a monumental dome and free of furnishings. Across the entranceway, the bar occupies an elevated open loggia, or *manzara*, which has been oriented to enhance breezes and to provide "a touch of intimacy", according to Dahan. Stairs have been minimised as architectural elements.

A concern for shade and light characterises the entire composition, including ample porches, covered seating areas and passageways. A high pergola admits light and shade to the entry courtyard, with fountain beneath. Covered with wooden *treillage*, the roof covering provides subdued, filtered daylight during the day, and at night reflects the artificial illumination.

Among the most explicit features with historical antecedents are the restaurant's arches, which in spirit recall the Fatimid arches of the tenth to twelfth centuries — shallow arches outlined in masonry supported by short columns — that characterise Fatimid structures. Other reinterpreted elements include shading devices based on ideas present in the *mashrabiyya*, the familiar bay windows shaded with turned wood, the previously mentioned *manzara*, and the *shokhsheikha*, an octagonal wooden lantern topped by clerestory windows. Materials are not superficial, but integral, carrying their own weight. All facing stone, typically *hashma* stone (limestone rich in sand — saw-cut, trimmed, and hand-faced by local craftsmen) is load bearing, as are all domes, vaults, and wooden roofs. Only the basement relies on concrete framing, a structural underpinning that actually rests on over two hundred piles, driven thirty-five metres into the soil of the former landfill. Floors of marble or ceramic consist of new interpretation of old patterns; few industrial materials appear throughout the construction.

Following the course of the hillside down from the Hilltop Restaurant, visitors follow a pathway that the landscape architects Maher Stino and Laila Elmasry Stino describe as "a spine like a *casbah*". The path proceeds through a series of gardens along the spine, accompanied by trickling water, aromatic plants and local materials, providing a series of experiences in which outdoors and indoors merge, from one structure through sunken gardens like outdoor rooms towards the next building. After changing direction towards the south-west, the spine connects to the second major architectural component, the Lakeside Café.

Unlike the hillside restaurant, with its arches and domes, the Lakeside Café offers a contemporary counterpoint within the park. While the restaurant achieves its architectural effects through massing of architectural elements such as domes and arches, the café arrays a collection of simple cubic volumes around a series of open courts, stepping down to a lake. Cascading water and paving materials provide the unifying elements that convey the spirit of the Islamic garden.

Essentially a series of shaded platforms, the café serves as a mediating point between the open spaces within the park and enclosure, providing shade and resting places for park visitors as well as casual food service. Two distinct zones organise the venue: a square palm court surrounded by kiosks divided into quarters from a central fountain by water courses, offering shade and seating for visitors; and an intermediate space defined by service rooms and a cafeteria that extends from a cascade out over the lake as a terrace, offering the illusion of floating. Designed as a cluster of pavilions by the French architect, Serge Santelli, the café offers both enclosure and protection as well as a transparent aspect towards the city beyond.

The 'floating' terrace, which houses the cafeteria, culminates the pathway begun uphill within the garden. Oriented as a cross-axial courtyard, divided by fountains and a pond, tree-lined, and served by food kiosks, the terraces provide a dramatic conclusion to the garden progression, offering water, shade, and views, anchored by two larger pavilions at each end, with semi-transparent walls of wooden latticework.

Santelli, a former student of the late American architect Louis Kahn, came to the commission, like Dahan and Farid, through the invited competition for the hillside restaurant in 1999. A former winner of the Aga Khan Award for Architecture in 1983 for a project in Tunisia, Santelli describes one of his chief design concerns as "expressing Islamic tradition through contemporary language". Whereas the original plans for the park included only one restaurant, ultimately the plans changed to include another structure for food service along the artificial lake, with Santelli as architect.

In conceiving the underlying ideas for this Lakeside Café, Santelli reinterpreted historic Islamic designs in a more 'rationalist' vocabulary. According to the architect, his motivating ideas lay in a variety of Islamic traditions, including Mughal and Andalusian, where controlled watercourses define human versions of paradise. In contrast to the hillside restaurant, where the forms seem explicitly drawn from history, Santelli has employed a contemporary rationalism to reinterpret historic precepts.

While the hillside restaurant comprises a complex of upper and lower levels, from service and storage spaces to elaborate, mechanically cooled dining rooms, the lakeside pavilion relies on a more modest programme and budget. Simple pavilions follow a rigorous orthogonal geometry, composed of piers and bases of concrete block with wooden latticed roofs, and border the palm court — essentially an indoor/outdoor seating area. *Hashma* stone provides accents in the most important areas of the courtyard and terraces, beneath walls of concrete block with artificial stone coating. Service rooms, toilets and kitchen consist of plain rectangular spaces arrayed around the transitional courtyard, culminating in the open lakeside terrace.

Other reinterpretations of Islamic traditions include the use of wood for *mashrabiyya*-like effects. Santelli mentions *bourgalli* latticework, a technique he observed and used for its simplicity and low cost. However, he refers to the use of wood for windows and in kiosks, as inspired, "not in shape, but in spirit". Santelli employed a sophisticated paving scheme for the entire complex, using light cream Egyptian marble with green accents in patterns that reflect the Islamic interest in geometry.

In the initial planning for the park, landscape architects Stino and Stino of Sites International had positioned an entrance pavilion down the eastern hillside, allowing vehicles and pedestrians a moment's pause before gaining access to the park. Following their design for the Hilltop Restaurant, architects Dahan and Farid were asked to design

Fig. 99. Drawing by Serge Santelli of the Lakeside Café interior.

the entrance gates to the park, complementing the design of the restaurant with a similar design vocabulary. Their design for the entrance was a "strong, intuitive" one, according to the architects.

Their plan calls for two pylons, interlaced with a series of arches. Essentially the pavilion forms a portico with dual sections: the first section, roofed or covered; and the second, a semi-covered pass-through. As in the hillside restaurant, the architects returned to Fatimid antecedents in determining its scale. In the initial section, intersecting vaults cover the ticketing area; in the second, wooden trellis provides covering. Other materials include wrought iron for the gates, wooden tie beams, and marble and slate patterned floors.

These three primary structures join an ensemble of parkland structures and surfaces designed by Sites International, including paving materials, lighting standards, seating, and waste receptacles. In addition, play equipment and observation points on the summits of the hills will add architectural character to the natural setting, producing an effect of ordered openness throughout the thirty-one-hectare design.

Fig. 100. Master plan of the new AUC campus.

While relatively small in square-metre-coverage, these three structures should have a telling presence within Cairo proper, sited so prominently within Azhar Park. They may consequently provoke discussion and debate on architecture within Cairo and Egypt, a cosmopolitan city within a nation searching for additional strong architectural models. Egyptian architecture during the last decades has struggled to keep abreast of a burgeoning population, a scenario in which more than 350,000 persons join Cairo's ranks annually, rendering Cairo one of the world's fastest growing cities.

Although blessed with one of the world's greatest ancient architectural treasure-troves in its Pharaonic heritage, and a similarly rich Islamic treasury of urban architecture, contemporary architecture has followed international trends with mixed results. Although populated with a large number of architects, lax construction codes, lack of contemporary theoretical discourse, and varying client demand have resulted in few significant contemporary structures of note. In an article reported in *Archi-*

Fig. 101. A rendering of the main axis of the new AUC campus.

tectural Record, Paul Bennett summed up the situation: "A lack of building restrictions, outdated laws for licensure, and inadequate education reached a breaking point in 1992, when a number of poorly-built structures collapsed during a major earthquake". The demise of the architectural magazine, *Medina*, has constricted academic communication among architects practicing there.

Landscape architecture relied in large part on international sources: Maher Stino, together with his wife and partner, established the first office of landscape architecture in the country. The aforementioned Fathy, whose clientele included the poor, remains the country's most well known practitioner. Talented architects have been practicing in Egypt, however. Abdel Halim, the principal of the Community Design Collaborative, a Cairo-based architectural and planning practice located in Cairo since 1980, has witnessed his firm's growth to include comprehensive, multi-hectare projects. His work has regularly taken him throughout the region, to Saudi Arabia, Muscat and Oman, and to Jordan. His plans for a cultural park for children received the Aga Khan Award for Architecture.

In Cairo, Abdel Halim's work includes the Qasr El Funoun, or Palace of Fine Art, formerly known as the Nile Gallery—a thorough renovation and redesign occupying land on the grounds of the Cairo opera house. In that project, Abdel Halim employed light and enclosure, geometric planning and details that graft contemporary and historic motifs. His most recent significant project involves planning for an entirely new campus for the American University in New Cairo (AUC), a $250 million project for the university that includes a "series of interweaving spaces", he says. Originally award-

Fig. 102. A rendering of the new AUC campus by the architect Abdel Halim.

ed to a firm in Boston, Massachusetts, called Boston Design Collaborative, the team was enlarged to include Abdel Halim's firm as well as Sasaki Associates.

In addition to the planning, programming, and design work, the firm has analysed local resources, including indigenous industries that may provide materials and systems for the campus. An array of well-known international architects, including the firm Hardy Holzman Pfeiffer, Legorreta+Legorreta, and Ellerbe Beckett are signed to contribute designs for individual buildings within the campus.

While the AUC project involves an institution, Egyptian architects are frequently employed in the development of residential and hospitality structures for the satellite cities springing up on the outskirts of Cairo in Heliopolis or Nasser City. Sometimes confined to gated compounds, the residences within the new towns often reflect European or American housing trends, according to local architects. The question becomes how to establish a context where none had existed previously. International architects have often contributed designs for resort architecture, including such well-known practitioners as Michael Graves and Sasaki Associates, who associate with local firms in the implementation of their designs. Michael Sorkin describes the condition of houses reminiscent of Beverly Hills out on the edges of the encroaching desert land as both "surreal and familiar".

The architect Akram El Magdoub, together with two Italian architects, Maurizio di Puolo and Enzo Serrani, recently designed the Om Kalthoum Museum, situated near the famous Nilometer river gauge. Paul Bennett describes the museum as "richly textured", showcasing "one of the first uses of multimedia programming in the city".

Recently Egypt has been the setting for two prominent international competitions, both of which illustrate trends in the larger design culture. In the first, for the design of the Bibliotheca Alexandrina, a hitherto unknown firm called Snohetta received the commission, in contemporary form, for a site near the Mediterranean of the Library of Alexandria — what had been one of the premier institutions of human civilisation. Prior to the competition, no firm had existed; the principles cobbled together a group specifically for the Alexandrine effort, which they won.

The resulting 74,400 square metre structure, with its strong circular geometry reminiscent of the harbour, its tilted roof over an ellipse, and its powerful interior spaces, captured worldwide interest and brought international attention to new architecture in Egypt. Hamza Associates of Egypt was associated with the Norwegian firm. Subsequently, Snohetta acquired additional commissions, including the Oslo opera house and a museum for the work of the British artist J. M. W. Turner.

In 2003, in another example of international firms acquiring important Egyptian commissions, a small Irish architectural firm won the competition for the design of a new Egyptian Museum. Long a mainstay of urban life on Tahrir Square near the Nile, and a stopping place for generations of

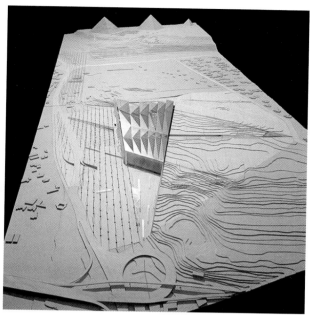

Fig. 103. Model of the Grand Museum of Egypt by Heneghan-Peng.

tourists, the Neoclassical museum will be relocated to the periphery, approximately nineteen kilometres out near Giza, and will be housed in a dynamic structure to be designed by the firm Henaghan-Peng. Decentralisation and internationalism continue to flourish in Egypt.

This injection of modernity on a large scale, produced under the spotlights of international competitions, may open Egyptian architecture to additional intellectual currents and broaden the professional dialogue. Until now, as Michael Sorkin has reported, "one of the surprises [...] is that architecture figures so little in the elaboration of this difference, that its symbolic import seems to have little or no weight" in the struggles facing Egypt as it grows and changes.

The Azhar Park project, constructed on land that is both two thousand years old, yet fundamentally changed — re-engineered, scoured three metres below grade — and reconstituted as urban parkland, may provide badly needed breathing room for the citizens of Cairo. But it may, in fact, serve as a spur for architectural discussion, offering alternative expressions of contemporary design sensibility and understanding, and questioning the role of modernity within a country in the act of defining itself.

A Decisive Moment for the Survival of Historic Cairo

NAIRY HAMPIKIAN

The Islamic heritage of Cairo was first introduced to the cultural map of Egypt by Edmé François Jomard, a member of the French scientific mission accompanying the Napoleonic Expedition to Egypt (1798 to 1801). In his work,[1] the then 'modern' Cairo was given special attention, receiving a much more detailed map than any previously available with individual buildings historically and architecturally documented and hand crafts surveyed. This encyclopaedic survey of Cairo can be considered a precursory form of large-scale conservation,[2] since it in fact paved the way towards extensive intervention on historic Cairo in 1882, when the Comité de Conservation des Monuments de l'Art Arabe was founded. The Comité developed a systematic set of actions for safeguarding the Islamic and Coptic heritage of Cairo: buildings with historic value were registered as monuments; monuments were rescued from urban invasions that would eventually have led to a risk of their expropriation and the parasite structures built in, on and around them were removed; damaged or missing elements of monuments were restored; details and decorations of historic buildings were documented, preserved, completed, and duplicated repeatedly; dialogue was established between the different bodies involved with the different aspects of monuments — such as ownership, craftsmanship, and financing; finally, the whole process was published in the *Bulletins* — yearly publications by the Comité. Without doubt, the programme developed and implemented by the Comité can rightfully be considered the greatest attempt at rescuing historic Cairo ever put into operation in modern times.

Today, at the beginning of the twenty-first century, we are witnessing another dynamic thrust aimed at salvaging Cairo's architectural history. Governmental bodies such as the Governorate of Cairo, the Ministry of Tourism, the Ministry of Housing, the Ministry of al-Awqaf (Endowments), the Ministry of Communication and Trans-

Fig. 104. View of historic Cairo from the Zuwayla Gate looking north.

Fig. 105. View of Azhar Park from the western minaret of the Zuwayla Gate.

port, the Ministry of Electricity, and the Water Supply and Sewage Companies are cooperating and combining their efforts under the umbrella of the Ministry of Culture,[3] in order to salvage the cultural heritage of historic Cairo. In 1998, the Ministry of Culture was allocated LE242 million by presidential decree to restore forty-seven monuments out of 450 for the whole of historic Cairo. In parallel, the Governor of Cairo has developed the Darb al-Ahmar Rehabilitation Project, which was initiated in cooperation with the Aga Khan Trust for Culture (AKTC) and, according to unconfirmed press statements, will be executed in five phases at a cost of LE300 million. The Ministry of Housing led the restoration work for al-Azhar Mosque, which was carried out in less than two years. All this newly aroused public awareness and acknowledgment of the importance of historic Cairo should give some satisfaction to those who, for more than five decades, have worried about its survival and the lack of any conservative action, although contrasting feelings do exist *vis-à-vis* this massive governmental effort.

HISTORIC CAIRO — CONTENT OF A LIVING LANDSCAPE

According to a United Nations Development Programme (and Supreme Council of Antiquities) report published in 1997, historic Cairo occupies a stretch of 3.87 square kilometres of urban fabric accommodating 310,500 inhabitants. Its boundaries are defined by the al-Futuh Gate to the north, Ibn Tulun Mosque to the south, Port Said Street to the west and Salah Salem Street to the east. To this area one must add clusters of monuments outside these borders such as the Citadel, the area around Ibn Tulun Mosque, the Madrasa of al-Zahir Baybars, and so on.

Harmony and discord simultaneously characterise the streets of historic Cairo thanks to its main components, the poles that have paradoxically fed on each other and coexisted through time: the frozen moments of history represented by the majestic domes, minarets, sultanic inscriptions, monumental portals and the mobile world of the living urban fabric represented by the ever-changing non-registered buildings, the people and their daily activities around the monuments. When dealing with historic Cairo, therefore, we have to refer to these essential components.

IMPLEMENTING AN INTERVENTION STRATEGY

Before initiating this extensive intervention scheme, a separate body was formed under the direct authority of the Minister of Culture and working in close collaboration with the Supreme Council of Antiquities (SCA). This new body, called al-Qahira al-Tarikhiyya (meaning Historic Cairo), established its headquarters in the old barracks of the Citadel. The group began by gathering the data necessary for the realisation of Phase I of the project. The scope of the scheme lies essentially within two domains:

- conservation of single monuments according to conventional practice;

- urban planning of the historic core of Cairo, as an attempt to deal with the context of single monuments.

To achieve these two goals, the planning committee was divided into two separate sections: the first deals with the conservation of single registered monuments and the second with the upgrading of the historic core and with the removal of undesired components.

JUSTIFICATION FOR THE INTERVENTIONS

Reasons for the emergence of the new restoration and urban renewal initiative are varied and complex. It is said by some that historic Cairo has surfaced on the agenda of Egypt for tourist and economic reasons with reports, for example that al-Muizz Street is going to be transformed into a tourist area of national importance, becoming commonplace in the media.[4] The impact of growing international awareness of conservation, national heritage and historic city concepts has surely also played a role. The sheer reality of the derelict state of historic Cairo rendered clear the necessity for rapid, large-scale action for precisely these reasons.

The current state of monuments in historic Cairo has been surveyed in the Ministry of Culture's publication of the conference, co-organised by the Ministry itself and UNESCO, which addressed this initiative.[5] Some of the current difficulties can be summed up as follows: a lack of available funds for conservation work; the disaster-prone state of the infrastructure; a malfunctioning refuse disposal system; pollution due to factories in the area; a lack of coordination between the different bodies; a gener-

Figs. 106, 107. Southern façade of the Zuwayla Gate before and after conservation work by the Comité.

al failure of the planning processes in conservation activities; a lack of qualified and conservation-conscious supervision on the projects; the absence of properly trained people to work on the conservation projects; a failure to follow up with the maintenance of registered buildings; the absence of a body that has systematically studied urban planning in historic Cairo; the unclear borders of historic Cairo; the absence of legal channels to safeguard the old city as a 'protected area'; the absence of efforts to register the non-registered buildings; authorities failing to adopt the idea of adaptive reuse of historical and non-registered buildings.

To overcome these and a wider range of technical, social, financial and administrative problems, this intervention was initiated through a separate body and with a new budget so that it could act independently and solve these issues. This new body was designed to pave the way for a general facelift of historic Cairo. The question remains as to whether it will be able to successfully tackle and overcome all the previous problems.

A PRELIMINARY ASSESSMENT OF CURRENT CONSERVATION PROCEDURES

Since Phase I has not yet been completed, any evaluation of it might be considered premature. Despite the problems listed above, some people are still tempted to ask whether this massive intervention was really necessary or not. The quantity of ailing monuments and the complexity of the problems facing these buildings do, though, show the necessity for such concerted action, especially as the slow pace of work over the past few decades added new problems to the existing ones. The advantage of a large-scale intervention also means an ability to 'think big', vital when tackling problems of infrastructure. Yet the personal touch when dealing with the individual elements, whether these are parts of the living city or monuments, should not be lost. All in all, I firmly believe that this is a golden opportunity for infrastructure conditions to be improved in historic Cairo, something that the project is already beginning to prove possible.

The press has often viewed these restoration efforts in a rather surprising way, varying between tones of excitement or aggression. To quote a few headlines: "A Fatimid Mosque Saved from Water"; "Wikalat Bazar'a Soon Renewed"; "Breaking the Silence"; "The Citadel Gets Rid of the Effects of Time"; "Making Room for History"; "Destruction of Wikalat al-Kharbotly to Build a Tower and a Commercial Centre"; "Historic Sites in Danger"; "The Legend of the Centuries"; "Endangered Façades"; "The Irresponsible Requisition of Islamic Monuments"; and likewise. An absence of updates from those responsible for project management meant that the media had free rein until the 2002 publication mentioned above (in note 5), which served as the first public review of the al-Qahira al-Tarikhiyya project. This publication explained the project in general and gave information on specific monuments either in preparation or under actual conservation, including the urban conservation project. In the future it would be desirable if project management documented and reported the progress of the work to the public in yearly reports, such as those produced previously by the Comité. Regular updates on the progress of the overall intervention would also encourage those who are participating in it.

Work has been initiated on many of the forty-seven monuments targeted by the project. To evaluate the practice of 'single monument conservation', the following questions must be answered. Are the basic problems being resolved? Are the technical shortcomings of previous conservation projects being studied, evaluated and overcome? In the case of the al-Darb al-Asfar project, the answer is yes, since the infrastructure in this alley has been completely renewed. If these standards of infrastructure were to be applied to the rest of the city, the 'large-scale project' would be able to achieve its goals.

Administrative problems seem to have been resolved at least in part. Direct dialogue between the different parties involved under the umbrella of the Ministry of Culture seem to be achieving miracles in some cases. Yet there is great controversy as far as conservation activities are concerned. The main

Fig. 108. Southern façade of the Zuwayla Gate during the ARCE conservation project in 1999.

criticism is the time factor. Conservation projects need to be allowed to establish a certain rhythm and time of their own if they are to be successfully carried out according to international standards, since conservation is painstaking and should not be attempted on compressed schedules. It is true that the main success of this massive intervention lies in the short time schemes it has proposed for the achievement of the whole plan, but modification of the timetable might relieve pressure and improve the quality of the work. It is also necessary to force contractors to include and respect proper conservation expertise. It appears that project management has been considering these issues and more time has been gained to rethink and improve methodology.

In this context, some urgent matters need to be addressed:

- the discipline of the conservation of historic buildings in Egypt makes no clear distinction between codes governing general construction contractors and specific constraints to be respected when dealing with conservation. In the meantime, international conventions have established unified codes and specifications for materials and methods to be used for historic buildings. These were based on an analysis of past errors, the inadequacy of certain types of materials in the context of the old fabric, their incongruity in the long run, and a number of other lessons learnt from

Fig. 109. Monuments, inhabitants, shops, conservation teams... A coexistence to be preserved.

Fig. 110. Election time around Bab Zuwayla.

earlier interventions. Since there is currently a great deal of reawakened emphasis on conservation in Egypt, it is impossible to ignore these international conventions and an Egyptian code for contractors practicing conservation must be urgently drawn up;

- as the discipline of the conservation of historic buildings is developing, and as the awareness of the range of problems facing old buildings is widening, new types of experts are joining the ranks of conservation specialists. A handbook listing reliable worldwide contacts to be consulted on special issue should be created;

- today, the extent to which high technology can be applied to the conservation of historic buildings is unlimited. But, for the past two decades, the new tendency in the West has been to use traditional materials and building methods whenever possible, rather than making unnecessary use of technology. Conservation of Cairo's historical buildings (and Egypt's antiquities in general) is torn between importing modern technology, and the traditional ways of restoring historical buildings. Training centres should be developed to upgrade the quality of traditional craftsmanship;

- the very term 'monument', used automatically to identify all buildings more than one hundred years old, needs to be questioned. In 1881, members of the Comité initiated a 'list of monuments' in which all buildings that were historically, aesthetically, and/or culturally, worthy of protection, were registered. The chosen buildings were identified as 'monuments' under one category, varying from each other only in the date of their construction. 120 years have passed since this chronological categorisation was drawn up and still monuments are classified according to this basic subdivision relating to the correspondence of their construction date to the different political periods of Islamic reign in Egypt. It is high time to rethink the categories of buildings worthy of protection. As viewed from conservators' and town planners' perspectives, the actual conventional subdivision is now meaningless;

- professionals in Egypt are torn between restoration and conservation, between introducing or excluding high technology, and selecting construction codes to fulfil the specifications for the conservation of historical buildings. A unified code should govern these dilemmas;

- in spite of a thirst for unified codes governing the practice of conservation, it must be stressed that through the practice of 'single monument conservation' a unification of interventions is taking place. Unified codes are important for preventing the use of forbidden materials and methods in conservation, but this does not mean that unified solutions to the apparently similar problems facing all monuments should be accepted. It is true that within similar types of buildings locat-

Fig. 111. Porch under the Zuwayla Gate; now a busy passageway in the street.

ed in the same past and present environmental conditions, similar problems are manifested. Yet each building has its own pulse of resistance and rhythm of ageing; accordingly, each has its specific problems. Therefore, it seems obvious that a tailored intervention must be found for each case. To achieve the goals of the project does not mean giving the same medicine to all the patients in the hospital.

A PRELIMINARY ASSESSMENT OF CURRENT PLANNING PROJECTS

As far as urban planning projects in the historic core are concerned, the intervention scheme is still in its initial stages, but indications from preliminary projects suffice to predict some of the future trends. For the first time in Cairo an organisation is in charge of the detailed study and proper management of the living urban fabric around single monuments, an element that previously did not exist. Until very recently, and with the exception of the AKTC projects in al-Darb al-Ahmar and the Zuwayla Gate, historic Cairo has been treated as an arena for historical buildings only with no attention being paid to the surrounding urban context that brings the city and its monuments to life. The non-registered buildings as well as all the commercial, educational, recreational and social activities, together with living conditions, were usually ignored. This approach is now changing and 'single monument conservation' projects, such as the 'al-Darb al-Asfar' and 'al-Fustat' projects, are already adopting wider urban perspectives and attending to both monuments and the living quarters around them. The existence of urban planners within the same decision-making body as the single-monument restorers is a major achievement, which, if managed properly, will enable proper area action plans to be established dealing with complete districts of the historic city — plans that will take into consideration both the body (the built environment) and the soul (the inhabitants) of historic Cairo.

There appears to be an attempt to focus on Fatimid Cairo (delineated by the first walled city of the Fatimids). This tendency can be seen in the attempts to connect the interrupted remains of walls marking the formerly non-existent borders of the Fatimids' al-Qahira, listed in the following observations:

- the project on the northern wall of al-Qahira, including the conservation of the al-Nasr and al-Futuh gates and the extensive rebuilding of the northern wall, will re-create the northern borders of Cairo;

- the western side of Fatimid Cairo is already bordered by Port Said Street, built on the same location as the former Khalij Misri canal. Port Said Street has lately been the object of much attention: the tram that passed down the middle of the road was eliminated and the road was widened accordingly; the monuments on this street are under conservation;

- on the eastern side, two projects are underway. On the southern side of al-Azhar Street, the AKTC is working on the thirty-hectare Azhar Park, described earlier in this book. This park, which is bordered on its western side by the remains of the Ayyubid extension of the walls, will act as a border to Fatimid Cairo. Meanwhile, a second project has already started to uncover the remains of the Fatimid walls, which run northwards to meet the eastern extension of the northern Fatimid wall. When finished, these two will define the core of Fatimid Cairo with respect to the rest of the historic city;

- on the southern side of the city, the modern Ahmad Maher Street marks the southern border of Fatimid Cairo. Remains of the southern wall are still visible behind and between the houses on the eastern side of the Zuwayla Gate, but no project has yet been launched there.

It must also be noted that major efforts are being made to define and enhance the points of access to Fatimid Cairo. This is clear from the following actions:

- the tunnel project running underneath al-Azhar Street from Salah Salem Street to Opera Square will turn al-Muizz Street into a pedestrian zone. This will allow the original main spine of the Fatimids' al-Qahira to be restored as a continuous internal (pedestrian) street;

- north of the new Azhar Park, near the entrance of the tunnel from Salah Salem Street, the AKTC, in cooperation with the Cairo Governorate, is building an 'Urban Plaza' with integrated underground car parking. This building, together with the neo-Islamic-style buildings of Dar al-Ifta on the other side of al-Azhar Street will mark the entrance from Salah Salem Street;

- at the entrance to the tunnel from the west, there is a project to rebuild the Old Cairo Opera House, which burned down in the 1970s. The present car parking structure will have to be demolished since it stands on the location of the former opera house;

- on the northern border of the isolated city, cemeteries of the al-Nasr Gate area were partially removed to make way for a motorway, a garden and, perhaps, hotels. This will be a pleasant approach to the old city from the north.

Figs. 112, 113. Bayn al-Qasrayn looking north before and after restoration of the al-Barqiyya *madrasa*.

Fatimid Cairo will thus be well delineated through the execution of these projects. The precise identification of the borders of an urban area marks the first step towards the preparation of a proper, controlled urban development plan. This project has the potential to create an access-controlled environment in which developers and planners will enjoy working. It is to be hoped that once the borders are identified, the areas inside will be re-documented and, with the help of new laws, any projects will be tightly controlled, so that whatever is planned is likely to be realised. This has been a major problem for urban planning in historic Cairo. Because things change so rapidly between the time they are documented in order to prepare plans and the time of execution of these plans, the documentation on which they were based no longer corresponds to reality. Consequently plans lose their efficiency and in some instances become unworkable and remain purely theoretical.

Once again, the mere existence of an urban planning body studying and working solely and systematically on feasible urban plans for historic Cairo is a major asset for the Old City, abandoned to neglect and dilapidation for more than a hundred and fifty years.

CONCLUSIONS

In conclusion, three main issues seem to be critical at this stage of decision-making.

Firstly, will historic Cairo lose its soul? Or should it be replaced by a new soul that is more appropriate to its historically justified, high economic value? Within the boundaries of historic Cairo, monuments, non-registered buildings and daily activities must survive and coexist together, although not everyone shares this belief. Some hope for a demolition of all non-historic structures, similar to what happened around the Pharaonic temples at the turn of the century. Others hope for a change in activities, with shopkeepers being given the opportunity to transform their daily activities into tourist ones, or of being removed outside the historic core of Cairo. A third voice suggests the partial evacuation of the city's historic core. Taking into consideration the segregated mix of activities in the historic core of the city, the creation of a 'node system' might ease the tension around these contradictory expectations for the historic core of the city. The concept is to subdivide the Fatimids' al-Qahira into 'tourist nodes' and 'community nodes'. Each type would develop its own living standards, needs, conservation codes, clientele, and so on. Use of the 'node system' would permit the whole city to be upgraded, with each area suited to the level of the needs of the clientele it serves. The fruit seller need not sell gold and Pharaonic statuettes, nor would the neighbourhood bakery be forced to sell baguettes. The 'node system' would allow the local community to abide side by side with the tourists: in segregation and yet in a continuous and pleasing connectedness.[6]

Secondly, is it enough to have registered monuments functioning only as 'monuments'? The fear of reusing historic buildings by adapting them to appropriate functions needs to be re-examined. Adaptive reuse is the only way to assure the maintenance of certain conserved buildings. The appropriate reuse of monuments has already become a part of the al-Qahira al-Tarikhiyya practice whenever possible as it is only by such reuse that buildings resulting from the intervention in historic Cairo will be protected in the longer term. More laws should, however, establish rules for the re-adaptation process during the conservation projects, the choice of the reuse, and the standards for maintenance after the project and during reuse.

Thirdly, was this massive intervention unavoidable? Yes, massive intervention was inevitable. The situation in historic Cairo was truly lamentable and it was inexcusable to justify the former lack of response by merely counting the huge number of monuments in a bad state, the lack of qualified personnel able to work on them, the infrastructure, and so on. It would also have been inappropriate to ask for the sufficient number of international professionals to deal with the magnitude of monuments in need of rescue. Under these circumstances, local, massive action was obligatory and I believe that this will also represent the chance to build up a new generation of conservators and architects alert to the process of conservation. Indeed, it appears that this is already happening.

Finally, all those who are involved in any way in historic Cairo need to be participants in some aspect of this work. Reasoned discussion is necessary in order to make the best of this intervention, and it is to be hoped that a new way of looking at the old city will emerge from this ongoing dialogue.

[1] The section describing Cairo is in the eighteenth section of "L'Etat Moderne" (pp. 113-535) in the second edition of *Description de l'Egypte* known as the Panckouke edition, Paris 1821 and 1829 (26 volumes).

[2] See Nairy Hampikian, "Cairo: The Seen and the Unseen in the *Description de l'Egypte*", in *Napoleon in Egypt*, Irene Bierman ed., Lebanon 2003, pp. 63-76.

[3] The Ministry of Culture heads this salvage team since the Supreme Council of Antiquities, a body within the Ministry of Culture, was, and still is, the main organisation responsible for all Egyptian antiquities.

[4] Al-Muizz Street is in fact one of the main Egyptian attractions in the Pan-Mediterranean 'Museum without Borders' project along with sites in twenty-seven other countries.

[5] Reasons for the intervention are mentioned in *Historic Cairo*, Ministry of Culture and the Supreme Council of Antiquities, February 2002, pp. 14-18. In the same publication, photographic documentation clarifies the depressing situation of the city's monuments, pp. 42-194.

[6] Nairy Hampikian and May al-Ibrashy, "Filling in Gaps Between a 'Monument' and Another 'Monument' in Historic Cairo" — Case study: Proposal for the Rehabilitation of the Area around the Southern Gate and Walls of Historic Cairo, Proceedings of the 5th International Symposium of the Organisation of World Heritage Cities (20-23 October 1999, Compostello, Spain).

A Changing Perception of Public Gardens

NAWAL EL MESSIRI

Green open public spaces are a major concern for urban planners all over the world, and with urban development becoming more and more interdependent the problems of over-crowding and the lack of open spaces have become ubiquitous, trans-national issues. In spite of the similarity of problems, the terminology used still varies from country to country and clear definitions are needed to make the best possible use of international experiences to promote exchange. Thus certain basic concepts such as 'park', 'garden' and 'public' need be discussed in the light of what they mean to different cultures. This article attempts to clarify the conceptual understanding of these terms in the Egyptian mentality and to highlight possible differences in approach between city planners and anthropologists.

TRADITIONAL OUTLOOK

Cairo is a city of infinite complexity and endless problems. It is overcrowded with people of vastly differing backgrounds, heterogeneous cultural values and rapidly changing class structures. It is difficult to understand the variations in contemporary lifestyles in Cairo without comprehending the importance of tradition. For every Cairene incorporates aspects of this traditionalism in varying degrees, and it is this basic phenomenon which provides the city with its identity.

The Western park concept as a more or less virgin piece of nature is nearly non-existent in Egypt, where there is little concern for natural vegetation nor any great interest in either indigenous or introduced species on the domestic level. Islamic literature does not manifest a great love of wild nature; rather it conceives gardens as walled and protected retreats from it. Also, subtropical agriculture is a primary source of disease, spread via irrigation channels.[1]

In Egypt, where ninety-five percent of the land is desert, every piece of arable terrain has been cultivated and irrigated and thus almost all plants are meant to produce edible or useful products. This horticultural practicality remains a keynote to attitudes towards green space. The fact that every area of green land is cultivated, planted and irrigated makes it distinct from natural parks in terms of size and the care required.

For many Egyptians the concept of a 'public garden' is comparatively new. It is a luxury, something the poor dream of and aspire to. It is a symbol of paradise, for, in Arabic, the terms 'garden' and 'paradise' stem from the same root. The ideal of the paradise-garden is imprinted in all Muslims' mental conceptions, since the Koran provides many detailed paradise descriptions, including the layout and kinds of fruit trees and shade trees to be found there, as well as the running water and favourable company. Thus the concept of paradise or the ideal garden has served as a model for the creators and planners of gardens throughout the Muslim world.

There is a general consensus among art historians that the Islamic gardens of the past were intended to be the terrestrial models of the Koranic description of a heavenly Garden of Paradise. But it must be pointed out that the Paradise of the Koran is an allegorical description for a psychic state. The mundane garden as a physical fact is not Paradise.[2] Most importantly a garden signifies private space, separated from public life and alien intrusion. Hence, the concept of 'park' has its own cultural implications in the Egyptian urban setting. Similarly, the concept of 'public' versus 'private' has other identifiable characteristics.

Since ancient Egyptian times gardens were the private possession of the ruling families and the elite. The royal palaces of Hatshepsut, Tutmosis III and Akhnaton incorporated gardens. The monks of Christianity surrounded themselves with walls inside which they had large gardens and orchards.[3] Muslim rulers, too, established their royal gardens, which were varied in their style, depending on the rulers' origin. Accordingly, these gardens served as royal retreats and their impact on the residents of the city was not significant.

The introduction of public gardens into the urban fabric of Islamic cities is a recent phenomenon. In most Muslim cities less than one percent of the total land surface has been utilised as public green space. Meanwhile, the need for open space has been fulfilled in many cases by the existence of private courtyard gardens.[4]

The rules of Islamic jurisprudence concerning the distinction between public and private property in the city were loosely interpreted in medieval Cairo and a number of controversies surrounding the rights of usage of public space resulted. On the whole the individual's right was more important than public policies. Historians supply us with numerous examples to validate this point. If an individual constructed a building which had some religious, social or economic value, it could encroach upon a public space irrespective of the existing laws. In spite of the fact that regulations governing roads, drainage, burial of the dead, and so on, were formulated, greater emphasis was placed on the freedom of the individual than on city planning.

In Egypt, there has developed over the centuries a feeling that public, government-owned space is 'no mans land'. For centuries, the Egyptian public was never involved in policy making. The idea of effective political involvement in city planning has never existed. This was, and continues to be, aggravated by the lack of correlation between taxpaying and public development. Traditionally, taxes went into the ruler's pockets and the individual's aim was (and is) to try to minimise or avoid this hazard as much as possible. There is hardly any criticism based on the principle of misuse of taxpayer's money addressed to the governing body — quite in contrast to what is a current practice in the Western press.

Government agencies also tend to rely on existing public open green spaces as an easy resource for locating public facilities. Moreover, the competition over the allocations

Fig. 114. In the Zoo.

of seemingly 'useless' open spaces arises among different ministries. Each claims its right to use such available vacant spaces for their own purposes. This traditional attitude is to a certain degree responsible for the progressive elimination of public gardens. Both the public and the government claim the right to encroach upon them. The logical justification is that there are more beneficial usages for a public green space which does not produce edible products.

Thus the competition over garden space in Cairo deals basically with problems of perception and usage. In addition, the basic issue of the mere existence and creation of a green space in the city of Cairo remains a contested domain. Gardens in Egypt require both intensive human service and physical infrastructure, the most important component of which is a reliable water supply. Since most of the public man-made gardens were not a part of the culture, most of the garden areas were confined to the walled courtyards of private ownership. However, with the advent of the nineteenth century and with attempts to modernise Egypt, new ideas for creating public gardens emerged. The following example will present the development of one of the first public gardens in the city of Cairo.

AZBAKIYYA GARDEN: A FIRST ENCOUNTER

In 1837, Muhammad Ali, in his attempt to westernise Egypt, promoted the establishment of a public garden. He decided to transform Azbakiyya Square, which was filled with ponds, into a garden. The ponds were considered a source of disease-spreading insects. Muhammad Ali's major concern in creating the garden, then, was one of hygiene. Secondly, the locality was the residential neighbourhood of the foreign community and a garden was considered fitting to their status. To accomplish this task, the ruler confiscated forty *feddans* (equal to 16.8 hectares) belonging to a wealthy family and ordered the officials to begin transforming it into a garden. The architect was Murton Bey, whom Muhammad Ali had sent to Europe for his education.[5] From its beginning the garden was reputed to meet the needs of the foreign community and its design followed a European model.

The new Western trend was further emphasised in 1867 by Muhammad Ali's grandson, Ismail, who was infatuated with European culture. He rearranged Azbakiyya Garden according to the French style, reducing it in size (10 *feddans*) and making it octagonal in shape, after Park Monceau in Paris. It was designed by a French architect, Barillet, and a German botanist was placed in charge of planting trees. The garden was encircled with iron railings punctuated by four entrances, where Nubian doormen were posted and entrance tickets sold. In addition, public officers supervised the garden's security.[6] Ismail's transformation of Azbakiyya Garden into a replica of a Parisian garden was not an end in itself; rather, it was part of a larger scheme to create a modern quarter suitable for the residences of the foreign community. The houses surrounding the garden were demolished and their poor residents compensated. In addition, Ismail offered this same land free to whoever would construct buildings on it that could meet this conception of a western quarter.[7] In short, Ismail created a western garden by a western designer in a western quarter for a western public. Its benefits were also shared by the elite Egyptian public who aspired to a western way of life and who could afford to pay the entrance fee.

With the expansion of the city, the shrinking of the foreign community and the development of elite quarters in other districts, the public coming to enjoy Azbakiyya Garden changed. For the ordinary Egyptian, Azbakiyya Garden was associated with freedom and western living: freedom meaning interaction between the sexes and liberty for the overt expression of traditionally restricted social behaviour. Thus Ahmad Amin describes the garden in the first decade of the twentieth century as a place for prostitution, vice, gambling and alcohol.[8] Ismail, when planning the garden, was thinking only of how he could impress his western guests by showing them a replica of their cities. However, since the garden was completely divorced from local culture, it became a symbol of western decadence, exemplified by its shift from being a meeting place for lovers to a place for prostitution. The railings around the garden itself became a famous space for the recycling of old books, as if the bookstands were erected to hide what went on inside it.

In 1948 licensed prostitution was abolished and with the advent of Nasser's regime admission to the garden became free. Its huge fence was demolished and a simpler one erected. The garden became a place for recreation for poor families from the surrounding areas. It also became, with the surrounding area, a space for peddlers and numerous other small moneymaking activities. According to the traditional conception of public spaces, economic activities take precedence over any other utilisation of public space. However, breadwinners were now confronted by a stronger rival; the garden became a contested space among different government agencies. Each tried to use the space for the construction of a building to house one of its activities. The Ministry of Culture built several theatres on its periphery, basing its argument on the fact that the garden was a place of recreation and entertainment, as were theatres. The Ministry of the Interior erected a building to house some of its offices, until a more permanent location could be found. Finally, the Municipality decided to ease the flow of congested traffic in the area by cutting a street through the middle of the garden and then constructing a flyover overlooking it. The public quickly gave up using this garden as a public place. The only complaints came from those who used the place for economic purposes. They were compensated with a less attractive location which they accepted unwillingly. Eventually the garden disintegrated to its present state.

Figs. 115, 116. Aquarium Garden: schoolchildren playing in the Grotto.

The history of Azbakiyya Garden, its design, function and actual use, denotes that public gardens are not static. They change with the changing fabric of urban development and pass through constant adjustments to satisfy the needs of their users. Attitudes towards entertainment also change over time. Consequently, for a garden to survive it should be suited to the changing social mores of its beneficiaries.

In his continuous efforts to beautify Cairo, Ismail Pasha established what is now called Horeyya Garden. The Aquarium Grotto Garden in Zamalek, the Zoo and the Orman Gardens in Giza also owe their existence to his perception. This trend continued for some time among the elite. Zulfugar Ali Pasha, an architect from Helwan, established both the Japanese Garden in Helwan, and

Andalus Garden in Zamalek. Zuharia Garden was also established during this period by the royal family. No other significant gardens were created until the 1980s with the exception of the Obelisk Garden, established during the rule of Nasser.

After the victory of 1973 more attention was directed to the internal affairs of the country. The infrastructure of the city received priority. Water, electricity, transportation and sewerage took precedence over the concern for gardens. The effect of the 'open door policy' was actually felt by the 1980s. Concepts such as pollution and the need for green spaces to relieve the city from its tainted air became important issues for discussion by policy makers and the media. The severity of the problem led to the creation of a new Ministry of the Environment. The last two decades of the twentieth century, and the few years following, have witnessed a boom in garden awareness, especially at the administrative level.

Fig. 117. Forbidden to sit on the grass in Horeyya Garden.

PRESENT HIERARCHY OF CAIRENE GARDENS
The organisational structure of the gardens of Cairo is diverse and complicated. Three Governorates and the Ministry of Agriculture are in charge of green public spaces accessible to the Cairene public. Each one is responsible for a number of gardens depending on their nature and/or location.

Users of public gardens are not aware of this administrative separation. Visitors to gardens, especially those coming from poor areas are not constrained by the distance of the garden but rather by the nature of activities provided in it.

The gardens controlled by the Ministry of Agriculture are in essence zoological, botanical and fish gardens. The Zoo (established 1891) is located in Giza Governorate, and referred to by the common people as "The Garden". When the family say "we are going to the garden", it means that they are going to the zoo. Other gardens are identified by their name. This garden ranks highest in the hierarchy of gardens in terms of public popularity and its attraction stems not only from its zoological appeal but also from its vegetation. This includes gigantic shade trees that allow the older members of the family to sit on the ground and enjoy themselves while the young play around or observe the animals. It satisfies a cultural enjoyment and habit of sitting cross-legged on the ground while eating or relaxing. It is a family garden in the real sense. In addition it receives groups of schoolchildren from all over Egypt. Going to the Zoo is a full day activity. The family equips itself with necessary sheets to spread on the ground to sit on and plenty of food is prepared; sometimes the food is cooked in the garden.

Orman Garden, also in Giza and nearly as old as the Zoo, is exclusively a botanical garden having rare species of vegetation. Due to its proximity to Cairo University its visitors are mainly university students who go there to study, or to meet friends, or play football. Because it is close to the Zoo Garden, its share of visitor numbers is much less.

Fig. 118. Andalus Garden: no visitors.

Aquarium Grotto Garden, in Zamalek (one hundred and thirty years old), is the most popular among groups of schoolchildren who enjoy viewing the man-made caves and fish species exhibited in it. It is also a favourite place among university students for romantic dates. In spite of the beauty of the garden and its location it does not attract the elite residents of Zamalek. They only appreciate views of it from their windows, and are conscious of the importance of greenery and are ready to fight for it. But when it comes to spending time in such gardens they find them inappropriate for their style of life.

So, although the Zoo and the 'Fish Gardens' are located in prestigious quarters, their visitors are basically from the mainstream of the population. The entrance fees to these gardens is 25 piastres. The Zoo in particular has very permissive garden rules and regulations and it is consequently very noisy with microphones and drums from the numerous cafés seeming to suit these particular visitors.

Until three years ago the gardens of the Cairo Governorate belonged to the Department of Beautification and Cleaning, a department found in all governorates. This department is overburdened with the task of cleaning an urban metropolis housing some sixteen million people. With the increasing concern of relieving the city's pollution, the Cairo Governorate initiated a new administrative plan for its public gardens. This plan was initiated in 1987 when the International Garden at Madinet Nasr was established. This garden acquired an international reputation since part of its initial budget came from donations from leaders of the different countries who visited the site and chose a location to carry the name of their country.

With the success of the International Garden, with the rising awareness of the need for green areas in the city, and with the appointment of a Governor who is an agriculturalist, the Governorate, in the year 2000, decided that a special organisational body needed to be created. In that year the Department of Special Gardens was established. It became responsible for twenty-three newly created or conserved gardens. This department has a special board of directors and a general director who reports directly to the governor. The remaining public gardens and other green spaces, such as squares and pavements continue to be one of the many responsibilities of the Department of Beautification and Cleaning of Cairo.

Whenever the Governor of Cairo finds that a new or a renewed garden has a special value, he designates it to the Department of Special Gardens. These special gardens can be identified as 'heritage gardens' which, because of their historical, cultural or artistic attributes can be regarded as being of local, regional, national or international significance.[9]

The gardens of the newly established Department of Special Gardens rank at the top of the administrative hierarchy. They receive the utmost care and arouse the jealousy of the directors of other gardens. They have a separate budget and the income is spent on the salaries and maintenance of the gardens. The main source of income comes from entrance fees (LE1.00). Seven out of the twenty-three gardens charge only 50 piastres because they are located in low-income districts. Another source of income comes from renting cafés, theatres and other entertainment activities. According to the director of the Department, these gardens are financially self-sufficient. The Department employs 1,321 people, 525 of them are agricultural workers and the rest are supervisors, accountants, mechanics and drivers. These employees are responsible for 851,961 square metres of gardens. Three of these gardens are of historic value and have artistic significance. Thus they deserve special mention for they are treated differently.

Horeyya Garden, in Tahrir Street, was established by Ismail Pasha in 1876 and at that time covered an area of about twenty-nine *feddans* (equal to 12.2 hectares). This garden is of great historical importance because of its size and central location. Entrance was free of charge and children's games and activities were abundant. But over the years parts of the garden were subject to intrusion by various organisations: the Cairo Club, the Presidential Security Headquarters, the Mokhtar Museum and the Sheraton Hotel. The garden was left with little more than seven *feddans*. Furthermore, during the construction phase of the underground railway the garden was used as storage for the construction equipment. In the late 1990s the garden was subject to an elaborate conservation project that safeguarded the historic botanical heritage and changed the architectural design and function of the garden. The design now combines both a natural and a geometric appearance, with curved lines following the historic trees and the symmetrical and identical organisation of the new development. The function of the garden has also changed: it is artistic and spectacular with no children's section. It is a place for adults to enjoy the serenity and beauty of the surroundings, relaxing on the one hundred benches provided. A number of restrictions are in force – no sitting on the grass, no food admitted, no peddlers inside. It accepts only two hundred visitors at a time, commensurate with the number of seats available in the garden.

Fig. 119. Fustat Garden: simple seating arrangements.

The second historic and artistic garden, Andalus, was established in 1929 by Zulfugar Pasha as a present to his wife. It overlooks the Nile and has three sections: the first, al-Ferdous with an arabesque design and architecture; the second, in an Andalusian style with mosaic steps and a royal hall; and the third, a Pharaonic section with replicas from ancient Egyptian statues. This garden covers an area of 8,400 square metres. Similar to Horeyya Garden, large visitor numbers are not appreciated in order to protect the garden's artistic value. To accomplish this end, the entrance ticket to the Pharaonic section is LE1.00, while an additional LE5.00 has to be paid to visit the more elaborate sections.

The Japanese Garden in Helwan is the third garden in this category. It was established in 1917 by Zulfugar Pasha, a resident of Helwan, as a present to Sultan Hussein. The Sultan used to spend time at the resorts of Helwan, located next to a rubbish tip. Zulfugar Pasha turned the tip into a beautiful garden in an Asian style, including many statues of the Buddha and mythical animals. The area of the garden was left intact, while a fence was constructed around it to control entrance fees. At present, the garden is surrounded by a less privileged neighbourhood, thus it charges only 50 piastres for a ticket. It also attracts many school groups thanks to its interesting statues.

The present conservation of heritage gardens and their maintenance demonstrates that over the years there has been a developing perception from the administrative bodies concerning the significance of green public spaces in the city of Cairo. Generally these gardens serve school trips and the middle classes. The upper middle and top-class residents prefer membership to exclusive clubs or have their own private gardens.

The success of the Department of Special Gardens aroused rivalry among other departments in the Governorate. The Department of Beatification and Cleaning in Cairo established a group of gardens which it called Distinguished Gardens. There are about ten of these gardens and their major characteristic is that they all are located in low-income quarters.

Fustat Garden, which is administered by this Department, is presently one of the most important gardens in the city of Cairo. It is of special importance to Azhar Park since it is the closest garden to it and is located in the midst of one of the poorest quarters in Cairo. It is the largest garden or man-made park in the city covering an area of two hundred and fifty *feddans* (equal to 105 hectares), not all of them fully developed yet. Like Azhar Park it was a dumping ground for refuse called

Fig. 120. Fustat Garden: children's area.

Abou al-Souod. This area was constantly self-igniting from combustion and spreading pollution all over the city. At first, the governorate wanted to relieve the city of this pollution and to have a green area, not necessarily a garden, instead. No special budget was allocated for this purpose; the governorate used the facilities of the Department and no outside contractors were involved. The first phase was inaugurated in 1989 and the entrance fee was 5 piastres. Unlike Azhar Park, there was only limited treatment of the garden soil. The initial idea was to create flat green areas: large shade trees with deep roots are not suitable for this soil so this shortcoming was compensated for by the construction of several kiosks with seats. The park is a real family entertainment park with all sorts of children's games and activities. Visitors are allowed to picnic on the ground and cafés serve *sheisha* (water pipe or hubbly bubbly) thereby encouraging fathers to accompany their wives and children. At present the garden entrance fee is only 50 piastres but it also makes a lot of income from various other activities. It is served by 247 employees, 102 of them are agricultural workers. According to the Director of the garden, the income of the garden during the last ten years was more than LE16 million .

AZHAR PARK AND THE CONSEQUENCES

So far we have discussed the various concepts of gardens and their historical, administrative and cultural applications in the city of Cairo. This will allow us to assess its newest addition, Azhar

Park, in relation to the other gardens in the city. Moreover, we must address measures and procedures which will need to be implemented in order to make the gardens of Cairo a sustainable reality. We need to learn from earlier mistakes to transfer successful mechanisms and to multiply the impact of approaches that are effective.

The Azhar Park project started from an acceptance of the present urban context with all its ruins, poor housing conditions and low-income residents. Its planners were

Fig. 121. Fustat Garden: a tour around the garden.

aware of the cultural legacy underlying these conditions and had the vision to uncover that legacy through a physical and socio-economic rehabilitation process of the Darb al-Ahmar district. Ismail Pasha, in Azbakiyya Garden, pursued a modern redevelopment scheme that was to replace the local community with a foreign one, providing it with a garden that suited foreign taste. Here, then, we encounter two radically different approaches. The expectations for the future of Azhar Park expect it to contribute to the upgrading of the adjacent neighbourhoods rather than destroy them.

As we have seen, in order to survive for long periods and to continue to be socially viable, gardens must suit the needs and social mores of their visitors. It is apparent from the above discussion that users of public gardens mainly belong to the lower levels of society. The upper classes are more interested in private clubs and their social milieu, although these clubs are overcrowded while many of the public gardens are actually much larger and nicer in terms of available green open space. Will Azhar Park be able to bridge this gap? Will the Hilltop Restaurant be able to attract the well-to-do residents from Heliopolis, Zamalek and Maadi to Azhar Park? The rehabilitation programme of al-Darb al-Ahmar aims at improving the socio-economic situation of the residents. To what extent will these improvements change their lifestyle? Entertainment and leisure activities are very much class oriented and are not necessarily related to economic levels. Clearly, Azhar Park will play a pioneering role in exploring and fostering new ways of coexistence and interaction between specific social modes of behaviour related to green open spaces.

Some gardens survived for long periods but did not continue to be socially viable because they were overprotected and treated as museum gardens. This indicates that there is still a tremendous need for all levels of society to change their perception regarding public gardens. Administrators are now convinced about the importance of having green spaces in the city. Educated and cultured people should be encouraged to visit the various gardens. For many years, Cairo did not witness the creation of any new gardens, while older ones were closed for conservation. This situation has changed significantly. The gardens which where under conservation have opened and many others have been created. Presently, with few exceptions, gardens are under-visited in comparison to the overcrowding in the private clubs.

To encourage usage of the gardens by the different strata of society there should be a minimum of mutual respect among them, without interfering with the cultural patterns of entertainment of the different groups. One way of achieving this would be to have some sort of soft zoning for the gardens. This is not meant to imply any form of segregation, but something like smoking/non-smoking zones. In other words, a section would be allocated to children, another to ball games, and a third for music... and so on. This is already practiced in certain gardens, especially with children's areas, but there are no restrictions on trespassing. The media should play a stronger role in informing the public of the nature and characteristics of the various gardens and increase public awareness to safeguard and protect their public gardens. So far, Azhar Park has maintained a very low profile in terms of propagating its existence through its different phases of construction. The inauguration of this park should be seized as an opportunity for involving the media in promoting a 'code of conduct' for the use of public parks.

How a garden should be managed and maintained depends on its use, on the number of visitors it is likely to attract, and on its historic, artistic and cultural significance. Azhar Park is not a haphazard idea but the outcome of comprehensive studies carried out to international standards. Its management during the construction phase and its management after its opening are discussed in other papers. Here, I would like to provide specific recommendations regarding maintenance and its relation to the type and number of visitors. Directors of different gardens have stated that there is a predictable pattern in visitor numbers. Ordinary days of the week account for the lowest number of visitors. That number is doubled or tripled during weekends but quadrupled on feast days. However, on 'Sham el Nasim', the spring festival, numbers go up exponentially, and there are no empty spaces whatsoever, on the grass or elsewhere. On that day, the International Garden receives an estimated 100,000 visitors. Visitors to the Zoo sometimes exceed 250,000 visitors, and Horeyya closes altogether. This indicates that after 'Sham el Nasim' provision needs to be made for a complete overhaul of garden spaces. Any strategy for garden maintenance should take this phenomenon into consideration.

Finally, will Azhar Park work as a catalyst for change in the old city? Undoubtedly the Darb al-Ahmar rehabilitation project should produce economic prosperity and raise levels of education and health. But it is essential that this development be accompanied by special programmes aimed at increasing public awareness regarding the protection of their monuments and their green areas. This type of education should start with schoolchildren, thus enabling future generations to derive the best possible benefits from their natural and cultural resources.

[1] John Brookes, *Gardens of Paradise: The History and Design of the Great Islamic Gardens*, New York 1987, p.199.

[2] Ralph Blakstad, "What is an Islamic Garden", in *Environmental Design*, J.I.E.D.R.C 1986, p. 22.

[3] Brookes, *Gardens of Paradise* cit., p. 168.

[4] Nader Ardalan, "Places of Public Gathering in Islam", in *Proceedings of Seminar Five in the Series of Architectural Transformation in the Islamic World Held in Amman*, 1980, p.5.

[5] Doris Abouseif, *Azbakiyya and its Environs from Azbak to Ismail*, Cairo 1985, pp. 87-92.

[6] Abd Al-Rahman Zaki, *Al-Kahira*, Cairo 1943, p.178.

[7] Ibid.

[8] Ahmad Amin, *Qamus al-Aadat al-Misriyya*, Cairo 1952.

[9] M. Sheena Goulty, *Heritage Gardens*, London 1993, p. XVI.

City of the Future

PHILIP JODIDIO

Debates about historic preservation are frequent. What exactly can be done to improve a city whose sedimentary layers are so complex as to defy any obvious clarification? In an area where day-to-day life and monuments are intertwined, should the two be somehow separated, allowing the historically significant to stand apart from the mundane, or is such a fabric too delicate to re-weave? This conundrum exists in the fullest sense in the Darb al-Ahmar area of Cairo, selected by the Aga Khan Trust for Culture (AKTC) as the site of one of its most ambitious rehabilitation programmes. The obviously integrated approach to al-Darb al-Ahmar's difficulties already presented in this book may seem to be derived from an almost inevitable logic, and yet, elsewhere in Cairo, storms rage over how the historic city can coexist with the demands of tourism and the rights of residents. The ambitious Historic Cairo Restoration Programme launched by the government in 1998 is meant to restore 157 monuments in an eight-year period. According to an internal report prepared for UNESCO by a monitoring mission sent to Cairo in August 2001 and published by *Al-Ahram Weekly* in February 2002, "this rapid undertaking also creates the imminent risk of making mistakes in a very delicate balance between the current needs of a fast-growing urban community and respect for authenticity and unique heritage values". When the nine-hundred-year-old Bab Zuwayla, one of the main Fatimid gateways to Cairo, was restored under the supervision of Nairy Hampikian recently (the project was carried out by the American Research Centre in Egypt (ARCE) with $2.8 million in funding provided by the United States Agency for International Development (USAID)), it was announced that the government is "planning to transform the whole area into an open-air museum, as part of the larger Historic Cairo rehabilitation project. One aspect of this project would involve the removal of slums and workshops, which it has been assured, would take place in cooperation with the area inhabitants and traders. 'Compensation will be provided for every family and trader because we do care about people, and not just about monuments,' a representative said."[1] The intervention of the AKTC in al-Darb al-Ahmar obviously does not espouse the view of the historic area as an "open-air museum". Instead, a substantial effort has been made to reintegrate monuments as complex as the long-buried Ayyubid wall into the life of the community. This is being done not only by opening connections into the new Azhar Park, but also by renewing housing and monuments that abut the wall or even sit partially on top of it at one point. And rather than seeking to move residents and local workshops to some undefined new location, this project takes on the training of local craftsmen in the traditional arts of carpentry and stonework that they no longer fully master.

Fig. 122. An image taken by K. A. C. Creswell of the Citadel, north side, in the 1920s.

Cairo has seen other rehabilitation projects that seek to deal with some of the underlying problems of the city. The Zabbaleen Environmental and Development Programme initiated in 1981 targeted the group that collects and transports a large part of the six thousand tonnes or more in solid waste generated by the city every day. Coptic Upper Egyptian agricultural workers who migrated to Cairo in about 1930 and settled in tin houses in Imbaba, the Zabbaleen, moved to Moqattam in 1970 and re-erected their squatter houses, gradually transforming them after that into stone structures. Without running water or much electricity, these people lived in appalling conditions, with their basic, essential skills unrecognised by most authorities. First conceptualised by the Governor of Cairo and the World Bank in 1976, the project was launched when Environmental Quality International (EQI) received a grant from the Ford Foundation to assist in upgrading the living conditions of the Zabbaleen. Another major participant in the Zabbaleen Environmental and Development Programme was the Zabbaleen Gameya, first established by the late Bishop Samuel, Bishop of Social and Ecumenical Services of the Coptic Orthodox Church, as an association that represented the interests of the settlement. The government of Egypt, in cooperation with the International Development Association of the World Bank, financed a concomitant project for the construction of basic infrastructure and facilities to upgrade the Moqattam settlement. A route extension programme devised by the NGO Oxfam added eight thousand homes to the routes of the Zabbaleen system. Despite the recent decision by the government to call on foreign refuse collection services to relieve the solid waste problems faced acutely in areas like al-Darb al-Ahmar, this attempt to improve the life of some of Cairo's poorest residents shows that the AKTC is not alone in seeking to carry out the delicate task of improving conditions while allowing people to live with their own heritage and neighbourhood. One interesting facet of this project is that it has served as the model for a similar initiative carried out in the Payatas squatter area located to the north of Manila in the Philippines.

Islamic, or medieval, Cairo is an area of narrow streets, covered markets and crumbling old buildings. Of all Cairo, this large neighbourhood most evokes its past, and, as photos taken in the nineteenth century show, it has in many ways changed little in the modern era. It has inspired many writings, from the *Arabian Nights* to the more recent works of Nobel laureate Naguib Mahfouz. It is in this area that the tradition of the city, from the Fatimids to the present, is concentrated. Although the northern part of the medieval city, where the Khan al-Khalili is located, has seen the arrival of many more tourists than the southern zone, historic Cairo has surely been greatly undervalued as opposed to Pharaonic Egypt. Instead of clearing the workshops and residents to make way for an "open-air museum", the AKTC and others have made a wager that their efforts can improve life and preserve an environment that is truly steeped in history. Although it was until recent years a centre for the drug trade, al-Darb al-Ahmar is home to a deeply rooted community. About eighty thousand people, many of them related by marriage, live and work in this area where real unemployment rates may not

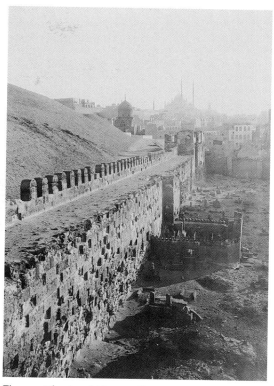

Fig. 123. The Ayyubid east wall, again photographed by K. A. C. Creswell in the 1920s.

be as high as most estimates imply. Studies carried out by Dina Shehayeb at the behest of the Aga Khan Cultural Services-Egypt show that, contrary to many assumptions, the population of al-Darb al-Ahmar consists mostly of persons born in the area (seventy-two percent) with only seven percent having been born outside Cairo. Their illiteracy rate (nineteen percent) is lower than the Egyptian urban average (twenty-six percent), and the male unemployment rate is about eighteen percent. Household income, on average $1,052 per year (based on the exchange rate of LE4.65 to the US dollar in June 2002) appears to be considerably lower than known averages for the city of Cairo: $2,570 in 1993, when the exchange rate was then LE3.50 to the US dollar.[2] With the arrival of Azhar Park it is certain that the circumstances of the Darb al-Ahmar residents will change. The obvious fact that they live in the very heart of Cairo, and not at its abandoned edge, has been underlined not only by the historic preservation work done on the Ayyubid wall and within the community, but also by the creation of the highly symbolic park at their doorstep. Rather than being recent immigrants as was long assumed, these people have their place in Cairo's future.

It might seem curious to think of the Zabbaleen when viewing the impressive thirty-one-hectare expanse of Azhar Park, and yet, as the texts of Cameron Rashti and Francesco Siravo in this book make clear, the site of the park was the rubbish heap of Cairo since late Mamluk times (the Burji

Fig. 124. From a 19th-century album devoted to views of Egypt by Maison Bonfils of Beirut (est. 1867): "General view of the tombs of the Caliphs and the Citadel of Cairo", 1870s.

Mamluks ruled Egypt until their defeat by the Ottoman Turks in 1517 under Selim I): five hundred years of rubble, forty-five metres high or more, the very stuff of history, the layered sediment of Cairo's life and past. From the rolling green hills of the site today, one monument stands out against the skyline, framed in the windows of the restaurants, aligned with the main axis of the park: Cairo's Citadel. Between 1176 and 1183, Salah al-Din (Saladin, AD 1176-1193), the founder of the Sunni Ayyubid dynasty, fortified the area to protect it against attacks by the Crusaders, and, since then, it has never been without a military garrison. Originally it served as both a fortress and a royal palace complex. Aside from the Moqattam Hills behind it, this location provides a strategic advantage both for dominating Cairo and for defending it against outside attackers. Moqattam is of course the home of the Zabbaleen today.

Azhar Park offers a view of the city almost as dominant as that of the Citadel itself and from its high points one has to look almost directly down to see partially unearthed remnants of the Ayyubid city wall, restored by the AKTC. This wall was also in part the work of Salah al-Din and it marked the eastern limit of the city. From these hills too, the visitor can clearly see the mosque and *madrasa* built for Sultan Hasan bin Mohammad bin Qalawun in AD 1356 as a complex incorporating a religious school for the four main sects of Orthodox (Sunni) Islamic thought and a hospital. Closer by still, north of the Citadel and close to the Zuwayla Gate, stands the Aqsunqur, or Blue, Mosque, built by one of al-Nasir Muhammad's amirs, Shams al-Din Aqsunqur, in 1346. Near the limits of the park a minaret recently restored by the AKTC marks the site of an unusual complex, built first as a mausoleum by the Mamluk prince Khayrbek in 1502. It was this prince who in 1517 betrayed the Mamluk army to the Ottomans, allowing them to take control of the country. Made governor of Egypt as a reward for his treachery, he built a small

Fig. 125. The east wall and tower of Bab al-Mahruq, K. A. C. Creswell, 1920s.

mosque next to the mausoleum in 1520. Left standing empty for decades before the recent restoration work began, Khayrbek Mosque is considered an important testimony to the Mamluk-Ottoman transition, and is remarkable because of its unusual architectural configuration. A more recent monument visible from the park on the same axis as the Sultan Hasan Mosque is the al-Rifa'i Mosque designed by Mustapha Fahmi at the order of Khushyar, mother of Khedive Ismail, and completed in 1912 by Max Herz Pasha. Though he was a justifiably

Fig. 126. An unsigned general view of the Citadel, *c.* 1880.
The site of Azhar Park is visible to the upper right of the Citadel.

controversial ruler it was Khedive Ismail who inaugurated the Suez Canal in 1869, erected the Royal Opera House where Verdi's *Aïda* was first performed in December 1871, and created the first all-Egyptian Cabinet in 1878. Tempted to create a 'Paris along the Nile', he also laid the foundations for modern downtown Cairo in the area originally named Ismailiyya. In the remarkable skyline visible from Azhar Park, al-Rifa'i Mosque, crypt of Egypt's last dynasty, might be considered a symbol of the transition of the country, however painful, towards the modern world.

As though this accumulation of great monuments would not have sufficed, it should be noted that the park is named after the great al-Azhar Mosque, located slightly north of the Darb al-Ahmar area. Al-Azhar was created by none other than Jawhar the Sicilian, Fatimid founder of Cairo just after his conquest in 969. Al-Azhar, meaning "the most flourished and shining" in Arabic, was dedicated to Sayeda Fatima al-Zahra', daughter of the prophet Muhammad, from whom His Highness the Aga Khan descends. It is only natural then, that this great new park in the heart of Cairo, close to its Fatimid roots and created by the present Aga Khan, should be called Azhar Park.

Despite its location so close to the wellsprings of Cairene history, it was a daring gesture to decide to build on top of more than five centuries of rubble. As Cameron Rashti explains elsewhere in this volume, the very nature of this sedimentary accumulation was a challenge to any construction or to the growth of plants. And yet, almost more than any monument, the debris of the great city is the trace of its life, not a burial ground but the natural accretion of human activity. As circum-

Fig. 127. A drawing by Sites International (Maher Stino) showing the Upper Meadow Zone of Azhar Park in the design development stage of the project. The Citadel is visible to the left.

stances would have it, the south-eastern edge of Azhar Park coincides with the Bab al-Wazir cemetery. Though this area is not visibly inhabited at present, it is a part of what Westerners have called "the City of the Dead". Built on the refuse of centuries, neighbour to the final resting place of countless Cairenes, almost literally encircled by traces of each major phase of the history of the great metropolis, Azhar Park is an affirmation of life and respect for the past. It is an invitation to view the future with a combination of optimism and respect for those who have gone before.

Turning the dusty, uninhabited sediment of Cairo into a living park has been a task of vast proportions involving many persons. Project leaders such as Stefano Bianca and Cameron Rashti of the Historic Cities Support Programme (see full list of acknowledgements at the end of the book) have led the way, but the architects and landscape designers are the ones who have truly left their mark on Azhar Park. Though others went before them, Maher Stino and Laila Elmasry Stino of Sites International have now assumed the task of the landscape design. The essentially axial layout, pointing views towards the Citadel in particular, was conceived before the arrival of Sites, but much of the peripheral architecture (kiosks, administrative offices, and so on) was designed by Maher Stino and his group who are based in Cairo. "We have sixteen million people," he says, "and we have almost no open space — nothing. We want to help the public understand what a park is and how to appreciate plants and nature. We also want something unique to Cairo. We don't want a copy of London's Regent Park." Limestone-block retaining walls that call on the expertise of local masons are a recurring element throughout the design, and great attention has been paid to the particularities of the site, where water supply and run-off are sensitive issues. On the eastern side where the topography is given to gentle slopes and there are no neighbouring residential areas, a design with large grass areas and flowers gives an oasis-like feeling of freshness and greenery. But the steeper western façade, near al-Darb al-Ahmar and the Ayyubid wall posed the problem of potential water accumulation and was thus planted with more desert varieties, including trees whose seeds were brought from Arizona by project horticulturalist El Saady Mohamed Badawy. Numerous fountains, especially near the two restaurants, undoubtedly recall the traditions of the Islamic garden, but here too Maher Stino avoids direct citations, preferring to allow modernity to be the guiding rule. The very scale of the landscape and horticulture effort speaks of the courage and will necessary to turn these hills into a real contemporary garden.

The two restaurants described in Robert Ivy's text in this book are the main architectural features of Azhar Park aside from its strong landscape design. It is interesting to note that the two facilities, respectively designed by the Egyptian architects Rami El Dahan with Soheir Farid and the Frenchman Serge Santelli, are quite different in their concept and aesthetic assumptions. Dahan, a disciple of Hasan Fathy, worked, amongst other projects cited by Robert Ivy, with the American proponent of post-modernism, Michael Graves, on El Gouna's Sheraton Miramar Hotel, a curious fantasy that Graves portrayed as "not Egyptian and not purely me". In describing the Hill-

Fig. 128. A street scene in al-Darb al-Ahmar in 2003 — where medieval Cairo meets day-to-day existence in the 21st century.

top Restaurant that Dahan designed in Azhar Park, the architect speaks of the architecture of Fatimid mosques as a source of inspiration, but stresses that even with its load-bearing stonework the heart of the structure is a functional, modern core. This warm architecture that he calls "monumental" will surely appeal to large numbers of park visitors who may look here for signs that their own traditions have been respected. Though 'post-modernism' or historicism are out of fashion in America, Europe or Japan, it was necessary in Azhar Park to make it clear that contemporary Egyptian ideas and workmanship have their place in the heart of Cairo.

The architecture of Rami El Dahan is one solution to the question of what to build today in Cairo in a modern environment that is surrounded by history. Another is offered by Serge Santelli in his Lakeside Café. Though not located as high above the city as the Hilltop Restaurant, the lakeside facility benefits from an even more spectacular view towards the Citadel, the Sultan Hasan Mosque and the other great monuments. Seemingly afloat on an artificial lake that is used as a reservoir for park irrigation, Santelli's structure is essentially modern in appearance with some reference to the principles of Arab design. It is almost as though the view from this vantage point offers enough history for the architect to be able to express himself in the vocabulary of today. A vista open to so much of the past of Cairo indelibly marks this as a point of transition between the past and the fu-

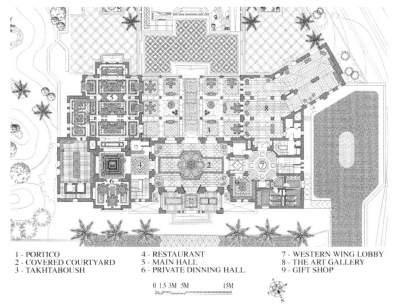

1 - PORTICO
2 - COVERED COURTYARD
3 - TAKHTABOUSH
4 - RESTAURANT
5 - MAIN HALL
6 - PRIVATE DINNING HALL
7 - WESTERN WING LOBBY
8 - THE ART GALLERY
9 - GIFT SHOP

0 1.5 3M 5M   15M

Fig. 129. Ground-floor plan of the Hilltop Restaurant
by Rami El Dahan and Soheir Farid.

ture. Not originally part of the park's design, Santelli's Lakeside Café aims to be its real gathering point. Though monumentality is not really an issue for Santelli, this location in itself is a concentration of past and present so powerful as to make the café a kind of monument in spite of itself — a monument of hope.

Yes, modern design, respectful of local tradition, can open new directions both for architecture and for thinking about the ancient city. In the face of projects like New Cairo, a recent development outside the capital that is nine times the size of Manhattan, it is essential to affirm that another vision of modernity can take hold here. Described by one critic as a "Middle-Eastern version of outer Houston, with mega-supermarkets, concrete apartment buildings and even a golf course blooming from the desert", New Cairo need not be the fate of the great city, whose historic core risks being converted into an 'outdoor museum', or razed to make way for soulless high-rise buildings. By daring to undertake the 'impossible', creating a modern park where before there was only dust and rubbish, and delving deep into the real problems of al-Darb al-Ahmar, affirming its life and character, the AKTC has done nothing less than to open a path between past and future that does not rob the people of their heritage in favour of some kind of sterile consumerism, or worse, an enforced exile in the desert of a New Cairo.

As the authors of this book demonstrate, the task is not an easy one, nor is each initiative assured of success, but the methodology employed here can surely be applied elsewhere. Moreover, the exemplary nature of the project is undoubtedly the issue at the heart of this work. Historic preservation and indeed construction as ambitious as that undertaken in Azhar Park require an investment in time, funds and energy that is considerable, but is there not today an urgency to use these sedimentary layers of past eras as a true foundation for understanding and future growth? As His Highness the Aga Khan asked at the recent inauguration of the Humayun's Tomb Gardens in India: "What, then, of the deeper values that we risk abandoning under the dust of our own indifference, or that might be crushed to rubble by our own destructive human forces? In the troubled times in which we live, it is important to remember, and honour, a vision of a pluralistic society. Tolerance, openness and understanding towards other peoples' cultures, social structures, values and faiths are now essential to the very survival of an interdependent world. Pluralism is no longer simply an asset or a prerequisite for progress and development; it is vital to our existence. Never perhaps more so than at the present time must we renew with vigour our creative engagement in revitalising shared heritage..."

In his text for this book, Seif El Rashidi quotes Gérard de Nerval (*Voyage en Orient*, 1842) who called Cairo "une cité du passé, habitée seulement par des fantômes, qui la peuplent sans l'animer" (a city of the past inhabited only by ghosts who fill it without giving it

Fig. 130. A photograph taken in November 2003 from Azhar Park looking towards al-Darb al-Ahmar and the modern skyline of Cairo. Here the past, present and future of the city meet.

life). Like other great cities of the world, Cairo has enormous problems, but its sixteen million inhabitants make it very much a city of the present. Built on the ruins of eras past, surrounded by the ghosts of Cairo's origins and history, Azhar Park and the Darb al-Ahmar rehabilitation project are investments in the future of the city. They are affirmations of the value and interest of a population and a place. Whatever their difficulties, al-Darb al-Ahmar and the Azhar Park site are so much a part of the heart of historic Cairo that there is no other valid solution but to breathe life into them as this project is doing. Other megalopolises may have been more 'efficient' at wiping out traces of the past, but most never had a past as rich as that of Cairo. The rehabilitation and construction undertaken by the AKTC in the Egyptian capital do not seek to 'clean up' the city but to open the way to what will come, while celebrating the past. For those who will follow and who understand, like the opening in the Ayyubid wall linking al-Darb al-Ahmar to Azhar Park, this is a gateway to the city of the future.

[1] *Al-Ahram Weekly*, 18-24 September 2003, Issue no. 656.
[2] Al-Darb al-Ahmar Neighbourhood Conservation Planning, AKCS-E, Bab al-Wazir Area, social survey of 840 inhabitants conducted in June 2002 by Dina K. Shehayeb.

Chronology of Cairo

COMPILED BY SEIF EL RASHIDI

EARLY ISLAMIC EGYPT (639-868)	TULUNIDS (868-904) AND IKHSHIDS (935-969)	FATIMIDS (969-1171)	AYYUBIDS (1171-1250)
639 'Amr ibn al-'As enters Egypt from Syria	868 Abbasid Caliph al-Mu'tazz appoints Bakbak as governor to Egypt; Bakbak sends Ahmad ibn Tulun instead	969 Fatimids enter Fustat with little resistance; Jawhar al-Siqilli founds al-Qahira in anticipation of the arrival of the Fatimid Caliph al-Muizz from North Africa. Al-Qahira becomes the seat of the Fatimid empire	1176 Salah al-Din al-Ayyubi becomes sultan, extends Cairo's fortifications and constructs citadel
640 Byzantine forces defeated at Ain Shams	869 Ahmad ibn Tulun rules independently from Abbasid caliphate, founds al-Qata'i	973 Al-Muizz arrives in Egypt	1187 Salah al-Din recaptures Jerusalem
641 Babylon (the Roman settlement near the later city of Cairo) capitulates and Muslim armies form the settlement known as al-Fustat (Tent City)	905 Tulunid dynasty collapses and Egypt reverts to direct Abbasid control	989 Al-Azhar becomes a centre for higher education under Ya'qub ibn Killis	1193 Salah al-Din dies and Ayyubid empire is fragmented
642 Arab armies take Alexandria	935 Muhammad ibn Tughj rules Egypt autonomously under the title of al-Ikhshidi given to him by the Abbasid Caliph	1073 Al-Mustansir summons Badr al-Jamali, governor of Acre, to quell violence in Egypt	1199 Al-Adil unites Ayyubid empire
644-645 Abortive attempt by Byzantine troops to reclaim Egypt	968 Kafur al-Ikhshidi dies; political and economic strife encourage Fatimid conquest of Egypt	1087 Badr al-Jamali, now the Fatimid vizier, consolidates Cairo's walls	1240 Al-Salih Ayyub builds up an army of Turkish slaves (the Bahri Mamluks)
750 Abbasids enter Egypt and found al-Askar		1096 First crusade begins	1250 Louis IX captured by Ayyubid army in Mansourah; al-Salih Ayyub dies and is succeeded by his son Turan Shah
		1099 Fall of Jerusalem to the Franks	
		1169 Salah al-Din al-Ayyubi takes control of Egypt	

BAHRI MAMLUKS (1250-1382)	CIRCASSIAN MAMLUKS (1382-1517)	OTTOMANS (1517-1805)	MODERN EGYPT (1805-)
1250 Brief reign of Shagaret El Dorr as Sultana	1382 Sultan Barquq seizes power, establishing Circassian Mamluk dynasty	1517 Khayrbek appointed first Ottoman governor	1805-1848 Muhammad Ali Pasha; virtual independence from the Ottoman court, comprehensive efforts to modernise Egypt
1258 Mongols capture Baghdad	1400 Tamerlane sacks Damascus, and economy deteriorates, plague and famine are rife	1768 Ali Bey al-Kabir revolts against the Ottomans, takes part of Arabia	1854-1863 Said Pasha; grants concession to the French to construct the Suez Canal
1260 Baybars defeats Mongols at Ain Jalut and reinstates Abbasid Caliph in Cairo	1412 Mu'ayyad Sheikh retakes Syria, rules until his death in 1421	1772 Revolt of Ali Bey al-Kabir suppressed	1863-1879 Khedive Ismail; construction of European-style districts of Cairo in anticipation of the opening of the Suez Canal in 1869
1283 Sultan Qalawun builds monumental complex including a maristan (hospital)	1422 Reign of Barsbay brings period of peace, cultural vitality and increased trade	1798-1801 French expedition to Egypt; Napoleon founds l'Institut d'Egypte	1936-1952 Farouk I; deposed and exiled by Revolutionary Command Council
1291 Ashraf Khalil defeats crusaders, who retreat to Cyprus	1468-1496 Cultural revival under Sultan Qaytbay	1805 Muhammad Ali expels Ottoman governor and is confirmed wali of Egypt by Sultan Selim III	1952-1953 Ahmad Fouad II; Regency Council rules until 1953, when a republic is declared with Muhammad Naguib as president
1293-1341 Three reigns of al-Nasir Muhammad	1488 Discovery of Cape of Good Hope has an adverse effect on trade in Egypt		1954 Gamal Abdel Nasser becomes president of Egypt
1340-1382 Descendants of Qalawun remain in power	1516 Sultan al-Ghawri loses battle against Ottomans. Khayrbek, governor of Aleppo, betrays the Mamluks		1958-1961 Egypt and Syria merge to form the United Arab Republic
	1517 Tumanbay II captured and hung, Ottomans take over Egypt		1970 Abdel Nasser dies; Anwar El Sadat becomes president of Egypt
			1981 Sadat is assassinated; Muhammad Hosni Mubarak becomes president

AKTC Projects in Cairo: Timeline

COMPILED BY WILLIAM O'REILLY

1984

His Highness the Aga Khan attends the international seminar entitled "The Expanding Metropolis: Coping with the Urban Growth of Cairo", organised by the Aga Khan Award for Architecture. The Award was created by the Aga Khan in 1977 to enhance the understanding and appreciation of Islamic culture as expressed through architecture. The ninth seminar in its series, "Architectural Transformations in the Islamic World", looks at the impact of population shifts into Cairo and its historic core and the consequent deterioration of its urban fabric. It examines measures needed to control and direct this urbanisation process.

On the occasion of his visit, the Aga Khan makes an offer to His Excellency the Governor of Cairo to build and operate a public park, placed at the disposal of the inhabitants of Cairo and its visitors, as a gift financed and developed by the Aga Khan Trust for Culture.

1986

After various studies, a thirty-hectare site on al-Darassa, owned by the Governorate of Cairo, is proposed. The Trust commissions a design team to prepare preliminary studies, following which it accepts the site proposed.

The site's location, the last vacant space in central Cairo, presents an enormous opportunity to provide green spaces to a city where they have disappeared over time, to enhance the quality of urban life, to provide a location for family and leisure activities, to generate cultural renewal and to provide a platform for viewing the core of the historic city.

Late 1980s

An initial Park programme is prepared, but needs to be adapted to new circumstances. The General Organisation for Greater Cairo Water Supply needs part of the site to build, under a grant from USAID, three large water tanks, as part of a municipal water reservoir and supply system for the surrounding district. In agreement with all parties concerned, a modified project incorporating the water works is submitted to the Governor.

1989

The Aga Khan Award for Architecture prize-giving ceremony is held in Cairo. In his address, His Highness notes that honouring the award-winning projects is not enough, and that we need to understand why, and how, these buildings and area developments 'work' for the communities that brought them into being.

1990

An agreement is signed by the Cairo Governorate and the Aga Khan Trust for Culture, whereby the parties agree to the definition of the project site and scope, the establishment of an Egyptian company as an extension of AKTC to deal with all matters concerning the park's planning, implementation and operations, and the constitution of the Azhar Park Authority Board to oversee the operations of the completed project. It also set out the conditions regarding the duration and termination of the agreement. It is agreed that the first works would start at the same time as current occupants — a horse compound of the Cairo police and the storage site of a major contractor — depart after completion of work on the water reservoir system.

1990-1992
The water reservoir system enters the design phase.

1992
The Historic Cities Support Programme is set up as the operational branch of the Aga Khan Trust for Culture, with the task of implementing conservation and urban revitalisation projects in culturally significant sites of the Islamic world. Along with its work in Cairo, the Programme undertakes projects in the northern areas of Pakistan and Zanzibar, to be followed by further interventions around the world.

1992-1996
A master plan for the park is drawn up with assistance from Sasaki Associates, Boston. GEI Consultants provide specialist advisory services in geo-technical engineering. Design work is coordinated with the ongoing reservoir system design.

1994-1997
Analyses and tests are undertaken to manage complicated soil and horticultural conditions. A preliminary on-site nursery is set up in order to establish an appropriate range of plant species for the park.

1995
A substantial part of the water reservoir system is built, although additional work is required prior to the commissioning of the system.

1996
The Cairo Governorate hands over the site to the Aga Khan Trust for Culture. Excavation and earthworks for general site re-grading begin. On behalf of the Trust, Stefano Bianca and Cameron Rashti are made responsible for the formulation of a project design development and implementation work plan.

Upon the rediscovery of the formerly buried Ayyubid city wall of Cairo during early excavations, the Trust expands the park project to include revitalisation of the fringe of the adjacent Darb al-Ahmar district and restoration of key monuments in the area. The project expands to become a broader sustainable development programme, based on the proposition that economic, cultural and environmental initiatives need to be elements of an integrated rehabilitation strategy in order to effectively improve the quality of life of communities.

Investigation of conditions in al-Darb al-Ahmar is carried out by a planning unit and planning proposals are generated. An interdisciplinary team from the Aga Khan Cultural Services-Egypt under the supervision of Mohammed El Mikawi is set up. Stefano Bianca and Francesco Siravo are made responsible for the project's development and technical coordination.

1997
Following survey and testing, a programme for the restoration of the Ayyubid wall is put in place, to be managed by specialists recruited by the Trust and its local affiliate, Aga Khan Cultural Services-Egypt, under the scientific direction of Professor Frank Matero, following principles conforming to modern conservation practice. The wall is perceived as a dynamic edge and meeting point between the Darb al-Ahmar community and the park. A physical survey of the Darb al-Ahmar district is undertaken.

1998
A detailed park design is established as the result of a collaborative effort led by Maher Stino and Laila El-masry Stino, principals of Sites International, Cairo, the lead design consultant and park landscape architect. A fifty-hectare off-site nursery is created, on land made available by the American University in Cairo. Native and xerophytic species appropriate to the environment are grown for later planting in the park.

A pilot study of the Darb al-Ahmar district is undertaken to ascertain what improvements are needed and how best to intervene. Pilot projects are undertaken to rehabilitate historic monuments and key buildings, and to formulate neighbourhood activities.

1998-1999
Design development of key architectural features of the park — the Hilltop Restaurant, the Lakeside Café, and various pavilions and plazas — begins.

1999
A design competition for the park restaurant facilities takes place. Rami El Dahan and Soheir Farid, principals of El Dahan & Farid Engineering, are chosen to design the Hilltop Restaurant and Entry Gate, while Serge Santelli, architect, and his associate, Karine Martin, are to design the Lakeside Café.

In al-Darb al-Ahmar, a variety of interventions which associate physical improvements in the area of housing and public open spaces with a number of socio-economic development projects are initiated. These include training and skill enhancement programmes, small enterprise promotion including micro-credit programmes, health clinics, women and childhood education. Other agencies of the Aga Khan Development Network involve themselves in this process.

2001-2002
The park earthworks, geo-membranes and infrastructure systems are constructed.

2002
An agreement is concluded with the Governorate to develop an Urban Plaza at the north-western end of the park. A commercial building with shops, offices and an integrated multi-storey car park is being developed, the plan of which is closely coordinated with the park design in terms of entrances, terraces and shared facilities. Tabanlioglu Associates of Istanbul are chosen as project architects.

2002-2003
The park facility buildings, plazas and finishes are constructed.

2003
A programme is prepared for comprehensive and adaptive redevelopment of the houses on the west side of the excavated Ayyubid wall, with residential use in the upper floors and commercial facilities at street level.

2007
Construction work begins on the Urban Plaza.

The main park project is completed. The management of the park is entrusted to Aga Khan Cultural Services-Egypt under the supervision of the autonomous Park Authority Board.

Preliminary Results of a Socio-Economic Survey in al-Darb al-Ahmar

COMPILED BY JURJEN VAN DER TAS

INCOME

MONTHLY INCOME PER HOUSEHOLD
OF FIVE PERSONS

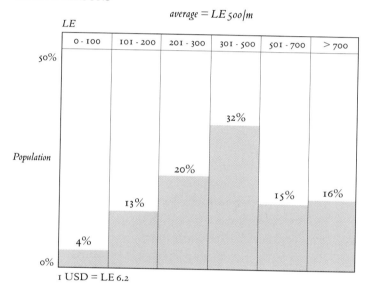

1 USD = LE 6.2

DURATION OF HOUSE OCCUPANCY
IN AL-DARB AL-AHMAR

Source: AKCS-E Darb al-Ahmar Baseline Survey, December 2003

EXPENDITURE

MONTHLY EXPENDITURE PER HOUSEHOLD
OF FIVE PERSONS

	as %	LE
Rent	3	16,2
Utilities	5	27
Food	54	291,6
Business	8	43,2
Education	17	91,8
Health	8	43,2
Savings	1	5,4
Debts	4	21,6
Other	0	0
	100	540

ASSETS
PER 100 HOUSEHOLDS

Colour TV	90
Electric water heater	19
Washing machine	10
Telephone/cellular phone	55
Satellite dish antenna	5

OTHER OBSERVATIONS

1. Ownership of land and/or buildings

Land owners	0%
Owners of buildings	5%
Owners of land and buildings	0%

2. Occupancy status of the houses

Single owner	13%
Partial owner	19%
Long-term tenant	68%
Short-term tenant	0%

Note between 1 and 2: there is a major difference between ownership of a building (consisting of 4.5 houses on average) and individual houses

3. Residents wanting to continue living in the area	84%
Residents unclear about residential preference	14%

4. Spread of population by gender and age

< 15 yrs: 28% of which 14 % female and 14% male
15-60 yrs: 65% of which 33 % are female and 32% male
> 60 yrs: 8% of which 4% are female and 4%male

Biographies

AUTHORS

Janet Abu-Lughod holds graduate degrees from the University of Chicago and University of Massachusetts and has been studying and writing about cities for more than half a century. Her teaching career began at the University of Illinois, took her to the American University in Cairo, Smith College, and Northwestern University where she taught for twenty years and directed several urban studies programmes. In 1987 she accepted a professorship in sociology and historical studies at the Graduate Faculty of the New School for Social Research, from which she retired as professor emerita in 1998.
She has published over a hundred articles and thirteen books, a number of which deal with the Middle East, including an urban history of Cairo that is, despite its age, still considered one of the classic works on that city: *Cairo: 1001 Years of the City Victorious* (Princeton 1971).

Jim Antoniou, RIBA MRTPI FRSA, is a British architect and city planner with international experience in conservation and urban design, the rehabilitation of squatter areas, the construction sector and education facilities, working with international agencies such as The World Bank, and various UN agencies. He has been involved in historic Cairo for a number of years as consultant to the Egyptian Supreme Council of Antiquities for UN-ESCO. He was also commissioned by UNDP as senior advisor on the Rehabilitation of Historic Cairo Project (1997). He has lectured at various academic institutions in the USA, Europe and the Middle East. He is also the author of numerous books, including *Environmental Management* (McGraw-Hill 1971); *Islamic Cities and Conversation* (UNESCO Press 1981); *Cities: Then and Now* (Macmillan 1995); *Historic Cairo* (American University in Cairo Press 1998). He has also written many articles, notably in the *Architectural Review*, the *Royal Institute of Architects Journal* and *Building Design*. As an illustrator and artist, his work has been exhibited widely, including at the Biennale of Venice.

Stefano Bianca is a Swiss architect and architectural historian (graduated from ETH Zurich) who has spent much of his research and professional life in the Muslim world working for various governmental institutions and international organisations. Since 1976, he has directed a number of major planning, urban design and conservation projects in cities such as Fez, Aleppo, Baghdad, and Riyadh. Since 1992, he has been the Director of the Historic Cities Support Programme of the Aga Khan Trust for Culture in Geneva, shaping the growth of this new Trust Programme. He has lectured and published widely, his most recent books being *Hofhaus und Paradiesgarten* (Munich 1991 and 2001) and *Urban Form in the Arab World* (London/New York 2000).

Nairy Hampikian is an architect who graduated from Cairo University and has enriched her professional formation in historic preservation, Islamic and Armenian history of architecture, and archaeology in different international Universities in Egypt, Armenia, Italy, Germany and the USA. Since 1985, she has been involved in different international excavation/conservation projects in different architectural and archaeological fields in Egypt. Having specialised in the conservation of monuments in Historic Cairo since 1998, she is the director of the USAID funded Bab Zuwayla Conservation Project. Simultaneously, she lectures widely, writes articles on various architectural and conservation subjects around the world, and teaches architectural conservation in the Architectural Department of Misr International University (MIU) in Cairo.

Robert Ivy, FAIA, architect and editor, became Editor in Chief of *Architectural Record* in October 1996. The author of numerous magazine articles, his award-winning book entitled *Fay Jones* was reissued in 2001. Ivy is currently a fellow of the American Institute of Architects, the Philippine Institute of Architects, the Institute for Urban Design, a former regent of the American Architectural Foundation, and a peer reviewer for the US General Services Administration. He received a degree in architecture from Tulane University. In 2002, the US Department of State appointed Ivy as US Commissioner to the Venice Biennale of Architecture. In 2003, Ivy was appointed Vice President and Editorial Director, McGraw-Hill Construction, with responsibilities for twelve publications.

Philip Jodidio was educated at Harvard University. He was the Editor in Chief of the leading French art monthly *Connaissance des Arts* from 1979 to 2002. He has written widely in magazines, and is the author of more than twenty-five books on contemporary architecture, including the *Architecture Now* series published by Taschen in six languages and distributed in seventy countries. His most recent book is a 500-page monograph on the Japanese architect Tadao Ando (Cologne 2004).

Frank G. Matero is Chair of the Graduate Programme in Historic Preservation at the Graduate School of Fine Arts as well as Director and founder of the Architectural Conservation Laboratory at the University of Pennsylvania. Since 1988 he has been on the faculty as lecturer in Architectural Conservation at the International Centre for the Study of Preservation and the Restoration of Cultural Property (ICCROM) in Rome and Senior Lecturer for Restore, New York City. He has consulted on a wide range of conservation projects including the archaeological sites of Mesa Verde, Casa Grande, Bandelier, and Catalhoyuk in Turkey.

His numerous publications include forthcoming books on the technical history of the stone industries of North America and a history of archaeological site preservation in the American south-west.

Nawal El Messiri received her Ph.D. in Urban Anthropology from Indiana University in 1975. From 1960 to 1980 she was a researcher and lecturer at the American University in Cairo. From 1980 to 1983, she was a Programme Officer at UNICEF. Since 1983, she has been working on the management of development projects related to traditional arts and crafts. She is in charge of several rehabilitation projects associated with the restoration of historic monuments.

Nasser Rabbat, B.Arch., M.Arch., Ph.D., is the Aga Khan Professor of Islamic Architecture at the Massachusetts Institute of Technology (MIT), where he has taught since 1991. His scholarly interests include the history and historiography of Islamic architecture and urbanism and post-colonial criticism. His books include: *The Citadel of Cairo: A New Interpretation of Royal Mamluk Architecture* (Leiden 1995); *Thaqafat al Bina' wa Bina' al-Thaqafa (The Culture of Building and Building Culture)* (Beirut 2002); and *L'art islamique à la recherche d'une méthode historique* (forthcoming, IMA, Paris 2004). He is currently finishing a book on the fifteenth-century Egyptian historian al-Maqrizi, which is slated for publication in late 2004, and is editing a book on the courtyard house to be published in 2005. Professor Rabbat serves on the board of various organisations concerned with Islamic cultures, lectures extensively in the USA and abroad, contributes to a variety of newspapers and magazines on art, architectural and cultural issues, and maintains several websites focused on Islamic architecture.

Seif El Rashidi graduated from the American University in Cairo with degrees in economics and architectural history, and from the London School of Economics with an M.Sc. in City Design and Social Science. He worked on a range of architectural and interior design projects for Ahmad Hamid Architects before joining the Aga Khan Trust for Culture's Cairo project in 1997. Since then, he has been a member of the Darb al-Ahmar neighbourhood revitalisation team and has been involved in urban conservation and preservation planning.

Cameron Rashti is an architect and project manager with extensive project experience on major projects in North America, Europe and the Middle East. He is a graduate of Dartmouth College, holds professional architectural degrees from Pratt Institute and Columbia University, and is a registered architect in the USA and the UK. He joined the Geneva-based Historic Cities Support Programme within the Aga Khan Trust for Culture in 1994 as Deputy Director, following his association as Vice President of Perkins and Will International managing projects in Canary Wharf and other sites in London and Europe. Within HCSP, he was (among other tasks) responsible for the implementation of the Azhar Park project.

Francesco Siravo is an Italian architect specialised in historic preservation and town planning. Since 1991 he has worked for the Historic Cities Support Programme of the Aga Khan Trust for Culture, with projects in Zanzibar, Cairo, Samarkand and Mostar. Previous work includes the preparation of plans for the historical areas of Rome and Urbino, Italy, and for the old town of Lamu, Kenya, as well as consultancies for UNESCO and ICCROM. He has written books, articles and papers on various architectural conservation and town planning subjects, including "Zanzibar. A Plan for the Historic Stone Town" (1996), and "Planning Lamu. Conservation of an East African Seaport" (1986).

ARCHITECTS

Rami El Dahan and his partner *Soheir Farid* are a husband and wife team who have been in private practice in Egypt since 1983. They have worked as planners, architects and engineers. As they say themselves, "our firm is especially experienced in vernacular architecture and the use of locally available construction materials". From 1979 to 1989, they worked with architect Hassan Fathy. Their latest project is the Ismaili Centre in Dubai (under construction). They have designed several resorts, centres and hotels in Egypt, such as the Mövenpick Hotel in El Quseir (1991); planning and design of the El Gouna Town Centre, including commercial and housing projects, the Mosque and several hotels (1993-2002); Hyatt Regency Taba and Sheraton Miramar Hotels, in association with Michael Graves (1996). They have also completed a considerable number of urban planning projects and rehabilitation of historic monuments. They are the architects of the Hilltop Restaurant in Azhar Park, Cairo (2004).

Serge Santelli was born in 1944 in Paris, and received a Master of Architecture and City Planning degree from the University of Pennsylvania in 1970. He worked in the atelier of Louis Kahn before becoming an assistant professor at the Institut Technologique d'Art in Tunis. Since 1973, he has taught at the Ecole d'Architecture de Paris-Belleville and has been responsible for the "Habitat au Maghreb" workshop since 1985. In addition to a number of projects in France, Tunisia and Senegal, Santelli has researched and published numerous articles on Arab and Islamic architecture and urbanism in North Africa and more particularly on the traditional and contemporary habitat of that region. He received the Aga Khan Award for Architecture in 1983 for the Résidence Andalous in Tunisia. Serge Santelli is the architect of the Lakeside Café in Azhar Park, Cairo (2004).

Maher Stino and *Laila Elmasry Stino* are the principals of Sites International, "a multi-disciplinary consultancy firm specialised in designing integrated environments where the built and natural environments blend to produce works of functional and visual harmony". Maher Stino graduated from Cairo University (1969) and received a Masters in Landscape Architecture from the University of Georgia in 1972 and a Ph.D. in Environmental Planning and Landscape Architecture from the University of Michigan in 1977. He is presently Dean of the College of Urban and Regional Planning at Cairo University. Laila Elmasry Stino had much the same educational background, obtaining her Ph.D. in Landscape Architecture in Michigan in 1983. She is currently vice Dean of Graduate Studies at Cairo University. Their work includes the Nubian Museum, Aswan, Egypt (site and landscape design, winner of the Aga Khan Prize for Architecture 2001); urban design of the historical precinct of Addiriyyah, Riyadh, Saudi Arabia; and the Mirage City & Golf Course (design, construction drawings & documents for a 160-hectare development in Cairo). They are the landscape designers for Azhar Park in Cairo (development and preparation of the final master plan, detailed final designs and construction documents and construction management).

Acknowledgments

We would like to extend our sincere thanks to:
HIS HIGHNESS THE AGA KHAN, the Sponsor
ABDEL RAHIM SHEHATA, Governor of Cairo
FAROUK HOSNI, Minister of Culture
ZAHI HAWAS, Secretary General,
    Supreme Council of Antiquities

OVERALL PROJECT DIRECTION

AGA KHAN TRUST FOR CULTURE, Geneva:
Stefano Bianca, Director,
    Historic Cities Support Programme
Cameron Rashti, Project Manager, Azhar Park
Francesco Siravo, Historic Wall
    and al-Darb al-Ahmar
Jurjen van der Tas, al-Darb al-Ahmar as of 2003
Nicholas Bulloch, Financial Director

CAIRO PROJECT ADMINISTRATION

AGA KHAN CULTURAL SERVICES (EGYPT):
Mohamed El Mikawi, General Manager (2001 to
date), Ossama Hambazaza, General Manager
(1997-2001), Sherif Zaki, Financial Controller,
Mohab Al Sayed Helmy, Hitham Mokhtar Amin
and Mohamed Mohy, Accountants, Walid Hegazy
and Amr Mahrous, Purchasing Officers,
Nahla Al Dessouki, Executive Secretary,
and Fatma Abdel Hamid, Secretary

*

1. THE AZHAR PARK PROJECT

Azhar Park is the product of a consortium of design
and technical consultants and trade contractors working closely with the management of the Aga Khan
Trust for Culture (AKTC) and its affiliate Aga Khan
Cultural Services, Egypt (AKCS-E). The following is
a list of key members of the project team:

AGA KHAN CULTURAL SERVICES (EGYPT):
Amr El Badry, Technical Coordinator, Hisham
Gameh, Park Manager, and the AKCS-E team.
Mohammed Hassouna, Legal Advisor, Hassouna
& Abou Ali, Attorneys at Law

CONSULTANTS:
Master Planning: Sasaki Associates (Boston):
    Don Olson, Principal, Maurice Freedman,
    Sr Engineer. GEI Consultants, Inc. (Boston):
    Gonzalo Castro, Principal

Park Architect: Sites International (Cairo): Maher
    Stino and Laila Elmasry, Principals, M. Abdul
    Monem El Sayed, Technical Director, Khaled
    Moustafa, Design Architect/Associate, Fathie
    Shehto, Specifications

Infrastructure Engineer: Misr Consult (Cairo):
    Sameh Abdel Gawad, Principal, Tarek Sabri,
    Project Engineer, Engineers, Ahmad Fathie,
    Electrical, Magdy, Infrastructure, and Moataz,
    Mechanical Engineers, Ashraf Shazli, Consulting
    Irrigation Engineer

Geo-Technical Engineer: Ardaman-Ace (Cairo):
    Mohamed Sheta, Partner, Ahmed Hosny, Project
    Engineer

Project Management:
Phase I: Earthworks, Geo-Technical Systems,
    Lighting Procurement, Piling, and Retaining
    Walls: Egyptian Project Management: Adel El
    Samadony, Managing Director, Ahmed Saleh
    Mokhtar, Project Manager, Mohamed Hassan,
    Project Engineer, Wahdan Annas, Project Control
Phase II: Hardscape, Roads, Lakeside Café and Park
    FF&E: Sites International: Maher Stino, Ossama
    Eid, Bassem Hussain, Khaled Gamea, Walid
    Ahmed, Ashraf Diallo, and others

Hilltop Restaurant & Entry Gate: El Dahan & Farid
    Engineering (Cairo): Rami El Dahan and Soheir
    Farid, Principals, Design Architects, Hassan
    Bakry, Bakry Associates, MEP Engineering, Yasser
    El Quedsy, Interior Designer, Rashad Tadros,
    Project Manager

Lakeside Café: Serge Santelli, Architect (Paris):
    Serge Santelli, Architect and Interior Design,
    Katherine Martin, Associate,
    Sites International/Production Architect:
    Ahmed Askan, Project Architect.

Lighting Design: Phoenix-Large/Lightmatters
    (London): Graham Large, Principal, Sharon
    Stammers, Designer

Restaurant Equipment Swiss Inn Hotels & Resorts
    (Cairo): Anton Good, President

CONTRACTORS:
(based in Cairo, unless otherwise noted)
Earthworks:
Phase I: AKCS-E team directed by Ossama
    Hambazaza: Initial Site Operations including
    Excavation, Grading, Geo-Technical and
    Horticultural Soils Testing.
Phase II: MEDCOM (Misr Engineering Development
    Company) General Contractor: Geo-Technical,
    Grading, Excavation, Tank Tops

Geo-Membranes: MEDCOM (Misr Engineering
    Development Company) General Contractor

Nursery/ Horticulture: AKCS-E team directed by
    Saady Badawy, Horticultural Engineer

Infrastructure: Main Infrastructure, Irrigation
    Systems, Power, Low Voltage, Communications:
    PICO (Projects Investment & Consulting Co.)

Electrical Supply: ABB (Egypt)

External Drainage: Al Fayrouz Housing
    Development

Retaining Walls: MEC (Misr Engineering
    for Construction)

Planting Soils: UNEC (United Company
    for Engineering & Construction)

Perimeter Fencing: Al Mashreq, Concrete Works,
    Saudi Metals/ Valley of the Kings, Metalwork

Lighting Systems: Grand International,
    Procurement / PHI Co., Installation.
    Manufacturers: Hydrel, We-ef, Kim Lighting,
    custom marble bollards by Sites International with
    DAL fittings, Concordmarlin, Group C,
    3 Brothers, Simes, Guzzini, Lumisphere, Airstar,
    and Hydrosphere

Roads: RIZKO (Rizko General Contracting),
    General Contractor

Hardscape Elements: RIZKO (Rizko General
    Contracting), General Contractor: Main Spine,
    Sunken Garden, North Tank Top Playground,
    Bridges, Benches. MEDCOM General Contractor:
    South and Central Tank Tops

Signage: Various

Lakeside Café: KAZ (Kamal El-Zoheiry
    Construction Co.), General Contractor: Building
    & Interiors / Basco: Kitchen equipment

Restaurant & Entry Gate: KAZ (Kamal El Zoheiry
    Construction Co.), General Contractor: Building
    &.Interiors/ Basco: Kitchen equipment

2. THE AYYUBID WALL PROJECT

The Ayyubid wall restoration project is being carried
out by a group of consultants, professionals and local
trainees under the direct management of the
Aga Khan Trust for Culture (AKTC) and its affiliate
Aga Khan Cultural Services, Egypt (AKCS-E). The
project team works closely with the authorities and
officers of the Supreme Council of Antiquities, in
particular, A. Abdel Sattar, General Manager,
and Magdy Soliman and Abdel-Khalid Mokhtar,
District Managers. The following is a list of key
members of the project team:

TECHNICAL COORDINATION:
Frank Matero, Chair, Graduate Programme
in Historic Preservation Programme, School
of Design, University of Pennsylvania

AGA KHAN CULTURAL SERVICES (EGYPT):
Zeiad Ahmed Amer, Ayman Abdel-Hakim
Al Gohary, Hazem Rashed (2000) and Mohamed
Said (1998-2000), Senior Architects, Noha Nael
Ahmed and Nadine Samir Fikry, Architects, and
Nora Abdel-Hamid Shalaby, Archaeologist

Project Manager: Elisa del Bono

Site Architects: Amr Mohamed Atta, Heba Foda,
Ehab Lasheen, Ibrahim Zakareya

Archaeology: Peter Sheehan, Sami El Masry (2002)

Conservators: Abdel-Rahman Abdel-Qader, Wael
Sayed Ahmad, Ibrahim Bahaa, Guy Derveux,
Catherine Dewey (1999-2000), Kecia Fong
(1998), Ikramy Ghareeb, Reda Ali Hassan,
Al Amir El Hefny, Essam Khatab, Rasha Ahmed
Korane, Ashraf Labib, Angelo Lanza, Melissa
MacCormack (2002), Tom Roby (1999), Debora
Rodrigues (2001), Abeer Saad-Eldin, Ali
Mohammed Saeed, Giovanni Santo, Noha Sayed
Abou Saqrah, Naser Sayed, Mahmoud Yahya

Foremen: Hamed Yousef, Ehab Shawky Besher,
Yehia Fahmy Hessen, Mohammed Husein,
Khamis Ali Qasem

Laboratory Testing: Engineering Laboratory of
Cairo University, Architectural Conservation
Laboratory University of Pennsylvania

Visitor Circuit Design: Robert Pilbeam, Phoenix-
Large/Lightmatters (London)

Masons: Mamdoh Ibrahim Abdala, Mostafa Abas Ahmed, Nasr Ahmad Abdel-Latif, Hassan Abdel-Rahman, Khaled Mohammed Ahmad, Ali Korani Ali, Mahmoud Mohamed Farahan, Farg Mohammed Ibrahim, Mauro Musolino, Laurino Saccucci, Salem Helil Salem, Mahmoud Sayed, Abdel Aziz El Shishiny

Materials: Hana Ghorab, Hassan Imam

Procurement Officers, Accounting and Storage: Mahmoud Abdel-Khaleq, Mohamed Alam Eldin, Tarek Galal El Din, Hamed Mohamed Hamed, Adel Sayed Ibrahim, Mohamed Yassin

3. MONUMENT RESTORATION ACTIVITIES

The restoration activities carried out in the framework of al-Darb al-Ahmar are the results of the efforts of project staff, consultants and contractors working closely with the management of the Aga Khan Trust for Culture (AKTC) and its affiliate Aga Khan Cultural Services, Egypt (AKCS-E). The project team works closely with the authorities and officers of the Supreme Council of Antiquities, in particular, Emad Osman and Wagdy Abbas, Inspectors. The following is a list of key members of the project team:

TECHNICAL COORDINATION:
Christophe Bouleau, Conservation Architect, HCSP, Wolfgang Mayer, Advisor

AGA KHAN CULTURAL SERVICES (EGYPT):
The Khayrbek Complex project includes Mohammed Said and Ashraf Ayad, Senior Architects, and Lara Iskander, Architect

Khayrbek Complex Project
STAFF/CONSULTANTS:
Architects/Engineers: ACE Moharram-Bakhoum, Bernard Maury (2001), Eman El Kilany, Saleh Lamieh (2000)

Contractors: EEC (Egyptian Engineering Company), Cintec International

Mosque and Minaret of Umm al-Sultan Shaaban
STAFF/CONSULTANTS:
Site Architects: ACE Moharram-Bakhoum, Saleh Lamieh (2000), Mohamed Lashin, Sandra Loucas, Christian Ubertini

Contractors: EEC (Egyptian Engineering Company), Cintec International

4. THE DARB AL-AHMAR PROJECT COMMUNITY DEVELOPMENT ACTIVITIES

The community development activities carried out in the framework of the Darb al-Ahmar Project are the results of the efforts of project staff and consultants working closely with the management of the Aga Khan Trust for Culture (AKTC) and its affiliate Aga Khan Cultural Services, Egypt (AKCS-E). Between 2000 and 2003, the social development activities were carried out under the supervision of the Centre for Development Services (CDS). The following is a list of key members of the project team:

AGA KHAN CULTURAL SERVICES (EGYPT):
Hany Attalla, Darb al-Ahmar Project Manager (November 2003 to date), Ashraf Boutros, Senior Architect, Kareem Ibrahim, Technical Manager for Housing, Khaled Khalil, Architect, Wael Sabry, Manager of the Training Workshop, and Seif El Rashidi, Planner

Housing Rehabilitation Team
STAFF/CONSULTANTS:
Documentation and Site Architects: Ahmad Al Biblawy, Nevine George, Mahmoud Qotb, Mohamed Abdel-Sattar Sayed

Community Liaison: Dina Shehayeb

Coordinators: Jeffrey Allen, Gina Haney (2002), CDS

Credit Officers: Mohamed Sayyed, Shaimaa Soliman

Foremen: Mohamed Hamdy Abdel-Sattar, Samir Saad Mustafa, Hani Mohamed Al Tayeb, Mohamed Al Tayeb

Legal Officers: Hussein Abdel-Kareem, Heba Al Batreeq

Masons: Awad Mohammad Awad, Abdel-Fattah Hanafy Hassan, Gom'aa Abbas Nazir

Community Surveys: Shahinaz Mekheimar (1999), Debora Rodrigues (1998-2001)

Structural Engineering: Khaled El Khouly, Ahmed El Khozami

Shoughlan Street School Project
STAFF/CONSULTANTS:
Site Architects: Heba Baragheet, Mohamed Ebaid, Mamdouh Sakr

Carpenters: Hamza Abdullah, Wolfgang Altenburg, Mamdouh Gamal, Khaled Abdel Hafeez, Issam Abdel Hafeez, Mohamed Hassan, Moustafa Hassan, Nasr Hosni, Moustafa Hussein, Tarek Ismael, Mosaad Mahrouss, Hisham Mohamed, Salahedin Mohame, Tamer Salah

Conservators: Nanis Adel, Ali Abdel Azim Ali, Paola Azzzaretti (2003), Ahmed Galal, Rasha Galal, Moustafa Hassan, Nabil Mikhaeel, Ashraf Mohamed, Yomna Mohammed, Housain Mohessen, Abdel Hameed Salah, Hanz Wagnar

Documentation Researcher: Seif El Rashidi

Foreman: Mohammed Abou Taleb

Masons: Gamal Abid, Yassin Ahmed, Sandro Amedoro, Ahmed Eid

Mechanical: Hassan Bakry, Hisham Basyoni, Karam Refaay, Sanitaire, Heinz Stemple (2002)

Plasterers: Said Farouk, Mohamed Hussein, Mostafa abd El Khalek, Khaled Mahmoud, Ahmed Said

Shoring: Gad Atta, Mohammed Atta, Fawzi Abdel-Megid

Planning and Open Space Unit
STAFF/CONSULTANTS:
Coordinator: Jeffrey Allen

Planners: Ahmed Essam, D'oaa Hatem (2003)

Community Development
STAFF/CONSULTANTS:
Arts and Cultural Activities: Marwa Ali Mohamed, Abeer Mohamed, CDS

Employment: Ahmed Abdu, Gehan Ali Youssef, CDS

Health Services: Hend Abdel Latif, Mohamed Moustafa, Nahla Abdel Naby, Ghada Moustafa, Nevine Said, CDS

Human Resources: Catherine Whybrow (2003)

Micro-Credit: Mohamed Abdullah, Mohamed Abdel Sadek, Ikromy Mohamed, CDS

Monitoring & Evaluation: Gina Haney

NGO Development: CDS

*

PUBLICATION CREDITS

Drawings, Plans, Maps and Models: AKCS-E, Janet Abu-Lughod, *Cairo: 1001 Years of the City Victorious*, Princeton University Press, Princeton 1971, Jim Antoniou and from *Historic Cairo: A Walk Through the Islamic City*, American University in Cairo Press, Cairo 1998, Rami El Dahan, Soheir Farid, Abdel Halim (Community Design Collaborative), Heneghan-Peng, Serge Santelli, Sites International (Maher Stino)

CAD Renderings: The MIT Design Computation Lab led by Professor Takehiko Nagakura with Andrzej Zarzycki, Kyoung Eun Kwon and Jun Oishi

Photography: AKCS-E, Stefano Bianca, Nairy Hampikian, Boulos Issaq, Barry Iverson, Nawal El Messiri, Gary Otte, Nasser Rabbat, Cameron Rashti, Randa Shaath, Robin Oldacre-Reed

Historic Photography: Courtesy the Creswell Archives, Fogg Art Museum at Harvard University, Barry Iverson, Kunstakademiets Bibliotek (Copenhagen), Library of Congress (USA), Royal Photographic Society (Bath), Dan Tassel

Photographic Research: Jeffrey Allen, Robin Oldacre-Reed, William O'Reilly, Seif El Rashidi

Archival Research: William O'Reilly, AKTC Librarian

Digital Image/Document Processing: Jeffrey Allen, Robin Oldacre-Reed, Marie-Martine de Techtermann, and others at AKTC and AKCS-E

EDITORIAL COORDINATION PHILIP JODIDIO (FOR AKTC), HARRIET GRAHAM (FOR UMBERTO ALLEMANDI & C.)

COPY-EDITING HARRIET GRAHAM

LAYOUT ALESSANDRA BARRA

PHOTOLITHOGRAPHY FOTOMEC, TURIN, ITALY

PUBLISHED BY UMBERTO ALLEMANDI & C., TURIN, ITALY

SECOND EDITION REVISED
PRINTED IN ITALY, JUNE 2007
ISBN 978-88-422-1235-5